Regionalism Across the North–South Divide

T0270812

Regionalism Across the North–South Divide charts the increasingly important trend of regional cooperation between the developed 'North' and the developing countries of the 'South'. It focuses on the responses and reactions of developing countries to the current wave of globalization and explores the state strategies adopted to create this 'new regionalism'. Introductory chapters introduce a theoretical framework, locating the semi-periphery in the context of globalization. Subsequent chapters then present in-depth case studies of the following countries and regions:

- Brazil and MERCOSUR
- South East Asia
- Eurasia and Turkey
- Sub-Saharan Africa
- Chile and the Americas
- North Africa
- China and East Asia
- Australia and Asia-Pacific

This study is invaluable for making sense of what regionalism means for the South and its insights contribute to a wider understanding of international relations, the relationship between globalization and regionalism and the possibility of cooperation within the developing world.

Jean Grugel is Lecturer in Politics, University of Sheffield, UK. **Wil Hout** is Associate Professor of International Political Economy, University of Nijmegen, The Netherlands.

European Political Science Series

Edited by Hans Keman, *Vrije University, The Netherlands* and Jan W. van Deth, *University of Mannheim, Germany, on behalf of the European Consortium for Political Research*

The European Political Science Series is published in association with the European Consortium for Political Research – the leading organisation concerned with the growth and development of political science in Europe. The series presents high-quality edited volumes on topics at the leading edge of current interest in political science and related fields, with contributions from European scholars and others who have presented work at ECPR workshops or research groups.

Sex Equality Policy in Western Europe
Edited by Frances Gardiner

Democracy and Green Political Thought
Edited by Brian Doherty and Marius de Geus

The New Politics of Unemployment
Edited by Hugh Compston

Citizenship, Democracy and Justice in the New Europe
Edited by Percy B. Lehning and Albert Weale

Private Groups and Public Life
Edited by Jan W. Van Deth

The Political Context of Collective Action
Edited by Ricca Edmondson

Theories of Secession
Edited by Percy B. Lehning

Regionalism Across the North–South Divide
Edited by Jean Grugel and Wil Hout

Also available from Routledge in association with the ECPR:

1. *Regionalist Parties in Western Europe*, edited by Lieven de Winter and Huri Türsan; 2. *Comparing Party System Change*, edited by Jan-Erik Lane and Paul Pennings; 3. *Political Theory of European Constitutional Choice*, edited by Michael Nentwich and Albert Weale; 4. *Politics of Sexuality*, edited by Terrell Carver and Véronique Mottier; 5. *Autonomous Policy-making by International Organisations*, edited by Bob Reinalda and Bertjan Verbeek; 6. *Social Capital and European Democracy*, edited by Jan W. van Deth, Marco Maraffi, Ken Newton and Paul Whiteley.

Regionalism Across the North–South Divide

State strategies and globalization

Edited by Jean Grugel and Wil Hout

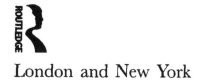

London and New York

First published 1999
by Routledge
2 Park Square, Milton Park, Abingdon, Oxon, OX14 4RN

Simultaneously published in the USA and Canada
by Routledge
270 Madison Ave, New York NY 10016

Transferred to Digital Printing 2006

Typeset in Baskerville by
The Florence Group, Stoodleigh, Devon

British Library Cataloguing in Publication Data
A catalogue record for this book is available
from the British Library

Library of Congress Cataloging in Publication Data
Regionalism across the North–South divide : state strategies in the
   semi-periphery / edited by Jean Grugel and Wil Hout.
      p.   cm.
   Includes bibliographical references and index.
   1. International economic relations. 2. Regionalism.
I. Grugel, Jean. II. Hout, Wil.
HF1359.R433   1998   98–25623
337–dc21   CIP

ISBN 0–415–16212–2 (hbk)
ISBN 0–415–16213–0 (pbk)

Contents

Series editor's preface

The post-war development of inter-state relations can be divided into different episodes. First, the establishment of a bi-polar world with two hegemons (the Soviet Union and the United States) which dominated the world system and the interactions between nation-states. The key concept was military security, which produced an often uneasy type of stability. Second, the emergence of a large number of new states due to decolonisation and of divisions between these states due to the competition between the two hegemons, forming the 'first' and 'second' worlds. In addition to these 'first' and 'second' worlds, a 'third' world came into existence, which was by and large dependent either on the richer capitalist countries or on the established communist states. Political adherence of third-world countries implied their economic dependence on one or other of the more developed 'worlds'. Third, in the wake of the OPEC crisis and the subsequent world-wide economic stagflation, international economic relations changed dramatically and affected all three 'worlds' in one way or another. The longer-term effects of these changes in relations can be observed in various ways: the disintegration of the Communist bloc or 'second world', the moves towards a more unified Europe, and the growing divisions of the third world in the 1980s. All these developments have been conducive to a re-ordering and re-orientation of the components that make up the complexion of the aforementioned three worlds. In other words, the existing world order was slowly reconstructed into a politically multi-polar world in which long-standing coalitions between blocs of states fell apart. This phenomenon is particularly visible in states with developing economies – the 'South' – and has, more often than not, been conducive to the formation of new coalitions between states that cut across the former 'worlds'. According to the editors of *Regionalism Across the North–South Divide*, this makes it imperative that international political economy be approached from a fresh perspective.

This perspective needs to take into account a two-tier development: the emergence of globalisation of the economy with more actors than nation-states alone on the one hand, and the emergence of regionalisation and concurrent regional cooperation between nation-states on the other hand. Such a perspective also implies that international economic relations are not only becoming more complex but also lead to new 'vulnerabilities' of national economies in the wake of a post-Fordist division of labour across the world economy.

In this volume, the contributors aim to shed light on these recent developments by investigating the emergence of regions, the strategic importance of regionalisation and the growing variation in the development of economies in the 'South' of this increasingly globalised society. To this end, the book is divided into two analytical parts. In Part I, the so-called semi-peripheral regions are studied by looking at the actions of the stronger economies of the South that are still dependent economically on the core of the capitalist world (i.e., the OECD-world) and how their strategies may enhance the political economic development of those regions. Part II examines those regions which must be regarded as underdeveloped and are most vulnerable within the world economy.

In essence, there are three factors which appear to direct the economic development of states within the emerging regionalisation of this globalising world economy: élite behaviour within and between nation-states, integration and co-operation within (geographic) areas, and the resulting position of states and regions within the global world market and related political economic hierarchy. These developments, which can be considered as the reconstruction of the world economy at this time, imply not merely a reconfiguration of international relations *per se* but foremost a repositioning of national economies and concurrent state strategies to cope with a globalising economy. This volume addresses these questions thoroughly and comes up with new answers based on evidence drawn from various parts of the world. The overall results are certainly challenging existing knowledge, making this book an important contribution to the study of international political economy.

Hans Keman
Weesp June 1998

Contributors

Marcelo de Almeida Medeiros is a researcher at the *Institut d'Études Politiques* of the University of Grenoble (France).

Daniel C. Bach is the director of the *Centre d'Étude d'Afrique Noire, CNRS–Institut d'Études Politiques*, Montesquieu University, Bordeaux (France).

Shaun Breslin is at the Centre for Globalization at the University of Warwick (UK).

Chris Dixon is professor at the Department of Geography, London Guildhall University (UK).

Mine Eder is a lecturer in the Department of Political Science at Bosphorus University (Turkey).

Jean Grugel is lecturer in the Department of Politics at the University of Sheffield (UK).

Wil Hout is associate professor of international political economy in the Department of Political Science at the University of Nijmegen (The Netherlands).

Derek McDougall is a lecturer in the Department of Political Science at the University of Melbourne (Australia).

David Seddon is professor at the School of Development Studies, the University of East Anglia (UK).

Acknowledgements

This book started out as a European Consortium for Political Research (ECPR) workshop on North–South cooperation directed by Wil Hout and Daniel Bourmaud, held at Bordeaux in April and May 1995. We would like to thank all the participants in that workshop for making it such an intellectually stimulating meeting. After the workshop, the project evolved towards a clear focus on new regionalism. This meant that several of the original contributions to the workshop did not fit in the book, but we would nevertheless like to acknowledge their contribution. Several papers were then commissioned at this stage, and we would like to thank those contributors to this book who adjusted their work to a framework which had already been established. We would also like to thank Caroline Wintersgill, Hans Keman and Patrick Proctor for their support and assistance in getting the book into press. Jean Grugel thanks her colleagues at the Department of Politics, University of Sheffield, and especially those in the regionalism cluster. Tony Payne deserves a special mention for reading sections of the book and discussing many of the ideas in it. Georgina Waylen also read versions of one of the chapters and offered extensive, and helpful, comments on it. Rob Collins and Chris Whittaker were particularly helpful with computers, so thanks to them. AIETI in Madrid, and Chris Feres especially, proved supportive and deserve thanks for assistance with research in Latin America. Most of all, Jean Grugel would like to thank Martin Smith, who not only read some parts of the book but also provided a supportive environment for finishing it. Wil Hout would like to thank the Netherlands' Organization for Scientific Research for providing him with funds as part of the project 'The Formation and Durability of Military and Economic Alliances', and to the British Council and the Netherlands' Organization for Scientific Research for a grant to travel to the University of Sheffield in 1996. He would also like to thank the Political Economy Research Centre (PERC) and the Department of Politics, University of Sheffield, for their hospitality during his stays there.

Part I

Theoretical framework

1 Regions, regionalism and the South

Jean Grugel and Wil Hout

This book examines the trend towards regionalism in the contemporary world order. Until quite recently, studies of regionalism tended to focus on developments in the industrialized areas and/or on the so-called Third World. However, the term 'Third World' has ceased to have much analytical significance and scholars have moved on to examining instead the political economy of an increasingly interconnected global order. As one leading scholar of international political economy has phrased it, a 'main source of academic uncertainty and confusion . . . has been the collapse of the Third World coalition of less developed countries' (Strange 1995: 162). Consequently, the focus of regionalist studies must also change. The concept of the Third World, pictured as a group of countries sharing important developmental features and similar linkages with the international system, needs to be reconfigured on the basis of their links (or absence of) with the industrialized world.

At the same time, the nature of regionalism itself has changed dramatically. The form the 'new regionalism' assumes has tremendous implications for international relations and for development studies. This book makes its contribution to the understanding of new regionalism by analysing regionalist developments and projects in the South. It examines the emergence of regionalism at the North–South interface, the semi-periphery, and within three distinct regions which group together peripheral countries. It tries to make sense of what regionalism means for the South and thereby to contribute to a deeper understanding of international relations, the relationship between the processes of globalization, regionalization and regionalism, the place of the state in international exchanges and the possiblity of cooperation within the developing world.

Developments in the 1990s have meant that region-building projects, as well as sometimes grouping together countries of roughly similar levels of economic development, also emerged between countries from either side of the 'North–South divide'. The form and content regionalism assumes in the South has undergone a radical transformation as economic and political elites, and in some cases sectors of civil society, responded to their changing position in the global order and to the weakening of state capacities in the

South by seeking new partners outside the state. Contemporary regionalism in the developing world is therefore very different from regionalist attempts in the 1950s and 1960s, when it was overwhelmingly political both in its aspirations and its forms. In contrast to that earlier period, 'new regionalism' is principally a defensive response to the economic marginalization of much of the South in the 1980s, its political reconfiguration during the political and economic turmoil at the end of the Cold War, and a fear of, or reaction to, the trend towards a globalized economy. States are the main actors in new regionalist blocs, sometimes responding to demands generated within society, sometimes in response to external pressures, and sometimes as a result of a particular regionalist vision of relatively autonomous state elites.

The book is organized in three sections. Part I provides some background to the changing position in the global order of the South and examines the competing theoretical perspectives on regionalism. This introductory chapter seeks to clarify some of the organizing themes around which the later chapters are constructed. Broadly speaking these are: the impact of globalization on the South; our conceptualization of the South, which we divide into the semi-periphery and the periphery, inspired by a world-system analytical framework; the terms 'region', 'regionalization' and 'regionalism'; and the term 'state strategy', which is used to explain certain regionalist trajectories. Part II looks at politics within some semi-peripheral states and the role they play in building new regions. Part III discusses regional associations within three developing areas, where the *region* is taking on a 'middle position' between the North and South.

Globalization and the South

Over the last decade, scholars of international relations, international political economy, North–South relations and development studies have noted a transformation of international economic relations taking place. The 'stretching' of social, political and economic activities across national frontiers and the 'deepening' of the density of patterns of global interconnectedness are generally referred to as globalization (McGrew 1997: 7). It is unnecessary for our purposes to enter into the debate whether this constitutes a radical break with past forms of global interaction or merely the intensification of certain trends which have long been present within the global political economy. What is not in dispute is that the contemporary forms of economic interconnectedness impinge on the relationship between the state and capital. The global patterns of trade, investment and production, and hence the choices state elites can make and the range of developmental options available, are being reshaped by: the liberalization of financial markets; the spread of information services and the concomitant mobility of service industries; and the shift from a fordist to a post-fordist system of corporate and industrial organization, resulting in the desire of the producers to locate close to the suppliers and their customers.

Globalization theories, though they draw on a variety of different and sometimes contradictory theoretical perspectives, all start from an awareness that knowledge, production and even diplomacy are no longer the exclusive preserve of the inter-state system. The significance of this lies in the fact that, until recently, the state was seen as the only, or at least the key, political actor in the international system. Many authors now seem to agree that, whereas the state remains an important unit of analysis in the study of the international political economy, it no longer can be the sole unit. Apart from the state, so-called inter-governmental, non-governmental and transnational actors merit attention (Strange 1995: 161). Within analyses which attempt to track the consequences of global structural changes, the tendency is to suggest that transnationalized production is leading to changes in the hierarchy of states and the dissolution of borders between states, in so far as they affect production, distribution and economic exchanges generally. New production techniques also contribute to the processes through which new cores and peripheries emerge which do not map directly onto the old state system. Cores and peripheries can now be regions within states or areas that cross state boundaries. Some scholars have mapped these new developments through identifying 'growth triangles', such as the SiJoRi triangle in South East Asia, which spans Singapore, Johore Province in Malaysia and the Riau Archipelago of Indonesia.

The tendency towards globalization is undermining the independent policy-making capacity of the state. But it does not affect the policy-making capacity of all states to the same extent. Globalization is an uneven process (Holm and Sørensen 1995: 4–7). It is to be expected that 'weak states' (Migdal 1988) have less means to hold globalization at bay, whereas 'strong states' may be more able to mitigate the effects of globalization. We agree with Hurrell and Woods (1995: 469) that

> globalization will not lead to the progressive global enmeshment heralded by liberal analysts. Existing inequalities make it more likely that globalization will lead to an increasingly sharp division between 'core' states, which share in the values and benefits of a global world economy and polity, and 'marginalized' states, some of which are already branded 'failed' states.

Thus, it is to be expected that the impact of globalization is greater on less developed countries than on the developed ones. In fact, it has a number of extremely broad-ranging consequences for developing areas. First, it has introduced a strong element of competition between developing countries for investment, the more so as developing states have chosen (or, as some would argue, have been pushed) to adopt neo-liberal, market-friendly macroeconomic and external policies. The 'competition state', identified by Cerny (1990), emerges in developing countries as well as in industrialized ones. Second, globalization may lead to a recomposition of, and renegotiation between, the interests the state represents. Third, the new globalizing tendencies almost certainly add more actors to the policy process, and, it could be argued, increase the power of 'external' actors over state policy. Apart from the state itself, and local groups, pressure may be brought to bear from, *inter alia*, foreign firms, foreign states and multinational agencies. The result may be a reduction in the 'autonomy' of the state and the range of policy instruments it commands. To use Peter Evans' (1995) term, the 'embeddedness' of the state may be reduced as a consequence of the increasing influence of external actors and this may result in a reduction of the developmental role the state is able to play. And fourth, the process of globalization brings into question the extent to which the rigid divisions between North and South, developed and underdeveloped, can be maintained in the face of an emerging global economy. It points to a separation within the South between those states which can adapt to the new global agenda and those which are unable to do so.

Globalization, therefore, would seem to presage a reconfiguration of the South, as the term was understood in the 1970s, and to pave the way for a reconstitution of a new international order in which some of the larger, more advanced states, the semi-periphery, those with an already established productive base, play a key role. According to Hettne (1995a), 'a rather selective group of countries are going to make the transition' to the new rules of the game. It is our contention that one way that semi-peripheral states try to make this transition, and thereby participate within the production structures of the global economy, is through adopting new forms of regional networks which bring in other states and which also lock in multinational producers within the alliance. Peripheral states may also try to participate in new regionalist associations as a way to avoid marginalization. Furthermore, it could be argued that, in an era of increasing globalization in which the international political economy is more dependent on government–firm and firm–firm diplomacy (Stopford and Strange 1991: 19–23), the states in the South will experience a further erosion of their negotiating power *vis-à-vis* transnationally active firms. In this light, the contemporary resurgence of regionalism might be seen as a reaction to the reduced leverage of states in the South. It should also be noted that it is the transformation of the international political economy which has made this new form of regionalism an option, by making it also attractive to some developed states in 'the North'.

The semi-periphery and the periphery

At the original European Consortium for Political Research (ECPR) workshop in 1995 from which this project emerged, a number of international relations and area studies experts posed the question of how the South is responding to the new global agenda of liberalized trade and globalized forms of production. The question was also raised whether the growing tendency towards globalization means that the state in developing countries has completely lost its power to shape national economic policies. While the answers seem to be complex, and to vary from country to country, and region to region, a common theme emerged for several of the states of the South, especially, though not exclusively, for the more industrialized ones: elites within some developing states and areas are trying to develop strategies for cooperation and integration and are seeking participation in some kind of new regional association or cooperation, with trade and investment links at its centre.

Clearly, then, in most developing countries at least, the state has some policy choices to make. To argue this is not to abandon the notions of inequality, stratification and subordination which are, in our view, at the heart of international exchanges and North–South relations. Rather we thought it important to probe how these regionalist strategies, which are seen as options for development, emerge in some Southern states and intersect with structured inequalities and historical patterns of subordination. We decided that it would make sense to focus more deeply on politics and development within some of these states in order to assess their potential as development strategies. In some cases, it made more sense to focus on the *region*, rather than the state, as the unit of analysis, and in these cases we tried to identify the inter-state and social alliances out of which regionalism is emerging.

Chapters 3 to 7 focus on the semi-periphery. It is important to note that we are using this term in a significantly looser way than its original formulation by Wallerstein (1974: 350; 1979: 23). In Wallerstein's world-system theory, the capitalist world economy is composed of a dominant developed core, a subordinate poor periphery and a political and economic 'buffer', called the semi-periphery. He argues that an international division of labour has gradually developed in which some units have come to produce predominantly primary products (agricultural produce and raw materials) while others have been able to develop technologically more sophisticated production processes. Over the last few decades, a 'new international division of labour' has come into being in which the traditional dichotomy between primary production and manufacturing has become blurred and parts of typical core production processes have been transferred to peripheral and semi-peripheral areas. Post-fordist production techniques and the growing importance of knowledge over labour intensify the tendency towards an ever more spatially diffused production.

Wallerstein's original analysis grew out of the study of the rise of the modern capitalist world economy during the 'long sixteenth century'. The semi-periphery was seen as a 'transmission belt' through which flowed the surplus that was syphoned off from the periphery to the core. In this era, the world system was largely undifferentiated. Apart from the European core and semi-peripheral states, a large 'external' area existed, which was only gradually integrated into the world economy. However, as a result of the changes in global production techniques and the dispersal of knowledge, the boundaries within the world system are blurring. Empirical analyses of the world system and its hierarchy have showed that the expectation of a simple trichotomy is not borne out (for example, Smith and White 1992). At the same time, the size of the semi-periphery appears to be growing.

Chase-Dunn (1989: 212) has attempted to overcome these problems by distinguishing analytically between two kinds of semi-peripheries: 'those states in which there is a balanced mix of core and peripheral activities' and 'those areas or states in which there is a predominance of activities which are at intermediate levels with regard to the current world-system distribution of capital-intensive/labour-intensive production'. This is an acknowledgement of the need to encompass analytically the increasing differentiation in the global economy. Quantitative-empirical researchers, such as Smith and White (1992), have, on their part, made a further empirical distinction of the semi-periphery and the periphery into 'strong' and 'weak' parts. The 'strong' semi-periphery is made up of mainly Western countries such as Denmark, Australia, Spain, Ireland and Norway, while the 'weak' semi-periphery is composed of countries such as Brazil, Korea, Thailand and Malaysia, alongside Greece, Portugal and Turkey. The 'strong' semi-periphery corresponds broadly to Chase-Dunn's first category, in which core and peripheral economic activities co-exist, and the 'weak' with his second, in which intermediate levels of capital-intensive/labour-intensive production predominate. Most of the chapters in this book deal with what Smith and White would call the 'weak' semi-periphery.

The level of analysis within the world-system approach remains steadfastly *global*. Phrased differently, the semi-periphery is analysed from the perspective of the *world system*, which remains the focal point and the unit of analysis. The role of the state in the semi-periphery, according to Wallerstein, is that of providing the capitalist world system with the means to function through the creation of a 'buffer zone'. This assumption makes it difficult – or, in some cases, even outright impossible – to understand the political and economic strategies adopted by semi-peripheral states in their own right. We do not deny that semi-peripheral countries may well play the role outlined by Wallerstein, but to make this role the defining characteristic of the state in the semi-periphery is to collapse all activity inside semi-peripheral states into one functionalist category and to deny the state any degree of agency.

So, rather than mechanically applying world-system theory, we have tried to retain some aspects of this theory which are most useful, without going so far with it that it operates as a theoretical straitjacket. As a result, we cast the semi-periphery in less functionalist terms. Our aim is to make the term less theoretically rigid. We use it to describe those states in which manufacturing, industrial or capital-intensive production occurs alongside the production of primary or semi-processed goods and in which there is domestic capital accumulation as well as foreign investment. As a result, the semi-peripheral state is, typically, far more complex in its functions and in the interests it represents than peripheral states, but the range of development choices, and the policy instruments at its disposal, are more constrained and limited than those of core states.

Chapters 8, 9 and 10 deal with smaller states than those in Part II. They have different levels of development and occupy a range of different functions within the world economy. They include the impoverished states of sub-Saharan Africa, the Maghreb states and the South East Asian region, where some states, for example Singapore, are relatively advanced. However, because of their size, their global position and/or their dependence on economic linkages within their region, it makes more sense to analyse the regional level, rather than the level of the state, in order to explain new regionalist outcomes. In the cases of the Maghreb and South East Asia, a focus on the region, rather than the state, allowed the authors to draw attention to the importance of actors from outside the region, whether state or non-state actors, in contributing to the shape of regionalism as it is emerging in the contemporary order. In the case of sub-Saharan Africa, this focus makes possible a discussion of region-building where the state is actually diminishing in sigificance and can no longer fulfil even the basic functions identifed by Weber in the nineteenth century. Hence we might conclude that one of the outstanding characteristics of the periphery, as opposed to the semi-periphery, is the more limited range of resources the state has at its disposal in building external relationships. New regionalism is certainly taking shape; but of the three variables which we identify below as determining regionalist outcomes – the world system, state–society interactions and the policies of other states/regions – the first two, and indeed especially the first, the position in the world system, chiefly accounts for political outcomes.

Regions, regionalism and regionalization

Although territoriality is a *sine qua non* of regions – they cannot exist without having a physical reality – they are not naturally constituted geographical units nor the straightforward 'common-sense' expressions of shared identities. Regions are made and re-made, and their membership and frontiers are decided through political and ideological struggle and the conscious strategies of states and social actors. Like Anderson's (1991) nations, they are above all 'imagined communities', brought into existence by human agency. It follows that their boundaries are not fixed and immutable; who is 'inside' and who 'out' is, above all, a matter of political negotiation. Some of the 'new' regions discussed in this book are being built on the foundations of identity politics of long-standing, for example in the Southern Cone of Latin America; but more are arenas where cultural and political identities, indeed even geography, are hotly disputed. A prior sense of belonging together, therefore, is not the only, or even the major, cause of region-building in the contemporary global order.

We argue that region-building is overwhelmingly the result of a set of strategic calculations by actors located inside states and societies who push for integration as a way of positioning themselves in response to global change. For the smaller, or poorer, states on the periphery, regionalism may sometimes be pushed by external actors and the changing global order more than domestic groups. In both cases, regionalism, as it is conceptualized in the studies in this collection, is a states-led project which has as its aim that of reorganizing particular geo-economic spaces. The role of the state changes – that is, regionalist policies are not static – as the strategies of state and state actors change in response to the demands of globalization and the interests of the groups they represent. This means that we assume that states, and state actors, are a key level of analysis in the global political economy, though not of course the only level of analysis. In some cases, state elites are driving region-building (Turkey); in others, we can identify a coalition between the state and actors from civil society (Chile and Brazil); and in a third set of countries, regionalism is being driven by social interactions across states and the state is trying to catch up and control the integration process (South East Asia and China). We conceptualize regionalism in a way that is analogous to Wyatt-Walter's definition (1995: 77), namely 'as a *conscious policy* of states or sub-state regions to coordinate activities and arrangements in a greater region'.

It is important, therefore, to distinguish regionalism from the historical and social processes of globalization and regionalization, which are not 'state projects but combinations of historical and emergent structures – a complex articulation of established institutions and rules and distinctive new patterns of social interaction between non-state actors' (Gamble and Payne 1996: 250). Regionalization, then, is a *de facto* process, in contrast to regionalism, which is the *formal* establishment of regions as political units. Regionalizaton refers to the regional expression of the global processes of economic integration and the changing structures of production and power. The result is to deepen the integration of particular regional economic spaces. But these spaces may well be different from the region-building projects undertaken by states since they are driven by a production rationale. They are not the result of conscious political projects. Nevertheless, regionalization influences, shapes and constrains the regionalist policies that states undertake. Globalization and regionalization – the processes of structural change at the global and regional level – determine the opportunities and parameters for state policy.

Hence 'new regionalism' derives its importance in the first instance in the context of globalization and regionalization. It is also a response to one of the key elements of the post-Cold War agenda, namely liberalized trade. It thus becomes a way of adapting to the new liberalism and is often described as 'open' regionalism, in order to mark the contrast with the closed nature of the 'old' regionalism in the 1960s which was based on either protectionist policies and the creation of internal markets or upon security communities which were brought together to counter a perceived external threat. For some states under consideration in this book, therefore, policies to promote 'new regionalism' reflect the adoption of conscious strategies to improve their global market position, or, more properly put, the market position of those companies with production sites within their geographical boundaries (for example, China). For others, it reflects a defensive strategy in the context of long-haul economic reform (for example, Brazil). In all cases, building regions is seen as functional for growth.

State strategies

If 'regionalism is a type of state project which can be distinguished from other types of state project' and emerges 'as the outcome of detailed bargaining and negotiation among domestic political actors' (Gamble and Payne 1996: 250), then the logical focus for researching particular forms of regionalism must be the state. Our argument is that region-building is occurring in the semi-periphery as a result, and forms a part, of conscious state strategies for development. But, although we can identify a number of semi-peripheral states and regions which have moved towards accepting new regionalism, they have not done so in the same way. The structural context in which regions are being built are different, the capacities of states vary and different social coalitions push for the adoption of regionalist policies. Hence the outcomes are very different indeed. One of the aims of the book is to illustrate and explain these differences. Our underlying assumption, then, is that state strategies will function as an explanation of new regionalism within the semi-periphery. As we argued above, it may still be of use for smaller developing states, but it must be employed closely in conjunction with a discussion of the world system.

In Part II, where the object of analysis is the state, we suggest that variables from the following three levels of analysis shape these strategies and determine their outcomes:

1 The *world system*, which can be taken as the structure limiting the independent actions of actors (be it states, transnational actors, non-governmental agencies or inter-governmental structures), in which manifestations of power can be of four basic dimensions distinguished by Strange (1988): security, production, finance and knowledge. Both the international division of labour and the inter-state system, as distinguished by Chase-Dunn (1989), can be seen as expressions of the world system at a certain point in time.
2 *State–society interactions*, or the relations between (formal) state structures and social, economic and political groups which emerge over economic and political processes and which vary according to context. Relations within the state in the semi-periphery are a key element towards the explanation of its role in recent regionalist projects. Although

the semi-periphery plays an important role in the functioning of the international division of labour as a whole, we do not interpret the decisions to adopt development strategies or to enter into regional cooperation schemes with core countries as a mere function of its position in the inter-state system. Rather, we see these decisions as the outcome of the political struggle, bargaining and negotiations which take place in each separate semi-peripheral country.

3   The *policies of the other states/regions* with respect to region-building. Domestic politics in the semi-periphery, as indeed throughout the global system, takes place in an environment which is conditioned not only by structural factors but also by the policies which emanate from other states and regional configurations. These, therefore, affect developmental and regionalist strategies.

Nonetheless, we must bear in mind the following:

> Development strategies are packages of policies aimed at steering economic activity into a particular mixture of ownership and sectors. Choosing development strategies as the object of analysis raises methodological problems, however. First, 'strategy' implies a purposiveness of state action that may not exist; imputing a central design requires caution. Strategies emerge by default, trial-and-error, and compromise; take years to crystallize; and are often plagued by internal inconsistency. Second, strategies consist of *packages* of policies. It is useful to disaggregate 'strategies' where possible, since different policies involve different political cleavages and conflicts.
>
> (Haggard 1990: 23)

It is clear from this that caution must be exercised when identifying state strategies. We should not suppose that strategies are successful merely because they exist. The emergence of a state strategy for regionalism does not necessarily imply the policy capacity to implement it. Nor should we assume that they are set in stone; changed priorities or altered alliances within states, and/or change at the global level, will probably result in a renegotiation of policy. Regionalism emerges as sets of state projects intersect (Gamble and Payne 1996: 250); but it may fail to coalesce if no common agreement can be reached. So, although state strategies for regionalism seek to modify or shape the process of globalization and regionalization, it should be borne in mind that they may fail to do so. It follows that not all the attempts at region-building that we identify here are successful. For almost all, it is too early to say with certainty which projects will be successful in the long term. Indeed, precisely what 'successful' means in this context is not completely clear. Does it signify the emergence of a regional bloc? Does it mean the transformation of the structured inequality of North–South relations? Does it mean more development for more people? These are questions which elites which engage in building new regions are themselves trying to answer.

To sum up, this book will suggest that, in the face of the current globalizing tendencies, one strategy which appears to have been taken up by elites and actors in some parts of the South is the adoption of cooperation and integration schemes. That is, the 'new regionalism' can be seen as an attempt by the state and/or domestic actors to impact on and influence the course of globalization within their regional sphere. The nature and effectiveness of their response will partly depend in turn on the position they occupy in the world system and on the policies of other states. Regionalism is conceptually different from regionalization and the pressure from transnationalized firms trying to maximize their market reach or their profitability. Furthermore, our work rejects the idea that state structures in the South are so weakened by globalizing tendencies that the design and implementation of economic and political strategies are impossible. What remains to be analysed, however, is how these strategies are decided upon, how far they constitute an option for development, and what kind of development they suggest.

2 Theories of international relations and the new regionalism

Wil Hout

Traditionally, the study of regionalism in international political and economic relations has been confined predominantly to the highly institutionalized forms of international cooperation among countries in the industrialized world. In the introductory chapter to this book, it was argued that recent changes in the international political economy have increased the importance of new forms of regionalism – most notably those involving developing (peripheral and semi-peripheral) countries, on the one hand, and a mix of developing and industrialized countries, on the other.

This chapter will serve as an overview of theorizing in international relations and international political economy with an eye to regional cooperation. For each of the theories discussed in this chapter, three themes will be focused upon. First, what is the role played by the state in regionalist projects? Second, what are the motivations of the actors that are involved in regionalist projects? Third, what forms of regionalism do the theories expect?

Many authors have indicated that the study of international relations has developed around a core of three dominant theoretical approaches (Holsti 1985; Gilpin 1987). The contemporary versions of these traditional theories are: neo-realism, neo-liberal institutionalism and neo-marxism. These perspectives will be discussed in the following three sections, with a particular view to their interpretation of regionalism.

Partly following upon and partly in reaction to the traditional perspectives on international relations and international political economy, several theories have been formulated in the last two decades. Four of these will be discussed in the subsequent sections, in particular with respect to their applicability to regionalism: world-system theory, the neo-Gramscian world order approach to international political economy, and the rival conceptions of globalism and regional governance. The main findings as to the three themes mentioned above will be summarized in a concluding section.

Neo-realism

Much of the debate on neo-realism has been inspired by Kenneth Waltz's *Theory of International Politics* (Waltz 1979; Keohane 1986; Baldwin 1993).

Waltz tried to develop a structural theory of international relations in which the relations among states (at the so-called systemic level) determine the behaviour of states to an important extent. In Waltz's view, the *distribution of power* is the main determinant of the behaviour of actors in any political system, including the international one. States are constrained in their relations with other states by their relative capabilities *vis-à-vis* these other states. States will try to avoid others becoming too powerful. Balance of power considerations therefore occupy an important place in neo-realist theorizing.

Some neo-realists have recently proposed that *relative-gains* considerations will influence state behaviour. They argue that even if a state is to derive an *absolute* gain from cooperation it will refrain from entering into a cooperative relationship if it expects that its partner will benefit *relatively* more from the relationship and will end up comparatively stronger. According to Joseph Grieco (1990: 220–227), relative-gain arguments are not limited to the realm of 'high politics': the outcomes of regional economic arrangements among both developed and developing countries can best be understood if states are seen as 'defensive positionalists' which are concerned about the distribution of the benefits accruing to the partners in the arrangement.

Robert Gilpin's (1987) hegemonic stability theory posits that cooperation among states is possible, but that a *hegemon*, a predominant state, is a prerequisite. When applied to regionalist arrangements, the hegemonic leadership thesis expects

> regionalism [to develop] more fully in those areas of the world in which there is a local hegemon able to create and maintain regional economic institutions, and . . . regionalism [to advance] at a less pronounced pace in those areas where local hegemonic leaderhip is less visible.
>
> (Grieco 1997: 173; cf. Lieshout 1992)

Neo-realist accounts of the role of semi-peripheral and peripheral countries tend to stress the conflictual nature of politics in the South when compared to relations among industrialized countries (cf. Goldgeier and McFaul 1992). One recent neo-realist analysis of alliance formation in developing countries stresses that the elites of developing countries prefer to form alliances with those of more developed countries. Levy and Barnett (1992: 23) have argued that many Southern countries lack the economic resources and domestic legitimacy that are needed to defend themselves adequately: 'there is an incentive for political leaders to ally with an economically more powerful state that might provide scarce resources, which, in turn, might help resolve internal economic and political problems'. In their view, security threats often stem from 'weaknesses in the domestic political economy' rather than from 'more narrowly defined and autonomously generated political threats' (Levy and Barnett 1992: 23). Alliances can provide developing countries with economic resources, military equipment and expertise they could not mobilize otherwise.

Along the lines suggested by Levy and Barnett, Steven David (1991) has proposed the theory of 'omnibalancing'. This theory agrees with the balance of power theory that states will try to resist threats from other states. The theory of omnibalancing 'departs from balance of power in explaining Third World alignment decisions as a result of the Third World leadership's need to counter *all* threats', no matter whether these threats stem from external or internal sources (David 1991: 233). In David's view, Southern politicians will try to appease 'secondary' adversaries so that they can focus their resources on their 'prime' adversaries (David 1991: 235). The conditions in developing countries are often such that primary threats are *domestic* and secondary threats are international. Therefore, politicians from these countries will often try to 'appease the international allies of their domestic opponents' (David 1991: 236).

On the basis of the literature reviewed in this section, it can be concluded that neo-realist theorizing leads to three expectations concerning regionalism. First, neo-realists expect that regionalist arrangements among countries in the (semi-)periphery or between these and developed countries will be predominantly security-related, and that the focus will be on warding off threats (internal or external). As was the case during the Cold War, such arrangements may result in military support in order to secure the country's allegiance in the global superpower contest. As in more recent cases – for instance, French involvement in African countries – the support may be motivated by the wish to protect economic interests in the country concerned. Second, neo-realists expect that the existence of a regional 'hegemonic' state will greatly facilitate the creation of regionalist arrangements, either because the dominant power will impose cooperation or because it will bear a disproportionate part of the burden of the arrangement involved. Third, and most importantly in regions without a clear hegemon, neo-realists argue that regionalist arrangements will be evaluated on the basis of the relative gains accruing to the different partners in the arrangement. In those regions where the distribution of power is not skewed in favour of a hegemon, regionalist arrangements that lead to disproportionate benefits for one or more of the partners will be opposed by states that fear that they will suffer a relative loss.

Neo-liberal institutionalism

Neo-liberal institutionalist approaches to international relations place much more stress on cooperation among states than do neo-realist ones. As Keohane and Nye (1977) have argued in their seminal formulation of the neo-institutionalist perspective, the international political economy is characterized by *complex interdependence*: in their view, the extent of dependence, and consequently the power, of states varies according to the issue area involved. Neo-liberals tend to see cooperation among states as the rule, rather than the exception, especially in those areas where policy coordination is necessary to realize the procurement of public goods, such as stable monetary relations, free trade or sustainable ecological development.

Neo-institutionalists assume that *regimes* – 'sets of implicit or explicit principles, norms, rules, and decision-making procedures around which actors' expectations converge in a given area of international relations' (Krasner 1983: 2) – exert substantial influence on the policies of governments. Neo-institutionalists do not accept the neo-realist claim that the existence of a hegemon is a necessary condition for the establishment of regimes. According to Keohane (1984: 78), the creation and maintenance of regimes depends, first and foremost, on the existence of shared interests.

The 'density' of 'policy spaces' is seen as an additional factor in explaining the decision to form international regimes. In a dense policy space, different issues will be closely linked, and decisions on one issue will have implications for other issues. In such a case, the creation of a regime can be seen as an efficient solution, for it will reduce the coordination costs involved in determining the effects of different agreements on one another. In Keohane's view, regimes are a reaction to so-called 'political market failures', which are interpreted as 'institutional deficiencies that inhibit mutually advantageous cooperation' (1984: 85).

Stephen Krasner (1985) has argued that the creation and modification of regimes offer possibilities for states from the periphery and the semi-periphery to influence the outcome of international political and economic relations. In particular, Krasner argues, non-core states will try to minimize the working of the market mechanism in selected issue areas and replace it with 'authoritative' allocation through international regimes. Thus, (semi-)peripheral states are engaged in a 'structural conflict' with the countries from the core, which tend to prefer market-based allocation, to change the 'rules of the game' in certain international political and economic issue-areas.

In the same vein, neo-liberal institutionalists tend to see regionalist arrangements as regimes through which the allocation of certain public goods can be established. In the case of the establishment of regimes that include countries from the core and from the (semi-)periphery, countries from the latter group hope to establish a 'double-bind' instrument through which they can obtain preferential entrance to core countries, on the one hand, and can try to set limits on the policies of these countries, on the other.

The specific expectations of neo-institutionalists as to different regionalist projects show considerable variation, which makes it more difficult to generalize than in the case of neo-realism. So-called *neo-functionalist theory*, which has been developed most clearly with respect to European integration (for example, Haas 1958), assumed that problems of increasing interdependence would lead governments to cooperation. Haas and others expected that policy coordination would spread from one issue area to another and the 'spill-over' effect would result in deepening integration.

Andrew Moravcsik's liberal intergovernmentalist approach to regionalism[1] starts out from the idea that explanations of international policy

coordination need to incorporate a theory of 'national preference formation' as well as a theory of 'intergovernmental negotiation' (1994: 36; cf.
Keohane 1993: 294–295). According to Moravcsik (1994: 43), neo-institutionalist theories of policy coordination need to take explicit account of
domestic political factors. Moravcsik argues that the level of interaction
among governments is undoubtedly important, but the possibility of
negotiating intergovernmental agreements is heavily dependent on the preferences of national social groups that either benefit from or are hurt by
these agreements.

An approach similar to Moravcsik's can be found in the work of Helen
Milner. In this approach, regionalism is perceived as the result of the
'demand' of domestic groups and the 'supply' by states of regional arrangements. Thus, the pressure for regional trade arrangements grows when
firms are more dependent on export, the level of multinational activity
of firms increases or the composition of trade shifts from inter- to intra-
industry trade (Busch and Milner 1994: 268–269). Also, firms that benefit
from economies of scale will tend to press for the creation of regional free
trade arrangements (Milner 1997: 80–86).

On the basis of this overview of neo-institutionalist literature, two main
conclusions can be formulated that are important for the study of regionalism. First, neo-institutionalists expect regional arrangements to be
negotiated in those situations where states have clearly defined common
interests – usually brought about by a high level of interdependence – in
creating mechanisms for policy coordination. Such regional arrangements
are seen as necessary to procure a public good or avert negative externalities resulting from interdependence. Second, neo-institutionalists tend to
stress the influence of (domestic) social groups, on whose support politicians
depend. Authors working in this theoretical perspective typically argue that
the creation of regionalist arrangements cannot be understood when the
pressure from domestic actors is not taken into account.

Neo-marxism

There is a wide variety of neo-marxist theories of international relations,
most of which deal with imperialism in one way or another. Most neo-
marxist theories draw heavily on classical theories of imperialism. Imperialism
is taken to be the domination (and exploitation) of one country or area by
actors from another country.

Most variants of the neo-marxist theory of imperialism have focused on
processes that are taking place in the developed, capitalist countries, and
ascribe the policies of these countries' governments to developments inherent
to the capitalist mode of production. According to neo-marxist interpretations, the capitalist mode of production will result in a downward pressure
on wages, because capital owners try to increase the margin of profit on
their investments. Moreover, it is assumed that this mode of production is

characterized by a trend towards the concentration of capital: as capitalism develops, firms tend to become bigger, as a result both of the accumulation of capital and of the take-over of and merger with other firms. This results in what Baran and Sweezy (1966), among others, have called *monopoly capital*.

International exploitation has been analysed predominantly in terms of the syphoning off by external actors of economic surplus produced in developing countries. On the one hand, Paul Baran (1957) has stressed the appropriation of surplus by foreign investors, who repatriate the profits. On the other hand, Arghiri Emmanuel (1972) has analysed the structurally disadvantageous effect of international trade on the developing countries as a process of *unequal exchange*. His central argument is that the value of commodities on the international market is formed in a different way from that on national markets, since labour, in contrast to capital, is relatively immobile across borders. In Emmanuel's view, the disproportionate inequality of wages, as compared to the value of labour power embodied in commodities, leads to a transfer of surplus from the developing to the industrialized countries.

Johan Galtung (1971) has described imperialism as a *structural* relationship between countries from the centre and periphery. He has described the relationship between the European Community (EC) and the developing world in terms of 'collective colonialism' (1973: 73; 1976). First of all, Galtung argues that the EC has created and supported a vertical division of labour: the former colonies of EC member states serve as providers of raw materials, labour and markets, while the EC countries supply capital and knowledge in the form of multinational corporations' investments and research. Second, EC policy is aimed at fragmenting the South: the EC enters into separate trade agreements with different groups of developing countries, such as the so-called African, Caribbean and Pacific (ACP) countries in the Yaoundé and Lomé treaties and the associated states. Finally, the EC tries to penetrate the developing world by forcing its 'Eurocentric' formula of development onto the local elites (Galtung 1973: 59).

Constantine V. Vaitsos's (1978, 1982) work on multinational corporations and regionalism bears a close relation with Galtung's. Vaitsos has argued that the activities of multinationals will, in many cases, impede effective regional cooperation among developing countries. Faced with attempts to establish regionalist cooperation schemes, multinational corporations will typically react negatively:

> First, they wish to avoid host government action which 'externalizes integration' by creating common fronts on the treatment of foreign factor inflows and on governmental intervention in industrial planning and control over the range of goods to be produced, the geographic allocation and composition of resources, and the structure of consumption patterns. Secondly, they wish to avoid a government induced rationalization of the structure of production. Thirdly, they attempt to

block integration among medium-size or large countries since, nowadays at least, multiple, parallel foreign subsidiaries – which often belong to the same parent TNE [transnational enterprises] – already operate in those countries.

(Vaitsos 1982: 10)

Two conclusions may be drawn about the position of neo-marxist scholars on regionalism. First, the creation of regionalist arrangements of the type that is studied in this book can be interpreted in the context of the more general neo-marxist understanding of imperialism, involving the subordination of the periphery and the semi-periphery to the interests of the core, for instance with respect to trade and investment opportunities. Such regionalism will have the intention of dividing the developing countries, by entering into distinct arrangements for different groups. Second, multinational corporations, which are considered to be crucial actors of capitalism, will try to block the establishment of regionalist schemes among developing countries, because of the risk that such schemes would place these countries in too powerful a position *vis-à-vis* international capital.

World-system theory

World-system theory is commonly associated with the work of a wide range of scholars, the best-known of whom are, for instance, Immanuel Wallerstein, Christopher Chase-Dunn and Giovanni Arrighi. As has been argued elsewhere (Hout 1993: 6–7), world-system theory has clear roots in the theories of dependency that were developed in the 1960s and 1970s.

World-system theory posits that, over the last few centuries, a system has come into being that can be categorized as a *capitalist world economy*. The system is a world system because it contains a single division of labour (which has expanded since the sixteenth century and now comprises all known parts of the world) and multiple cultural systems. It is capitalist in that it is based on production for the world market. It is a world *economy* because there is not one political structure that controls the worldwide division of labour (Wallerstein 1974: 347–348). In Wallerstein's view, the fact that there has never been one power centre that was successful in unifying the capitalist world economy into a single political system is the prime explanation of capitalism's persistence.

According to Wallerstein, the semi-periphery plays a very important political role: because it occupies a slightly better position in the world economy than the rest of the periphery 'it partially deflect[s] the political pressures which groups primarily located in peripheral areas might otherwise direct against core-states and the groups which operate within and through their state machineries' (Wallerstein 1974: 350). The fragmentation of the world system into separate political units enables economic transactions to take place on the basis of competition. If the system were to be transformed into one political unit – and thus become a *world empire* – decisions would be taken on political grounds, thereby giving rise to a redistributive instead of a productive economic order (Wallerstein 1984: 4).

A recent extension of world-system theory is what has come to be called the *commodity-chain approach* (Gereffi and Korzeniewicz 1990, 1994; Gereffi 1995). The idea behind the approach is that production and international trade have led to 'the emergence of a global manufacturing system in which production capacity is dispersed to an unprecedented number of developing as well as industrialized countries' (Gereffi and Korzeniewicz 1990: 45). Industrialization and core status are no longer synonymous because of the dispersion of parts of the commodity chain – 'a network of labor and production processes whose end result is a finished commodity' (Hopkins and Wallerstein 1986: 159) comprising raw material supply, production, export and retail marketing – across the world. Economic activity in the countries of the core tends to shift to the service sector and to technologically sophisticated parts of manufacturing, both of which produce relatively high value-added products. The semi-periphery, and certainly the periphery, tend to end up with the comparatively low value-added activities.

The further development of commodity chains should have a regionalizing effect. Arrighi (1994: 347–348) has argued that this process will involve a change of the 'space-of-flows' – the realm of economic transactions – to include new parts of the world and result in a new 'regime of accumulation'. Examples of the regionalization of economic activities are the creation of new types of *maquiladora* plants in Mexico in the 1980s, the formation of export-processing zones (EPZs) in other countries in Latin America and the Caribbean, and the creation of 'triangle manufacturing' in the 1970s and 1980s involving US buyers, manufacturers from the newly industrializing economies (NIEs) and affiliated offshore companies in low-wage countries (Gereffi 1995: 118, 134–135, 138). With respect to East Asia, Mitchell Bernard and John Ravenhill (1995: 183) have argued that

> we may now speak of *regionalized* manufacturing activity in a number of industries. . . . It is the interaction between firms linked by chains of production, exchange, and distribution that now constitutes the basic organizational 'unit'. Firms, or even decentralized divisions within firms, maintain a degree of autonomy in the production chain, but all significant activity is in some way coordinated with other organizations in the network.

Thus, the position of world-system scholars is that changes in the international division of labour make possible regionalist arrangements. Such changes lead to the effective *regionalization* of economic activities, with the creation of new ways of accumulation in the form of production networks, export-processing zones and the like. The interpretation of regionalization and regionalism is no exception to the more general argument of world-system theory, which sees political arrangements predominantly in terms of the function that they have for the process of accumulation.

Neo-Gramscian theories of world order

The neo-Gramscian world order approach is associated most clearly with the work of Robert W. Cox (1981, 1987, 1995) and Stephen Gill (1995a, 1995b). The fundamental assumption in this approach is that production and the social relations deriving from production are crucial to the building of political power, the formation of state structures, and world orders. States are central to Cox's analysis because they, in conjunction with the structure of the world political economy, are 'coordinators and regulators' (Cox 1987: 103) of social relations of production. The actual forms the state will take is dependent on the so-called historic bloc, 'the configurations of social forces upon which state power ultimately rests' (Cox 1987: 105). The inter-relationship between forms of states and social groups is what Cox has called the 'state–society complex' (Cox 1981). A world order 'consists of a relatively persistent pattern of ideas, institutions and material forces which form historical structures over time, where structures can transcend particular societies or civilizational forms, in both space and time' (Gill 1995b: 68).

Cox comes quite close to world-system theory in his explanation of world order. In his view, the modern state system and the world economy developed together since the fifteenth or sixteenth century. Cox (1987: 107) has distinguished several periods in the history of the world economy. During the age of mercantilism international economic relations were heavily influenced by political boundaries. The *Pax Britannica*, which came into being during the nineteenth century, was a period in which Great Britain, the 'hegemonic state' at the time, allowed the world economy to become autonomous from the states and thereby caused economic laws to become constraints on state policies. The period of the *Pax Americana*, starting at the end of the Second World War, has been characterized by a 'trans-nationalization' of the organization of production. In this period, Cox argues, international production and finance has presented both constraints on and opportunities for states.

Recent changes in the world order, according to Cox (1987: 298–308), concern the abandonment of multilateral regulation of the world economy and a concomitant increase of competition, first in military–strategic relations, and later also in the economic realm with respect to raw materials, capital goods and manufactures. States are pressed, by different domestic groups, to adopt 'offensive strategies' in world markets in order to help national industries obtain a larger share of foreign markets, and to implement protective measures in order to shield companies from international competition. The changes in the contemporary world order are manifested in an 'ontological shift', a change of the way the world is conceived

(Cox 1995: 36), which leads to, among other consequences, a restructuring of global society under the influence of economic globalization. This implies that 'the market appears to be bursting free from the bonds of national societies, to subject global society to its laws' (Cox 1995: 39).

Stephen Gill has interpreted the changes that were identified by Cox as 'a shift towards a neo-liberal, disciplinary world order' (Gill 1995b: 69), based on 'a neoliberal discourse of governance that stresses the efficiency, welfare, and freedom of the market, and self-actualisation through the process of consumption' (Gill 1995a: 401). The discipline imposed by neoliberalism, Gill argues, leads to an emphasis on economic deregulation, the combating of inflation, the reduction of state activities and cuts of government expenditure, on the one hand, and to a 'new constitutionalism', on the other. This 'new constitutionalism' is seen as a political effort, 'especially by the forces of the right and those of neo-classical economists and financial capital' (Gill 1995b: 78), to establish rules and institutions that would promote the policies desired by firms and capital owners. Examples of such rules and institutions are the conditionalities and structural adjustment programmes imposed by the IMF and the World Bank, regional arrangements such as the North American Free Trade Area (NAFTA) and the European Union (EU), and the regulatory framework of the World Trade Organization (Gill 1992, 1995a: 412). Regionalism is perceived by Gill (1995b: 72) as a way in which 'the autonomy of even the most powerful states [is] subordinated to the interests of large capital and a *rentier* view of monetary policy', as in the EU, or as a means 'to "politically lock in" neo-liberal reforms', as with the creation of NAFTA. A similar position has been assumed by W. Andrew Axline (1995: 33), who argues that

> [s]trategic regionalism, as embodied in NAFTA and the other blocs, provides a regional mechanism for insertion into the global economy. But it also serves as the mechanism for globalizing the neo-liberal ideology that defines the form and direction of sub-regional policies chosen for this insertion.

Andrew Gamble and Anthony Payne (1996: 249) have argued that regionalism, defined as a state-led project to reorganize the political and economic relations in a certain area, has been on the rise in recent times as a consequence of the decline of US hegemony, the world economic recession and the increase of globalization. In their view, regionalism is witness to the fact that a global hegemony around one state is no longer possible. Gamble and Payne expect that the 'weight' of regional cores will enhance the asymmetry of relations and that a deepening of integration will result in increased polarization. They argue that the 'ideological hegemony' of regional economic great powers such as Japan and the US will remain limited, because their dominance is based more on traditional power differences than on moral or political leadership.

Thus, regionalism appears to have a clear meaning for the neo-Gramscian world order theorists. Regionalist arrangements are seen as instruments that promote the interests of distinct state–society complexes, most notably those in the US, Western Europe and Japan. These interests are not perceived as completely homogeneous, although some authors, most notably Stephen Gill, have argued that regionalist arrangements serve to discipline other actors (such as states, business groups and social actors) and force them to subscribe to the principles of deregulation and limited state interference in economic activity. Seen from this perspective, regionalism is a tool for achieving the regional 'hegemony' of neo-liberal economic principles. In order to serve their own economic interests, the political–economic elites in the semi-periphery will try to 'lock in' the semi-peripheral economy with that of the core.

Globalism

One of the staunchest exponents of *globalism* is undoubtedly the Japanese author and former management consultant Kenichi Ohmae (1985, 1995). His view on economic relations at the end of the twentieth century is based on the assumption that economic ties across the world have become so strong that political boundaries have lost much of their meaning. To an important extent, Ohmae's world view conforms to what Björn Hettne (1995b: 8–9) has termed the 'fundamentalist liberal perspective', according to which 'change is the transformation of an incomplete world economy still regulated by political actors into a fully integrated and self-regulating world economy'.

According to Ohmae, the dominant force in the contemporary era is *globalization*, which is bringing about a 'borderless' economy. The forces behind this process of globalization are believed to be 'the irreversible effects of technology – in particular, modern information technology – on the structure of business processes and on the values, judgements, and preferences of citizens and consumers in all parts of the world' (Ohmae 1995: vii).

Ohmae sees the nation-state as an antiquated political instrument that can only get in the way of economic actors without contributing much to their performance. The influence of politics on the economy is particularly nefarious for Ohmae: politics means serving vested interests and opposing change, especially where market liberalization, privatization and deregulation are concerned. In many respects, for Ohmae, politics is Mancur Olson's (1982) 'distributional coalition' writ large: 'What began as a system to serve, fairly, the interests of the people inexorably becomes little more than a system to conserve centralized power' (Ohmae 1995: 52, 54).

John Naisbitt (1994: 43) has followed in the footsteps of Olson and Ohmae as he envisages the 'end of politics', amounting to the obsolescence of '[t]he idea that the central government – one huge mainframe – is the most important part of governance'. Naisbitt considers the new forms of regionalism as building blocks of global free trade: 'What is evolving around the world is not protectionist trading blocs designed to isolate any given region from the rest of the international players, but economic alliances that promote development within regions, while making all borders more porous' (Naisbitt 1994: 234).

Along the lines set out by Olson, Naisbitt argues that the examples of the Association of South East Asian Nations Free Trade Area (AFTA), the Common Market of the South (MERCOSUR) and NAFTA will show politicians and the general public alike that a country's economic well-being does not hamper another's wealth: they will come to realize that '[t]he global economy is not a zero-sum game, but an expanding universe' (Naisbitt 1994: 243).

Regional governance approaches

A growing number of scholars brought together here under the tentative label of regional governance take a position opposite to globalism. Without exception the scholars grouped here share a normative concern about the purported tendencies towards globalization, which, they feel, undermines the political – often democratically legitimated – process aimed at regulating society. Moreover, some scholars are worried about the potential implications of the further globalization of economic activities on the national state, which is still seen by many people as the prime object of political allegiance.

A rather idealistic position on regionalist governance can be found in the work of world-order advocate Richard Falk. According to Falk (1995: 12), regionalism could ideally serve as a means of 'mitigating pathological anarchism', which results from the claims of national sovereignty by national states over their respective territories, or as a complement to global governance in the United Nations system. Because of the resilience of national states, however, a more promising avenue for Falk (1995: 13) appears to be 'positive regionalism', which has resulted – 'of course, in Europe, but also in Asia-Pacific, Latin America, Africa and the Middle East' – in the protection of human rights, the resolution of conflicts, the promotion of environmental policies and the protection against deteriorating standards of living and economic marginalization. Falk (1995: 14) argues that

> [f]rom a world order perspective the role of regionalism is to help create a new equilibrium in politics that balances the protection of the vulnerable and the interests of humanity as a whole (including future generations) against the integrative, technological dynamic associated with globalism.

Charles Oman (1994: 99), the head of the OECD's Development Centre, has pointed out that regionalist arrangements might supply the instruments of policy coordination for developing countries, which are required in order to mitigate the potentially negative effects of increasing competition for foreign investment. Moreover, regionalist cooperation can serve as an instrument to limit the influence of domestic special-interest groups in developing countries by enlarging the domestic market and stimulating competition. Thus, regionalism might strengthen the effectiveness and credibility of the state in developing countries (Oman 1994: 15, 99).

To date, Paul Hirst and Grahame Thompson (1992, 1996) are the most outspoken supporters of regionalist governance.[2] They argue that the marked inequality of the contemporary international economy contrasts sharply with the assumptions of globalists such as Ohmae. According to Hirst and Thompson (1996: 53), the international economy is oligopolistic, with strategic alliances characterizing relations among multinational companies. Moreover, trade and investment are highly concentrated in the 'triad' of North America, Europe and Japan. They, therefore, expect that a trilateral regime will prevail, based on the three main blocs and supported by a system of 'minilateralism': 'bilateral negotiations that are emerging between the three main players on important issues, and between them and other minor players' (Hirst and Thompson 1996: 129). The main issues will be the maintenance of the international financial regime, trade relations, investment and labour migration, economic development and economic transition.

Regionalist arrangements have, in the view of Hirst and Thompson, an important role to play in the governance of the open international economy, alongside multilateral, national and regional (that is, sub-national) attempts at regulation. Such governance is needed, because markets alone cannot provide the levels of 'interconnection and coordination' that are necessary to ensure the functioning of today's complex international division of labour. Regionalist projects, such as the EU and NAFTA, 'are large enough to pursue social and enivironmental objectives in a way that a medium-sized nation state may not be able to do independently, enforcing high standards in labour market policies or forms of social protection' (Hirst and Thompson 1996: 121). Futhermore, they consider the EU to be 'the most ambitious project of multinational economic governance in the modern world' (1996: 153). In their view, it should be willing to take up economic governance for the European continent as a whole. By pursuing a 'continental Keynesianism', the EU countries can keep the wealth gap from growing, both in the EU and in the wider Europe, and can thus prevent the intensification of conflicts and the growth of migration (Hirst and Thompson 1996: 163).

On the basis of the 'regionalist governance' literature discussed in this section, several conclusions can be drawn about its perceptions of regionalism. First, politics and the national state are still seen as highly relevant objects of study. It is felt that the regulation of markets has remained a necessity, because the increase of internationalization has produced a higher level of interdependence and has, thus, increased the need for international policy coordination. States remain important, because they are still the major objects of political allegiance and are the only practically effective way to organize popular control over policy-making. Second, authors who stress the need for regional governance tend to see regionalist arrangements as instruments for national states to protect their political autonomy with respect to market forces. Third, regionalism can be interpreted as a means to 'pool' political resources and 'upgrade' the national interest of the cooperating states, in a way that would not be possible when the states decide to go it alone.

Conclusion

Seven contemporary theoretical approaches in international relations and international political economy have been analysed with respect to their views on regionalism. From the overview, it is clear that contemporary theories of international relations and international political economy contain highly different assumptions and expectations about these three themes, so that it is not unwarranted to speak about seven different *images of regionalism.* These images are summarized in Table 2.1.

The authors of this book will not attempt to 'test' the theories presented here. Rather, the theories are seen as analytical tools that highlight central features and regularities of the international political and economic order. The theoretical perspectives under discussion here are not able to offer full explanations of the topic of this book, new regionalism across the North–South divide. First, the developing world appears to be almost completely absent from most theories as a theoretical category. More often than not, there is hardly any acknowledgement of the fact that the countries from the South occupy a position structurally different from that of many other states. Second, most theories do not recognize the changing meaning of regionalism in the present era. Most see this phenomenon as cooperation among sovereign territorial entities, and do not appreciate the extent to which regional relations among states and other relevant actors are in a state of flux.

Despite these obvious shortcomings of the theories, we argue that it is very useful to study theories alongside peforming empirical analyses. To an important extent, the study of empirical processes informs theory, just as much as theory offers the tools to interpret the world. The academic study of international relations and international political economy should benefit from empirical insights, if only to broaden the scope of its understanding of international reality.

Notes

1   Actually, Moravcsik (1994: 32) has presented his approach as a critique of neo-functionalism, which 'lacked a theoretical core clearly enough specified to provide a sound basis for precise empirical testing and improvement'.
2   The summary of Hirst and Thompson's approach relies heavily on Hout (1997: 102–104).

Table 2.1 Images of regionalism

	Role of (semi-peripheral) state in regionalist projects	Motivations of actors involved in regionalist projects	Expected forms of regionalism
Neo-realism	The existence of a (regional) hegemon will enhance the success of regionalist projects.	State interest is the primary interest. Entry into regionalist projects is subject to 'relative-gain' considerations.	Mainly security-related forms of regionalism. Other forms will be evaluated in terms of future security (relative gains).
Neo-institutionalism	The state will act as a negotiator at the inter-governmental level, limited by national political considerations.	Procurement of public good, avoidance of negative externalities from interdependence.	Regionalism as the creation of institutions and regimes for policy coordination.
Neo-marxism	Subordinate *vis-à-vis* industrialized countries.	Exploitation of the developing countries. Maintenance of the privileged position of the industrialized countries.	Regionalism that enhances the role of the 'market' and institutionalizes unequal exchange and investment relations.
World-system theory	Subordinate to the core, but playing a political 'buffer' role. Taking in a middle position in the division of labour.	Make possible new forms of capital accumulation. Adapt the international division of labour to new needs.	'Market-led' regionalism, subordinate to the creation of regional production networks.
Neo-Gramscian world order approach	The semi-peripheral state will be the instrument to 'lock in' the semi-peripheral economy with the core.	Achievement of hegemony of the neo-liberal principles of economic order.	Regionalism as a disciplinary tool for the achievement of deregulation and limited government interference in the economy.
Globalism	Declining role of the state as compared to transnational actors. State as an essentially conservative force.	Regionalist projects are a counterweight to 'distributional coalitions'.	Regionalism will stimulate regional free trade and will be a building block towards globalization.
Governance approach	State is the prime mover in politics, the central unit of decision-making. State is the object of political allegiance.	Regionalist projects are attempt to protect values and maintain state autonomy *vis-à-vis* economic forces.	Regionalism as a programme to 'upgrade' the national interest by grouping with likeminded states.

Part II

State strategies and the semi-periphery

3 Australia and regionalism in the Asia-Pacific

Derek McDougall

The purpose of this chapter is to consider the way in which Australia's involvement in Asia-Pacific regionalism has been related to the country's own changing political and economic circumstances. Given the framework of the book, it starts off by examining briefly the extent to which Australia can be seen as part of the semi-periphery. It then looks more specifically at the way in which Australia's position in the world has changed in more recent times. Finally it discusses Australia's approach to regionalism as part of a strategy which has emerged for dealing with its changed position. Essentially the argument presented is that the increased emphasis on regionalism in Australia's international strategy is very much related to the country's changing political and economic circumstances. Australian regionalism, however, needs to be seen in the context of a number of other strategies which have been adopted or considered within the state. At a domestic level these have included various attempts to make the economy more internationally competitive. At an international level Australia joined with other 'like-minded' agricultural free traders in the Cairns Group and has also seen some potential in pursuing bilateralism with its major trading partners. The focus, here, however, is on the strategy of regionalism. Although there have been differences of emphasis among various groups in society, these have been largely to do with the appropriate combination of policies through which to achieve a set of goals which, in themselves, have been widely supported.

Australia as part of the semi-periphery

As a Western country on the edge of Asia, Australia has often been seen as an anomaly in world politics. This is also true in relation to its economic position, where Australia combines high living standards with a structure of exports which is similar to that of many Third World countries. In terms of the world-systems approach, with its division into core, periphery and semi-periphery, Immanuel Wallerstein (1979: 100) has written that the latter category 'includes the old white Commonwealth: Canada, Australia, South Africa, possibly New Zealand'. According to one characterization of the world-systems approach (Lange 1985: 186–187), the location of a state in relation to these categories is determined by the following broad criteria: 'gross national product (GNP) per capita; the structure of national production; the structure of trade; the class structure; the wage structure; and patterns of development and political response under conditions of world economic crisis'.

The semi-periphery has an intermediate position between the core and the periphery in relation to these various criteria. Wallerstein (1979: 23) suggests that this economic role has a political purpose in the sense that it reduces the polarization which would otherwise exist between the core and the periphery. Semi-peripheral countries have a bridge-building function which ultimately works to the economic benefit of the core, but can also be seen in the way in which those countries identify with the core on a range of more general political issues.

Whereas Wallerstein sees the semi-periphery in terms of its intermediate role, Chase-Dunn has suggested that the semi-periphery should be seen in terms of two possibilities: a weak and a strong semi-periphery (Chase-Dunn 1989: 210–214). The weak semi-periphery does conform to Wallerstein's definition in having an intermediate level of economic activities. In the case of the strong semi-periphery, it has a mixture of both core and periphery activities.

In terms of this categorization, Australia is part of the strong semi-periphery. It is core in the sense of having a high per capita income. It is more akin to the periphery in that its export income derives largely from the export of raw materials going predominantly to core countries. At the same time, Australia, like core countries, does have a complex economy, including a significant manufacturing sector. Politically, it has also identified with the core for the most part, originally with Britain and in the period since the Second World War with the United States. Within the Asia-Pacific, Australian governments have seen themselves playing an important role alongside the core Western countries.

Australia's changing political and economic circumstances

Having developed as six separate British colonies during the nineteenth century, Australia became a federation within the British Empire in 1901. The economy was based largely on the export of primary produce such as wool, wheat and beef, and also minerals such as gold, copper, silver, lead and zinc. Britain was Australia's major trading partner and source of investment.

In the post-1945 period, Australia became more open to developing its economic links with the Pacific region. While initially Britain remained as Australia's single most important trading partner, the development of the trading relationship with Japan in particular assumed increasing importance.

However, insofar as Japan can be seen as part of the core, what was involved was a change in the direction of Australia's trade, rather than a weakening of Australia's role as part of the strong semi-periphery. In 1949–50 the UK took 38.7 per cent of Australian exports and provided 51.9 per cent of Australian imports; Japan took 4 per cent of Australian exports in that year and provided a negligible proportion of Australian imports. However, by 1974–5 Japan absorbed 27.6 per cent of Australian exports as compared to 5.5 per cent for the UK; in the same year Japan provided 17.6 per cent of Australian imports and the UK 15.0 per cent (Higgott 1989: 140–141). Australian exports were still predominantly agricultural products and minerals. Australian coal and iron ore were important for Japan's economic development at this time.

Apart from the diversification occurring in Australia's pattern of trade, there was also more emphasis given to the development of manufacturing industry. Historically, protection had developed not just as a means of assisting manufacturing industry, but also as a way of ensuring the continued maintenance of high living standards. In a sense it was a device to spread the benefits of Australia's high earnings from agricultural and mineral exports to the population at large. Tariff levels were increased significantly during the Depression of the 1930s, and in subsequent decades Australia had one of the highest levels of protection in the Western world. Political support for this regime came from both organized labour and manufacturing industry. One should also note that traditionally the state in Australia has played an active role in the management of the economy, not just in terms of tariff policy but also in providing infrastructure to facilitate economic development and in regulating the labour market through the system of industrial arbitration. At the same time the state gave support to the ideology of private enterprise and for the most part did not become involved directly in productive enterprises itself.

In the post-1945 period, protection was extended to enable further development of manufacturing industry, again largely on an import-substitution basis. Beginning in the late 1940s, Australia embarked on a massive immigration programme which, among other things, helped provide the labour needed in the development of manufacturing industries at this time. A situation of full employment prevailed right through to the early 1970s. Labor was in power for most of the 1940s, handing over to a conservative coalition government between 1949 and 1972. Nevertheless both governments saw the state as playing an active role in promoting Australia's economic development. In terms of foreign policy, Australia's main link with the 'core' was now through its alliance with the US (gradually superseding its earlier link with the UK); this complemented the economic relationship Australia was developing with Japan as an emerging 'core' country.

From at least the early 1970s, Australia has faced more difficult economic circumstances. This situation has coincided with both the end of the long boom in the international economy and the onset of the era of increasing globalization. Australia has become less and less significant in the international economy, with its share of world trade declining from about 2.5 per cent of the total to 1.1 per cent during the postwar period (Higgott 1992: 128). There has been less international demand for Australia's traditional exports. The oil crisis in the early 1970s encouraged the search for more efficient manufacturing methods, requiring less reliance on minerals and making more use of synthetic substitutes. Agricultural protectionism in other parts of the world was also a problem for Australia, particularly in the European Community (EC) as a result of the Common Agricultural Policy, but also in Japan and to some extent the US. The declining relationship with Britain was confirmed by that country's entry to the EC in 1973, one effect of which was the virtual cessation of Australian agricultural exports to that traditional destination. At the same time, Australia (and again this might be taken as evidence of a peripheral characteristic) has continued to have a high proportion of manufactured goods in its total imports (some 84 per cent in 1985 as against a 64 per cent average for the advanced market economies in 1985) (Higgott 1992: 128).

At the political level, the task of responding to Australia's increasing marginalization in the international economy has fallen to both Labor and Coalition governments. The long conservative hegemony in Australian politics ended with the election of the Whitlam Labor government (1972–5). However, one of the problems of this government was its slow realization that the boom in the international economy had come to an end, thus jeopardizing its ability to implement expansionary social democratic policies. The Fraser Coalition government (1975–83), based on the majority Liberal Party and the rural-based National Party, adhered largely to status quo policies in dealing with the situation. It was left largely to the Labor governments of Bob Hawke (1983–91) and Paul Keating (1991–6) to attempt more adventurous policies designed to reposition Australia in the international economy.

One aspect of these policies involved an attempt to integrate Australia more closely with the economies of East Asia, with a greater emphasis on regionalism as part of this strategy. Before focusing on the issue of Asia-Pacific regionalism, an attempt will be made to delineate the key components in the Labor government's policy for repositioning Australia in the international economy. Apart from the economic dimension, it is also worthwhile drawing attention to the Labor government's attempts to redefine Australia's position in the world more generally. While Australia saw itself retaining a close relationship with the US, it also embarked upon a more independent foreign policy in the Asia-Pacific in particular, playing a leading role in the formulation of a peace settlement in Cambodia, for example. The policy of multiculturalism, which went back to the period of the Whitlam government of 1972–5, was an attempt to come to terms with the changing composition of Australia's population resulting from the large-scale immigrant component, including a significant proportion of Asians in more recent decades. The issue of reconciliation with the indigenous peoples came to the fore with the High Court's 1992 Mabo judgment (overturning the previous doctrine of *terra nullius*) and the enactment of the Native Title Act. Australia's changing international position was also highlighted when Paul Keating raised the issue of moving to republican status, a complex constitutional and political exercise which would involve severing the Australian relationship with the British crown.

While Keating argued that these foreign policy and identity issues were a vital part of Australia's attempts to redefine its role in the world, at an economic level policy developed on a more pragmatic basis. The tradition of an active state has meant that the thinking prevalent within government circles has exerted a powerful influence on economic policy. In the 1980s and 1990s this thinking has been very much influenced by the ideology of economic rationalism. Tariff barriers were to be dismantled and the focus was to be on the development of manufacturing industry which was internationally competitive. While opposition came from unions and industry which were adversely affected (for example, in textiles, clothing and footwear), this was insufficient to undermine the dominant ideology. The support of organized labour was won through the Accord which gave unions unprecedented access to governmental decision-making during the period of the Labor government from 1983 to 1996; nevertheless this was at the expense of a decline in real wages (with a fall of 12 per cent between 1974 and 1994 (Bell 1997: 234)). Richard Higgott (1991) has argued that the approach adopted can be seen in terms of the logic of 'two-level games'. This means that Australia has undergone a process of restructuring its own economy while simultaneously attempting to reposition itself in relation to the international economy. At the domestic level the agricultural and mining industries were already very efficient in world terms. The focus instead has been on developing other sectors of the economy to make them more able to compete internationally. This has involved dismantling the structure of protection which had developed during the first seventy years of federation. It was recognized that less complex manufacturing industry (for example, textiles, shoes) would find it more difficult to compete with cheaper Asian imports in these circumstances. But it was also argued that in certain industries and services the skills and technology available in Australia might give the country some competitive advantages.

With 'economic rationalism' increasingly swaying policies in Canberra (Pusey 1991), there have also been attempts to develop an industry policy. This has involved attempts to ensure that certain industries producing largely for the domestic market (for example, car manufacturing) are able to survive in the new environment. It also involves giving infrastructural and other kinds of non-tariff backing to industries which are judged to have some chance of competing internationally. In supporting a liberal international trading system, the Labor government also moved to deregulate the financial markets in Australia, with foreign banks now being able to compete for the first time. These various changes represented a significant volte-face in the attitudes traditionally associated with the Australian Labor Party. The main *quid pro quo* for the unions, linked as they are to Labor, was the development of a series of Accords whereby wage increases were related to changes in the cost of living. Some increases in wages were forgone in favour of increases in the 'social wage'. In the mid-1990s, the emergence of Hansonism (named after independent federal parliamentarian Pauline Hanson), with its platform of support for protection, restricted immigration and the dismantling of special programmes for multiculturalism and the Australian aborigines, has indicated some disaffection among workers adversely affected by Australia's economic liberalization.

At the international level, apart from the promotion of regionalism, Australia supported the extension of the liberal economic order through participation in the Uruguay Round of the General Agreement on Tariffs and Trade (GATT) (1986–93). As a medium-sized power, it stood to benefit from the recognition of a liberal rules-based system, but clearly it had limited leverage on its own. However, insofar as major powers, particularly the US, supported such a system, this was in Australia's interests. In addition, Australia took the lead in establishing a coalition of countries with a common interest in promoting the cause of agricultural free trade within the context of the Uruguay Round. Known as the Cairns Group, its membership consisted of five Latin American countries (Brazil, Argentina, Uruguay, Chile, Colombia), one North American country (Canada), one Eastern European country (Hungary), four Association of South East Asian Nations (ASEAN) countries (Indonesia, Malaysia, Philippines, Thailand), and three South Pacific countries (Australia, New Zealand, Fiji). The most comprehensive assessment of the Cairns Group concludes that it did play an important role in the early stages of the Uruguay Round even though the final stages were characterized more by the attempt of the US, the European Community and Japan as the major players to reach a settlement on the issue of agriculture (Cooper *et al.* 1993: 82). While this compromise, with its emphasis on the reduction of export subsidies and non-tariff barriers, might not have gone as far as Australia would have liked, it did at least mean that agriculture was now a sector which would come more clearly under the provenance of the new World Trade Organization. This, however, would provide very limited leverage for Australia in overcoming its differences over issues of agricultural protection with Japan, the European Union (EU) and the US, through the Export Enhancement Program.

Asia-Pacific regionalism

Apart from this attempt to advance its position in the multilateral global context, Australia has also devoted considerable energy to promoting regionalism within the Asia-Pacific context. The strategy pursued needs to be located in the context of the evolution of Australia's general political and economic circumstances. The argument presented here is that the emphasis on regionalism in Australian policy has been a strategy to avoid political and economic marginalization in the context of the changing patterns of the global economy and global politics. As Australian links to the Western 'core' have become more attenuated, so Australia has attempted to position itself more firmly as part of the Asia-Pacific region. In this context, countries such as Japan and China might be seen as economic core, although the US also retains a vital role as a core country in this region. Apart from the core countries in the region, Australia has also fostered relations with the ASEAN countries (particularly Indonesia) and newly industrializing economies (NIEs) such as South Korea, Taiwan, Hong Kong and Singapore (also an ASEAN member). All of these countries are seen as economically and politically important to Australia, particularly in terms of maintaining and strengthening Australia's economic position. In reference to Chase-Dunn's categorization, based on closeness to the core and the complex mix of economic activities, these countries could be classed with Australia as part of the strong semi-periphery. The traditionally active role of the Australian state in determining the parameters of economic policy was reflected in the role it played in the development of this regional policy. While this strategy suited the interests of the export-oriented sectors of the economy such as mining and agriculture, the bureaucracy essentially acted independently in fostering this approach. The emphasis on encouraging export-oriented manufacturing and service industries (such as education), particularly from the 1980s, also came primarily from within the state apparatus. Regionalism was seen as a way of maximizing the benefits for a more outward-looking Australian economy. As previously indicated, negative responses to the strategy of economic liberalization (extending here to the economic dimension of regionalism) have been piecemeal and have mostly come from industries which have previously enjoyed high levels of protection; Hansonism suggests a more widespread opposition, although so far it is only represented by one federal parliamentarian. The evolution of the strategy underlying the various phases in the development of regionalism will now be considered in more detail.

'Old' regionalism

The more recent Australian approach to regionalism needs to be seen in relation to how Australia has approached its region in the past. At one level, Australia has always given considerable attention to the implications of its regional location for its foreign policy. As a Western country on the edge of Asia, the region was seen essentially as a potential threat. The White Australia Policy adopted in 1901 reinforced this sense of distance from Asia. For much of the first half of the century, Japan was seen as the major source of threat; Australia relied on its membership of the British Empire to provide protection. With the fall of Singapore in early 1942, this strategy experienced a severe setback. While Australia had always seen the US as another potential protector, this strategy now came increasingly to the fore and was reinforced with the conclusion of the ANZUS Treaty in 1951. At the same time, Australia became more politically assertive within its own region. Although its attempts to exert more influence over Allied wartime strategy in the Pacific were largely ineffective, Australia did take the initiative in establishing the South Pacific Commission with the colonial powers in the South Pacific in 1947. The Labor government also showed some sympathy for the Indonesian nationalists in their struggle against Dutch rule in the 1940s.

During the period of conservative rule in the 1950s and 1960s, there was a strong emphasis on security considerations in Australian approaches to the Asia-Pacific. A strategy of 'forward defence' was developed whereby Australia was willing to undertake military commitments in South East Asia alongside either Britain or the US. Australia cooperated with Britain in the former instance in relation to Malaya and then Malaysia, and with the US in Vietnam. SEATO (the South East Asia Treaty Organization), formed in 1954, was very much military-oriented in emphasis with Australia participating alongside the US, Britain, France, New Zealand, Thailand, the Philippines and Pakistan. While security issues were foremost in Australian government thinking at this time, there was also an increasing emphasis on developing trade relations with the Asian countries, symbolized most clearly in the 1957 trade agreement with Japan.

The British withdrawal from 'east of Suez' in the late 1960s and early 1970s and then the failure of the US in Vietnam encouraged new thinking in Australia about how to relate to its region. The development of the *rapprochement* between China and the US was also important. The Whitlam Labor government (1972–5) favoured a less military-oriented approach. In general terms it wanted to encourage the further development of economic links and to promote regional cooperation, but regionalism involving Australia remained underdeveloped. ASEAN, established in 1967 by Indonesia, Malaysia, Singapore, Thailand and the Philippines, excluded Western countries such as Australia. Australia did, however, become a 'dialogue partner' of ASEAN in 1974. The conservative Coalition government of Malcolm Fraser (1975–83) placed even more emphasis on security issues and the global context. Issues within the region tended to be seen in terms of how they might affect the global balance of power. This was the case, for example, with the Vietnamese invasion of Cambodia in 1978; this was seen by Fraser as related to renewed Soviet expansionism. A strengthening of the relationship with China provided a means of countering the USSR.

'New' regionalism under Labor governments, 1983–96

It was mainly during the period of the Labor governments led by Bob Hawke (1983–91) and Paul Keating (1991–6) that a commitment to a new type of regionalism emerged. This can be seen both at the level of government policy in general and in relation to APEC (Asia-Pacific Economic Cooperation) in particular.

The renewed emphasis on Australia's region during the period of the Labor governments was partly an attempt by those governments to develop some distinctive emphases in their foreign policy as compared with that of their conservative predecessor. Whereas Fraser was accused of global 'grandstanding', Labor believed that Australian interests would be best furthered by developing a stronger regional focus. This can be seen in relation to both security and economic issues. In terms of security, an important development was the Dibb Report of 1986 (Dibb 1986), which argued for a policy of defence self-reliance (confirming the trend away from dependence on a major protector). Regional defence cooperation figured prominently in the Defence White Paper of 1994 (Australian Department of Defence 1994).

At an economic level, a good statement of the Labor government's thinking was the Garnaut Report of 1989 (Garnaut 1989). This drew attention to the economic dynamism occurring in North East Asia in particular and argued that it was in Australia's interests to take advantage of this situation. Essentially this involved further development of export activities where Australia already had comparative advantages, such as minerals and primary produce, but extending also to relatively new areas such as education services. According to Ross Garnaut, Australia would be in a better position to further its own economic links with North East Asia if it accelerated the process of domestic economic reform, with a view to eliminating tariff barriers and developing a strategy of export-oriented industrialization. Garnaut's argument could be seen as representative of the economic rationalism which was dominant within the Australian bureaucracy by this time. Opposition from adversely affected manufacturing industry and unions was relatively weak.

Australia's new regional policy was also related to the issue of Australian national identity. Traditionally Australia had seen itself as a Western country on the edge of Asia, a region of potential instability. Later the idea developed that Australia's location might enable it to act as a 'bridge' between the West and Asia. During the 1980s and 1990s the emphasis has been on Australia integrating itself with the region. This has been influenced by the abandonment of the White Australia Policy beginning in the 1960s, and leading to an increasing level of Asian immigration. In 1994, for example, some 29.3 per cent of immigrants to Australia were from Asian countries; out of a population of nearly 18 million, some 826,100 people were born in South East, North East and South Asia, with Vietnam, the Philippines, Malaysia, Hong Kong and India being the most important sources (*Year Book Australia 1996*: 103, 105). Demographically, however, Australia has remained overwhelmingly a European country. Without abandoning its Western orientation, it has increasingly thought of itself as an Asia-Pacific country. In promoting this new way of thinking about Australia's place in the world, the Labor government was influenced by the pragmatic considerations which have been referred to previously, but also believed that the changing nature of Australian society did warrant some reconstruction of Australian identity. One might note in passing that the fostering of links between Australia and East Asia runs contrary to Samuel Huntington's widely discussed 'clash of civilizations' thesis (most recently in Huntington 1996); Huntington in fact sees Australia as an example of a 'torn country'. Politically the promotion of a new Australian identity was promoted very much by Prime Minister Paul Keating (1991–6) and wide sections of the intelligentsia in Australia; Keating's conservative successor, John Howard, has not made the issue a key focus, even though he too has had to deal with the changing nature of Australia's population and the evolution of its international circumstances.

APEC

Developing a new regional policy is not necessarily the same as promoting regionalism. Closer links with the Asia-Pacific could have been pursued without also attempting to develop new forms of Asia-Pacific regionalism. In the Australian case, however, regionalism was seen as an important dimension of its regional policy. In this sense, regionalism involves conscious attempts to promote new forms of regional groupings rather than simply relating to other countries in the region on a bilateral basis. The new focus on regionalism can be seen most clearly in relation to Australian involvement in the establishment and development of APEC (see Cooper *et al.* 1993: 85–105). Australia had participated in various non-governmental initiatives designed to promote the concept of an Asia-Pacific economic community going back to the 1960s. These included the Pacific Basin Economic Council (PBEC) in 1967, the Pacific Trade and Development Conference (PAFTAD) in 1968, and the Pacific Economic Cooperation Conference (PECC) in 1980. PECC, involving business, academic and government representatives, was the most significant of these initiatives. Although Japan took the lead in the establishment of PECC, Australia was also a key participant. PECC encouraged further thinking about an Asia-Pacific economic community, and in that sense prepared the way for APEC. Interestingly it was Bob Hawke who took the initiative when, in a speech in Seoul in January 1989, he called for the establishment of an intergovernmental body with the aim of promoting economic cooperation in the Asia-Pacific (Hawke 1989: 5–7).

As explained by Hawke (1994: 431), Australia's motivation in promoting the establishment of APEC was very much related to a perception of its international economic interests:

> What I had in mind for APEC . . . was a framework of effective regional co-operation which could improve the Uruguay Round's chances of success. In addition, APEC could provide a forum for openly discussing obstacles to trade within our own region.

Essentially, then, there were two motivations for the Australian initiative. One was to do with using APEC as a vehicle for promoting the Australian position in support of trade liberalization at the Uruguay Round. The other was to support trade liberalization within the Asia-Pacific region, a goal consistent with Australia's desire to promote its own trade links with the region. In both cases APEC provided a useful means for countering Australia's economic marginalization.

Of course Australia as a 'middle power' was not the decisive influence in establishing APEC and determining its subsequent development. The positions adopted by Japan, the US and the ASEAN countries were more important. Japan itself had been involved in initiatives to develop regionalism since the 1960s; Australia was able to take advantage of Japan's positive approach to further Australia's own strategy for developing regionalism. The US, while generally preferring to focus on its key bilateral relationships in the Asia-Pacific, did not wish to be excluded from a development such as APEC. Despite earlier American reservations about multilateralism in the region, once it became clear that the US did want to take part in APEC the Hawke government lent its support.

The ASEAN countries as a whole were sympathetic to the inclusion of the US within APEC as a means of avoiding a situation where the new grouping would be Japanese-dominated. The main exceptions were Thailand and Malaysia. Malaysia developed a proposal for an East Asian Economic Grouping (later Caucus) which would have excluded the US as well as Australia and New Zealand, but this was not accepted in East Asia, let alone outside the region. The Malaysian proposal emphasizes the point that 'regions' should not be thought of as necessarily self-evident. In promoting APEC, Australia was giving support to the view that the region should be thought of as the 'Asia-Pacific' rather than 'East Asia'. A region restricted to East Asia would have excluded Australia, whereas a definition in terms of the Asia-Pacific was more inclusive. Again, Australia's concern about becoming marginalized was a major factor in explaining the approach it adopted on this issue.

In the subsequent development of APEC, the two objectives identified by Hawke have remained central to Australian policy. As a force working in favour of global trade liberalization, APEC could be seen as augmenting what Australia was trying to achieve through the Cairns Group. With the conclusion of the Uruguay Round, it could be argued that APEC's role as a force for global trade liberalization has become less, but this is only the case in the sense that that particular set of negotiations is now over. The issues arise in many other contexts and APEC can continue to play a role there. Relatively speaking, APEC has in recent years given more attention to promoting trade within its own region, focusing in particular on the goal of 'open regionalism'. The aim is to reduce trade barriers among APEC members but in a way which does not discriminate against non-APEC members. Again this is consistent with the Australian goal of promoting global trade liberalization and discouraging the formation of restrictive economic blocs. APEC's profile received a fillip when President Clinton instituted APEC heads of government meetings, beginning with the Seattle summit in November 1993 (and followed by Bogor [Indonesia] in 1994, Osaka in 1995 and Subic Bay [Philippines] in 1996). An Eminent Persons Group (EPG) had been appointed by the APEC ministerial meeting in 1992. Led by the American economist Fred Bergsten, its report in favour of 'free and open trade and investment in the region' had been accepted at the Bogor summit in 1994 (*Achieving the APEC Vision* 1994: 39). Developed countries were to achieve this goal by 2010, newly industrialized economies by 2015, and developing countries by 2020. At Osaka the focus was on what would be done to implement this goal. The outcome indicated that the objectives adopted were more statements of intent rather than firm commitments. From the Australian perspective this might appear disappointing, but APEC continued to be important as a forum where Australia could attempt to win support from other Asia-Pacific countries for the goal of trade liberalization both within the region and on a global level.

Other examples of regionalism

Apart from APEC, Australia has very few options as far as regional economic groupings are concerned. In 1992 John Hewson, the then leader of the opposition Liberal Party, raised the issue of Australia joining NAFTA (Baker 1993: 300). John Elliott, Treasurer of the Liberal Party, had even proposed that Australia should join the European Community. These proposals could be seen as responses to Australia's increasing marginalization, but, unlike APEC, they were not within the realm of practical politics. Within another part of Australia's own region, Australia has given tentative support to the establishment of an APEC-type organization for the Indian Ocean. A 'Look West' strategy was developed by the previous Labor government and Australia responded positively to the Mauritian initiative in March 1995 which led, after a series of meetings (including the International Forum on the Indian Ocean Region or IFIOR held in Perth in June 1995) to the establishment of the Indian Ocean Rim Association for Regional Cooperation (IOR-ARC) in September 1996. From the Australian perspective the IOR-ARC has potential for developing Australian trade links with India in particular. Generally speaking, it has much less potential for Australia than does APEC, but it could be seen as another example of Australian support for regionalism as a means of mitigating its economic marginalization.

Some other examples of Australian involvement in regionalism should also be mentioned. In some instances these are part of attempts to reduce economic marginalization. A closer relationship with ASEAN might be useful to Australia in terms of developing economic complementarities, but politically it does not appear to be on the agenda either for Australia or for the

South East Asian countries. However one defines the Asia-Pacific, Australia is simply not regarded as part of South East Asia. Australia has been involved in the ASEAN Regional Forum (ARF) since that body was established in 1994. Despite the name, this forum has the Asia-Pacific as its scope and meets annually for an exchange of views on security issues within the region. As a security forum it is not directly relevant to the goal of reducing Australia's economic marginalization as pursued by Australian governments. However, it does provide another setting within which Australia can engage in multilateral diplomacy within the region. ARF reinforces the perception that the Asia-Pacific should be seen as a region, and this is helpful from Australia's perspective, whether or not the issues being dealt with are explicitly economic. Although blocked by Malaysia so far, Australia would also like to join the Asia-Europe Meetings (ASEM), which began in 1996 in Bangkok and provide a forum for the countries of East Asia and the European Union to discuss various political and economic issues.

One more limited example of regionalism which does have direct relevance to Australia's economic situation is the Closer Economic Relationship (CER) with New Zealand. CER was established in 1983 as a successor to the New Zealand–Australia Free Trade Agreement (NAFTA) which had been set up in 1966. The Antipodean NAFTA only applied to certain products (with agriculture excluded) and was therefore not a full free trade agreement. CER involved a stronger commitment to the establishment of free trade between the two countries, with trade in merchandise becoming fully free by 1990. There is also a commitment to economic integration in relation to services and the labour market. Integration has not been achieved in investment and currency matters; an agreement on a common aviation market was unilaterally abrogated by Australia in October 1994. In 1995 New Zealand took 7.2 per cent of Australian exports and provided 4.6 per cent of Australian imports. For New Zealand, Australia took 20.3 per cent of its exports and provided 21.6 per cent of its imports (based on International Monetary Fund 1996: 106, 333). In many respects the political and economic relationship with New Zealand is the closest Australia has. CER is helpful in expanding Australia's market but can only be a minor element in coping with Australia's marginalization in the international economy.

Australia is also involved with New Zealand in South Pacific regionalism. The two main regional organizations are the South Pacific Commission (SPC) and the South Pacific Forum (SPF). The SPC was established by the colonial powers in the region in 1947 and was long dominated by them. It still has representation by the metropolitan powers, but also includes the independent states and dependent territories in the region. Explicitly political issues are excluded from its agenda and the SPC functions mainly as a channel for multilateral aid to the region. The SPF was formed in 1971 to act as a political voice for the independent island states of the South Pacific, but with Australia and New Zealand also invited to join. Neither the SPC nor the SPF is of any great significance in reducing Australia's economic marginalization. Both organizations have provided means for Australia to exert an influence in a region where it has important strategic interests. It would be oversimplified to see the region simply as an Australian sphere of influence since a number of other powers are involved (New Zealand, France, US, Japan, and Britain [to a declining extent]) and the island states are not simply subordinate. Australia has attempted to assist the island states through aid and preferential trade agreements such as SPARTECA (South Pacific Regional Trade and Economic Cooperation Agreement), but the region (apart from New Zealand) is not important for the Australian economy.

Having discussed APEC and other manifestations of Australian involvement in regionalism, some assessment of the value of this involvement for Australia's position in the international economy is important. The argument presented here is that regionalism has not had a major impact, but that APEC in particular does enable Australia to be in a better position to argue for a liberal world economic order. Should the global economy collapse into competing economic blocs, APEC might provide one option for Australia as the basis for another such bloc. It is also worth drawing attention to the variety of manifestations of regionalism involving Australia. While APEC might have received the greatest emphasis as a basis for protecting and promoting Australia's economic position, the IOR-ARC is clearly far less significant. The CER with New Zealand is important as a move in the direction of economic union, but cannot substitute for a more outward-oriented economic strategy. The SPC and the SPF are primarily manifestations of Australia's multilateral involvement in South Pacific affairs, rather than being of any great significance for Australia's economic position.

Bilateralism as an alternative

Insofar as the hopes placed in regionalism might have been exaggerated, alternative strategies such as bilateralism need to be considered. This appears to be the direction in which the conservative Coalition government, elected in March 1996, is moving. Regionalism remains important, but it is not necessarily seen as a panacea. Bilateralism would involve attempting to improve Australia's economic position by concluding agreements with individual trading partners. Given Australia's role as part of the semi-periphery, the leverage it has available to engage in this type of strategy is limited. There are normally other sources for the various items Australia can supply to its trading partners. Even when Australia is in a stronger position as a major supplier of a particular commodity (such as coal), it does not always coordinate its strategy for obtaining the best price for that commodity as well as it might (Beeson 1995). Ravenhill argues that Australia has tended to side too much with countries such as Japan in their trade disputes with the US. In campaigning for better market access, the US has not normally done so on the basis of this access benefiting the US alone (Ravenhill 1996: 11). While there have been fears that bilateral trade agreements negotiated by the US will adversely affect Australia, this has not necessarily been the case. In many cases there could be benefits for Australia deriving from the bilateral strategies pursued by the US. In general, however, bilateralism as an Australian strategy can only supplement what is being attempted in relation to regionalism. And, as has been argued, the prospects for regionalism as a strategy for reducing Australia's marginalization remain strictly limited.

The shift towards a greater emphasis on bilateralism in Australian strategy does help to put regionalism into perspective. An emphasis on its regional location will continue to be an important part of Australian policy, irrespective of the party in office. Some attention will also continue to be given to the promotion of regionalism. However, if regionalism proves limited as a means of dealing with Australia's economic predicament, one can expect that attention to lessen. Regionalism has a value as a means of promoting Australia's relations with other countries in the Asia-Pacific, but the economic dimension is of particular importance. Judgements about the value of regionalism in this respect are made within the bureaucracy and the associated political elites, whether from the Labor or the conservative side of politics. This corresponds to the way in which Australia has approached regionalism in the past; while Labor might have had a stronger commitment to regionalism in terms of rhetoric, this is essentially a matter of emphasis. The relationships with 'core' countries have been modified by the emergence of regionalism. However, regionalism has complemented the relationships with those countries (often involving members of the 'core' in fact, with APEC being the clearest example), rather than providing a completely different focus.

Conclusion

In this chapter I have argued that the Australian approach to regionalism has been a pragmatic one relating to Australia's changing political and economic circumstances. At one level the concept of the strong semi-periphery does draw attention to the relationship Australia has had with 'core' countries. However, Britain and indeed the US have become less important to Australia; Asia-Pacific regionalism involves not just the US but also 'core' Asian countries such as Japan and China and a range of other countries, most of which could be classed as 'semi-periphery', whether strong or weak. While Australia in the past might have identified with 'core' Western countries, in more recent times it has been concerned about the possibility of becoming economically and politically marginalized. Regionalism has been an attempt to deal with this situation, but should be seen as one of a number of strategies and should be placed within the broader framework of economic liberalization. Regionalism, and economic liberalization more generally, have been largely fostered by state elites, with opposition (largely ineffective) coming mainly from employers and workers in selected manufacturing industries which have been adversely affected.

4   Brazil and MERCOSUR

Jean Grugel and Marcelo de Almeida Medeiros

Regional integration has been an objective, at least formally, within Latin America and the Caribbean (LAC) almost since Independence in the nineteenth century. Contemporary schemes for LAC integration, however, rooted in economic cooperation as a means to industrial development, date from the 1960s. Brazilian participation, in view of the size of the economy and its position as sub-regional power, was vital for the success of these initiatives. But Brazil was not fully committed to integration in the 1960s, thus weakening the drive for hemispheric economic cooperation. Yet in the 1990s Brazil endorsed a new and imaginative attempt at integration, the Common Market of the South (MERCOSUR). This chapter will explain Brazil's new enthusiasm for region-building in terms of its changing position within the global economy and as a consequence of changes within the state. The transformation of Brazilian policy towards the rest of LAC was partly the result of state elites' altered perspectives on national political interests, alongside pressures to adjust the economy to the terms of an increasingly open but regionalizing world economy. Understanding the nature of the state is therefore central to understanding Brazilian regionalist policy. The second part of the chapter will analyse what state elites hope to gain from membership of MERCOSUR.

Brazil as semi-periphery

Brazil exhibits some of the 'classic' signs of semi-peripheral development. These include: uneven development; capital, technological and market dependence on developed countries; and an 'intermediate' state. The Brazilian economy grew rapidly, especially after 1967, but increased manufacturing capacity did not bring autonomy in financial and investment terms. Brazil was also unable to break into the protected markets of the US and the European Community (EC), despite its productive competitiveness in the 1970s. The effects of industrialization were spread unevenly through the country and growth distanced the major beneficiaries of 'dependent development' (Cardoso 1973), located in the public and private sectors, from the rest of society, allowing for the reproduction of massive inequalities between the rich and the poor in terms of both income and political resources. In turn, this has generated a particularly complex set of social and environmental problems which undermine the economic achievements, threaten the stability of the political system and present a serious challenge to the authority of the state.

Despite the tendency of some analysts to emphasize the weight of the Brazilian state in its relationship with social groups, attributing it to Catholic tendencies towards organic responsibility and collectivism (Badie 1993: 28), in fact, state autonomy has historically been limited. The power of the landed elites, in particular, weakened the centralizing authority of the state throughout the nineteenth century. The result was that early centralism was challenged by regional elites, leading to the imposition of a federal constitution in 1889. Since then, the struggle between centralizing authority and dispersing it regionally has been a major determinant of Brazilian politics. When General Vargas took power in 1930, the central state had few effective powers compared to those of regional bosses and the landowners. By 1945, Vargas had brought a far more modern state into being through the promotion of industrialization, spurred on by the impetus for internal development which Brazil received as a result of the Depression of the 1930s and the Second World War. The establishment of Ministries for Labour, Industry and Trade, along with those of Education and Health, the foundation of federal sector institutions and the suppression of the inter-state trade tax were among the measures which reduced the powers of the regions. By the end of the Second World War the emergence of labour unions and a middle class had effectively transformed national politics and the central state had taken on the role of outlining development goals and pursuing structural change.

The military coup of 1964 inaugurated a new phase of politics. Brazilian capitalism and the Armed Forces decisively rejected the populist model of industrialization associated with Vargas, which emphasized 'the right of popular preferences to determine the character of national economic policy' (Sheahan 1987: 187). Instead, a model of growth through concentration of income was pursued which, especially after 1967, became known as the 'economic miracle'. The political framework in which this occurred has been termed 'bureaucratic authoritarianism' (O'Donnell 1973) or 'managerial capitalism' (Sheahan 1987: 188) in order to capture both the repression of labour and populism and the *dirigisme* which characterized state activity in the economic sphere. Between 1967 and 1974, the economy grew by an average of 10 per cent a year. These growth rates were fuelled by unprecedented levels of foreign investment along with state investment in infrastructure, heavy industry and petrochemicals, leaving domestic capital a poor third in investment terms. State elites saw their role as one of nurturing domestic industry through protection, subsidies and infrastructural investment as well as one of stimulating trade. While production for the domestic market remained important, the export market also began to expand and the transnationalized sectors of the economy were the most dynamic. State policy actively sought to shape the conditions for growth through, for example, control of labour, tariff controls and active encouragement of foreign trade missions. As a result, Brazil was increasingly placed alongside the Asian newly industrializing economies (NIEs) as a rapidly industrializing economy.

Rather than a 'developmental state' along the lines of Japan, Korea or Taiwan (Johnson 1982), however, Evans (1992, 1995) suggests plausibly that the Brazilian state moved towards 'intermediate' status, with characteristics of both the developmental and the predatory state. On the one hand, there were pockets of efficiency such as the National Development Bank (BNDE) and the foreign trade sector, but, on the other, patronage remained a major determinant of state employment and the operation of personalist and clientelist networks explained many areas of state activity. Smith (1992) goes further, to argue that the Brazilian state has actually more in common with other LAC states than with the Asian developmental model. In particular he focuses on the question of state autonomy, which, he argues, is

> modest, at least by Asian standards. They [LAC states] have been subject to constant pressure from within and without; their decisions have been susceptible to veto by power groups at home, such as the landed aristocracy or organized labour or abroad such as the US.
>
> (Smith 1992: 54)

Certainly the links between state elites and the landed aristocracy, despite the relative decline of the coffee planters, were able to limit the effectiveness of policies of industrialization; and it is hard to deny the overarching influence of US security and trade concerns in determining the parameters of Brazilian external policy. As Haggard (1990) and Grindle (1986) observed, industrialization did not signify a defeat for the landed class, only a loss of relative power. 'Large landowners benefited. ... [D]espite unfavourable pricing policies, the drive to industrialization was accompanied by efforts to modernize agriculture because of its continued and even heightened importance in generating foreign exchange' (Haggard 1990: 36).

Neither industrialization under Vargas nor the 'miracle' of the 1960s and 1970s, then, came about through the actions of a 'developmental state'. But they were not simply a reflection of global growth nor a response to the demands of international capital either. The agency of Brazilian domestic actors was important in explaining the aggressive industrialization policies pursued after the military coup (in comparison to other LAC states) and the precise nature of the policy package, which was different from elsewhere in LAC. In order to explain the mode of industrialization in Brazil and the changing distribution of benefits from industrialization, it is important to focus on changes within the state and the make-up of political coalitions in power. This changed from an alliance between state elites, labour and agricultural and manufacturing domestic capital (populism), to one between the state, foreign investors and domestic capitalist groups in which the political privileges of the landed class were also protected (the dictatorship). This line of analysis is associated with the work of Evans (1979, 1995) and Haggard (1990). Evans identified a triple alliance between the Brazilian state, transnational corporations (TNCs) that were the dynamic centre of the economy (petrochemicals, pharmaceuticals, the automotive industry), and domestic capitalists. Access to technology, international markets, skilled management, and so on, placed the TNCs in a position of leverage *vis-à-vis* both the state and domestic business; but state investment remained important in oil, steel, infrastructure and electricity, for example, assuring it of resources in negotiating with domestic business and with TNCs. And the state continued to direct firms towards industrial production. Following Cardoso's pioneering work on dependency and industrialization, therefore, Evans (1979) termed this 'dependent development'.

Dependent development increased Brazil's global profile, turning it into an important producer of consumer durables within LAC. By 1991, it was the world's tenth largest economy. It also embarked on a pro-active policy of seeking markets outside LAC, including attempts to enter the European markets in the 1970s, though these were not particularly successful (Gomes 1990). But as Lamounier (1995: 145) commented, the pattern of economic development means that 'medieval economic inequalities exist side by side with a dynamic and increasingly sophisticated society'. The benefits of development have been extremely unevenly distributed. Brazil is a dual society, with most of the population materially excluded from the possibilities of capitalist consumption. It remains the country with the most inequitable distribution of income in LAC and social welfare provision is negligible. Moreover, welfare indicators actually worsened during the 1960s and 1970s. And if urban workers fared badly, the rural poor were even worse off. Access to land for the poor was steadily reduced throughout the 1960s until by the 1970s more than a third of rural workers were completely landless. The development of agrarian exports was partly responsible; but the political power the landowners exercised allowed them to leave uncultivated up to 2.8 million square kilometres despite a growing population in the country-side and declining opportunities in the cities (Oxfam 1991). Indeed Hagopian (1992) identifies the privileged access of traditional elites to arenas of power and decision-making as a major obstacle to development and democracy. Although, since 1985, they have increasingly operated formally within the democratic 'rules of the game', they benefit from, and reproduce, 'anti-democratic political practices ... ingrained in national political culture' (Hagopian 1992: 283).

In sum, Brazil forms part of the semi-periphery due to its uneven and dependent industrialization and its patterns of state–society interaction. Brazil's intermediate position was reproduced, not overcome, as a result of the way industrialization proceeded. For example, investment was dependent upon a favourable tax regime for TNCs and control over labour. In the 1960s and 1970s, this was achieved through the imposition of an authoritarian regime. The dictatorship could not separate itself from the operation of traditional, oligarchical and patronage networks which allowed it to function and survive, although this simultaneously limited its capacity to set goals of rationalization and efficiency (Cammack 1982; Hagopian 1992). Consequently, the pattern of uneven and impoverishing development went unchecked. One major problem resulting from this was the persistent 'fiscal inadequacy' of the state (Fishlow 1992) due to its inability to tax either foreign investors or the landed class. After 1974, this led to a growing dependence on international financial markets. During the period of the 'miracle', state elites focused their attention on the dynamic performance of exports, which increased from 15 per cent of Brazil's total production in 1964 to 42 per cent in 1974. But after 1974, maintaining these production levels in the face of oil price rises meant borrowing on a massive scale from international lenders. By 1980, the total external debt was US$60 billion. The causes of the economic collapse of the 1980s, as international interest rates rose making debt servicing an impossibility, lie in the 'dependent development' pursued through the 1960s and 1970s. Like elsewhere in LAC, the 1980s and 1990s have brought policies of economic liberalization. But these are mediated in Brazil by the determination of state elites to continue to shape national economic policy. The state is now more prepared to recognize the constraints imposed by the outside world – the trend towards a globalizing world economy and the policy decisions of other states for example – than in the 1960s and 1970s, when it was thought that Brazil could achieve autonomy through economic growth.

Life after debt: restructuring politics and the economy

It might have been expected that the transition to democracy after 1985 would result in a redistribution of political power and perhaps even economic resources. But the transition in Brazil came about chiefly as a result of the defection of economic elites from the dictatorship during the debt crisis after 1982. Institutionally, this had the advantage that the movement towards an elective presidency, the legalization of independent political parties and the inauguration of competitive Congressional elections came about peacefully. It also meant, however, that the transition was appropriated by the traditional elite, leading to a 'compromised consolidation' (Hagopian 1992). Democratization in Brazil has therefore been limited by obstacles in the way of deepening representation and citizenship and dominated by the presence of politicians from the previous authoritarian regime. This has been facilitated by a weak system of national parties (Mainwaring and Scully 1995).

The result has been continuity in terms of the composition of state elites, and a failure to broaden the network of relationships built up between economic and social elites and the state. During the transition, the Party of the Brazilian Democratic Movement (PMDB), the only legal opposition party to the dictatorship, was flooded with political heavyweights from the Democratic Social Party (PDS), the official party of the dictatorship, creating a number of conflicting power centres within it as it became the institutional agent of the transition. In the 1970s and early 1980s, therefore, despite the presence in the party of populist or social democratic politicians, including the present President, Fernando Henrique Cardoso (who later left), the PMDB was forced to accommodate powerful social and economic interests. This was possible because of the long-standing separation of political society from civil society and the failure of traditional parties in Brazil to play the democratic role of mediation between the state and society. The net result is that the composition of state elites in the new democracy remains *essentially* the same as under the dictatorship. Consequently, the democratic state continues to promote growth while it marginalizes issues of redistribution, poverty and landlessness. State elites remain receptive principally from pressure from the landed class, at least on the domestic front, and see their role as that of sponsoring a model of industrialization in which domestic entrepreneurs are to some degree protected from competition. Economic disparities remain as great as ever, with the richest 20 per cent in possession of more than thirty-two times the income of the poorest 20 per cent (United Nations Development Programme 1994).

Nevertheless, the transition to democracy has also created some new spaces for political activity on the part of the workers and the rural and urban poor, including the formation of a new political party which challenges traditional patterns of patronage, the Workers' Party (Alves 1993). The political conflicts which have developed as a result, between the state's continued pursuit of economic growth and popular demands for redistribution and social justice, have been played out in an arena of changed domestic expectations. It was evident that the era of easy growth was over. In particular, Brazilian strategies for economic growth were constrained by the debt overhang and by its late adjustment to the new global agenda of liberalization. As a result, the economy plummeted through the 1980s. Structural adjustment was, however, slow and partial. Because the economy had done so well through import-substituting industrialization (ISI), state elites distrusted liberalization, and the generation of trade surpluses in the 1980s allowed them to resist forced restructuring (Sola 1994). Consequently, Brazil has been the slowest of all LAC states in adopting policies of economic liberalization, and it was only with the failure of the two heterodox stabilization plans, the *Plano Cruzado* and the *Plano Bresser*, introduced by the first democratic government of José Sarney (1985–90), that the need to incorporate elements from a new paradigm was recognized as necessary for growth and stability.

According to Sola (1994: 154), state technocrats were the first to accept that reform was necessary. Liberalization was piecemeal, however, even under Collor (1990–2), the first government to attempt to open the economy through systematic reform. The reforms were hampered by weak political leadership and were poorly supported within the new democratic institutions. Corruption within the political system and a widespread disenchantment with Brazil's political leaders also hindered the process. There was, therefore, no domestic consensus behind liberalization. It was, in fact, chiefly Brazil's massive dependence on foreign investment, plus the domestic costs of avoiding adjustment, such as hyperinflation – 2,500 per cent in 1993 – which forced adjustment onto the political agenda at all, at least before 1990. Payne (1995) found in 1992 that business elites objected strongly to the instability of the economic climate under Sarney, making them eventually prepared to accept elements of liberalization as a lesser evil. Most, therefore, set about using 'their considerable political resources (significant economic power and social ties to key economic decision makers) to influence economic policy' (Payne 1995: 225) and shape the timing and pace of liberalization.

The short-lived Collor administration attempted a more systematic and comprehensive programme of adjustment than did Sarney's. Nonetheless, in comparison with the way economic liberalization proceeded in Bolivia, Mexico, Argentina and Chile, imports tariffs were relaxed only gradually and the capital goods sector in particular was protected from rapid competition. The importance of this is two-fold. First, it indicates that state elites remained receptive to pressures from domestic industrial producers, although since 1990 especially policies have been introduced to limit monopolistic practices in an attempt to push domestic industry into a more entrepreneurial and competitive mould. Second, since the reforms have been partial and it is accepted that there are exceptions to them, it has enhanced the power of technocrats who take decisions within the state. State bureaucrats have not been able to insulate themselves from social pressures, however. Industrial deregulation has proceeded slowly and privatization has been opposed, and on occasion even obstructed, by managers of public companies, labour unions and even suppliers. At a formal discursive level, the executive is committed to pushing for liberalization, partly as a result of increased external pressure due to continuing debt problems and partly from exhaustion with the search for alternative models of development. But in practice policy outcomes are more complicated because the state is permeable to pressure from agricultural and manufacturing interests.

The need to reform the state was more widely accepted by the early 1990s than a few years earlier. By 1992, when Collor was impeached amid a series of corruption scandals which damaged the standing of important sectors of the political and entrepreneurial national elites, privatization was increasingly seen by the public as a way of curtailing state excesses. Collor was replaced by his Vice-President, Itamar Franco, and Fernando Henrique Cardoso became Finance Minister in 1993. Cardoso introduced a programme of fiscal reform to match the previous trade liberalizations. The *Plano Real* succeeded in the important task of stabilizing inflation. According to the Brazilian Research Institute of Applied Economy (IPEA) of the Ministry of Planning, the *Plano Real* also had important secondary benefits. It was claimed that it generated around an extra US$ 7.3 billion in public resources. This was spent, according to the government, in compensating the poorest sectors of Brazilian society for the costs of stabilization, allowing Cardoso to claim that stabilization was achieved without forcing the poorest sectors of society to bear the greatest burden (*Veja*, 6 March 1996). In turn, this allowed Cardoso to win the presidential elections of 1994 as a candidate committed to moderate reform *and* economic modernization.

As President, Cardoso has pursued policies of modernization through social pacts. In contrast to the earlier corporatist pacts between the state, labour and employers, Cardoso has sought non-institutionalized support from capital, labour and the middle classes for a long-term project of state modernization and global integration. Change requires economic reform, including trade liberalization and an active state to regulate the market and to prevent social fragmentation. But it also requires the generation of growth, an efficient state to claw in some of the benefits of economic expansion, and a commitment to some form of redistribution in order to preserve social peace. Cardoso has also linked modernization with new regionalism. Membership of MERCOSUR, which demands economically orthodox policies from its members, has become a stick with which to push domestic entrepreneurs towards greater competition and into accepting the modernization of the state. At the same time, it is a carrot, offering manufacturers the possibility of an enlarged market, protected to some degree from competition from outside MERCOSUR by a common external tariff (CET). As a result of these policies, growth began again in 1995, when GDP grew 6 per cent and the industrial sector expanded in the order of over 8 per cent, although this has not prevented unemployment from continuing to rise, as indeed it has done every year since the beginning of the 1980s.

Brazil in the global order: linking globalization and regionalism

Although Brazilian state elites have been slow in pushing liberalization, they eagerly embraced new regionalism. Where economic liberalization has essentially been a question of 'muddling through' (Sola 1994), regionalism is the result of a thought-out and planned set of initiatives aimed at protecting national interest. Brazilian regionalist policies differ sharply from those of Mexico and Chile, for example. In Mexico and Chile, new regionalism is a step along the route to economic liberalization; in Brazil, it retains a significant component of nationalist-oriented development. There is, therefore, some continuity in Brazilian policy that underlies the apparently radical changes which MERCOSUR introduces.

By the 1960s, Brazil's foreign policy was structured around two competing logics. Like those in other large developing states, such as India or China, Brazilian state officials were conscious that the country possesses an economic and critical mass which compels the international community to take into consideration its existence (Lafer 1994: 222). Within the Americas especially, the size of the Brazilian economy makes it difficult to ignore: in 1994 Brazilian GDP was in the region of US$450 billion, while the Canadian GDP was US$493.6 billion (*Almanique Abril* 1996). But Brazilian state officials are aware that, especially since 1964, the economy depends upon foreign investment and follows a logic of dependence. As a result, foreign policies have reflected this duality. Brazil shifted from 'foreign policy independence' (1956–64) to 'automatic alignment' with the US (1964–74). This changed once again, to 'responsible pragmatism' after 1974 (Cervo and Bueno 1986).

These shifts express interlinked changes in Brazil's policy towards both the global environment and its neighbours in LAC. In other words, the attitude of Brazilian elites towards the rest of LAC, and especially towards those countries bordering Brazil, has been shaped in part by how they view their position in the global order more generally. The pursuit of rapid economic development in the 1960s meant the adoption of a strategy of political and economic aggression towards those neighbouring states that were economically weaker. The aim was to link Bolivia, Paraguay and Uruguay into the Brazilian economy as satellites. Argentina, which had too powerful an economy at this time to become a satellite of Brazil, was to be neutralized and its own ambitions to dominate the Southern Cone curtailed. During the period of automatic alignment between 1964 and 1974, state elites tried to win the support of the US for these regionalist ambitions (Becker and Egler 1993: 154). Partly in order to support their goals within the sub-region, Brazilian state elites also sought to deepen their country's relations with Southern Africa and Portugal, placing it at the head of an international Portuguese-speaking community. By 1974, Brazilian foreign policy had acquired a markedly more globalist tone. Brazil sought to take on a leadership position within the South more generally, and moved towards adopting a critical stance towards the US, and especially US protectionism, which was seen as blocking Brazilian export initiatives. In turn, this indicated the need for improving relations within LAC in order to strengthen Brazil's case against the US.

Democratization throughout LAC created further opportunities for foreign policy cooperation within LAC. In particular, Brazil and Argentina put an end to their traditional rivalry in the Southern Cone, partly in order to impede a nationalist backlash in both countries. As a result, an Act of Integration was signed between Brazil and Argentina in 1986. This was a reflection too of a new realism within LAC international affairs, which meant, effectively, that both countries abandoned their dreams of sub-regional domination. But the economic difficulties which beset both economies in the late 1980s prevented the adoption of policies of cooperation which lay at the heart of the Integration Act. Instead, the Act was used mainly to push internal reform. In 1990, both countries agreed to a programme of reduction in tariff protection and the abolition of non-tariff barriers, which was seen as a way of backing up trade liberalization in both Brazil and Argentina. Marcos Azambuja, Under-Secretary of State at the Ministry of Foreign Affairs, argued that the Collor administration used regionalism to push for a 'competitive integration of [Brazil] at the international economy as a basic device for the structural reform of the Brazilian economy' (Azambuja 1991: 1). As a result, Brazil's foreign policy was tied into the drive for liberalization.

Deeper integration, beyond that laid down by the Integration Act, was partly the result of the trend of intra-American affairs after 1991. The announcement in 1990 of an Enterprise for the Americas (EAI) on the part of President Bush led to a flood of initiatives on the part of LAC states couched in the language of 'open regionalism' aimed to secure for themselves tariff-free access to the US (Grugel 1996). But few LAC states pursued a development model that was a mix of state-driven and market elements in the way that Brazilian state elites still favoured, and accessing the US market, therefore, implied the need for a more rapid liberalization in Brazil than elsewhere and than had hitherto been contemplated. At the same time, it rapidly became obvious that despite the Americas-wide rhetoric of the EAI, the US was chiefly interested in promoting a new agenda of relations with Mexico and perhaps with a hinterland of other states located geographically close to the US and therefore within Washington's newly defined reduced security arena. The Southern Cone was relatively far from Washington and therefore hardly a priority for post-Cold War security. Hence the chance of Southern Cone states, including Brazil and Argentina, being included in any first-stage trade deals with the US were poor. The result was the revival of sub-regional integration centred on LAC and the Southern Cone. It was seen either as an alternative to EAI-type integration, or as a means through which to pressurize the US to include the Southern Cone in its free trade negotiations. The first position was basically that of Brazil; the second was favoured by the Argentine government under President Menem (1989–).

MERCOSUR emerged in 1991, when the Treaty of Asuncion was signed by Brazil, Argentina and two smaller neighbouring states, Paraguay and Uruguay. It created a market of 200 million people, with 80 per cent of the population in Brazil. Unlike the North American Free Trade Agreement (NAFTA), which created no barriers to trade with third parties, MERCOSUR established a common external tariff (CET), to come into force from 1995. It promoted a liberalized trade and investment climate, therefore, but within a restricted geographical space. This was important for Brazil, since its slow progress towards liberalization and the size of its industrial sector meant that there were important areas of the economy where a staggered adjustment to international competition was necessary both to protect domestic industry and to preserve social peace. According to one index, the degree of openness of the four member states was 13 per cent (Brazil), 18 per cent (Argentina), 43 per cent (Paraguay) and 37 per cent (Uruguay) in 1990, just prior to the start of integration (Brand 1992). Establishing the CET was therefore more important to Brazil than to any other of the members. The need for industrial protection was one reason why Brazilian elites sought to create MERCOSUR, rather than pursuing attachment to the North American economy through the EAI – even if it would have been welcome, which is in doubt. 'For Brazil, because of its higher tariff and the importance of non-US trade, joining a free trade association would have costs similar to a non-discriminatory unilateral liberalization' (De Paiva Abreu 1994).

After signing the Treaty of Asuncion, the four economies agreed to introduce tariff reductions and to eliminate non-tariff barriers towards other members of the pact by 1995. The policy-making technocrats in Brazil remained receptive to pressures from Brazilian industry, however, with the consequence that a number of trade barriers remained in place. For example, state licences were required in order to import flour, chemicals, wine and certain seeds for agricultural production (Bouzas 1996: 92). Government procurement was not liberalized either. And Brazil was consistently identified within MERCOSUR as the member most likely to resort to protectionism through the use of non-tariff barriers. Indeed Brazilian protectionism led to pressure within Argentina for the deployment of the safeguard formula and MERCOSUR's anti-dumping legislation in order to prevent Brazilian goods coming into Argentina. So liberalization did not proceed in a linear fashion after 1991, with the result that it was not complete when the CET came into effect.

Yet, despite these problems, the formation of MERCOSUR acted as a stimulus to growth in the two principal economies and to cross-border investment. Once again, Brazilian firms benefited the most. More than 300 Brazilian firms had invested in Argentina by 1994, in contrast to only thirty Argentine firms in Brazil (Goulart *et al.* 1994). The Brazilian firms were made up of those which had a history of investment abroad along with some others for which it was their first foreign venture. To some degree, therefore, the Brazilian strategy of internationalizing the business class through MERCOSUR, and hence preparing it for competition when and if trade is eventually liberalized in the Americas, had some positive results.

MERCOSUR, therefore, straddles 'old' and 'new' regionalism. It is 'old' in terms of its concern with retaining some degree of tariff protection. It is also 'old' in its grand – and grandiose – declarations of intent and policy and its attention to formal and juridical detail and to the mechanisms of inter-governmental consultation. All member states are aware that the integration in LAC failed in the past because of a lack of real economic interests between LAC firms, despite the complex *de jure* structures of integration that were created. MERCOSUR is committed to reducing the bureaucratic weight of integration; as Ruben Barbosa, Brazilian diplomat and one-time coordinator of the Brazilian policy towards MERCOSUR, put it: 'the function must preceed the form' (Barbosa 1994). Nonetheless, the formal mechanisms of consultation and policy-making through the individual ministries of states are actually quite cumbersome. Yet, despite this, MERCOSUR is also about updating those concerns in order to adapt to a liberal trading order. For Brazil, it functions both as a means to effect a gradual integration for Brazilian industry into a liberalized international system and as a way to preserve traditional claims to leadership with LAC.

Preliminary results: Brazil in MERCOSUR

One of the chief benefits Brazilian elites see in MERCOSUR is the possibility of expanding exports. Brazil's export performance suffered in the 1980s due to a combination of protectionism on the part of the developed countries (US and the EC) and the inability of Brazilian domestic manufacturers to adjust to competition. The great advantage of MERCOSUR is that Brazilian industry does not need to restructure to compete within it, for Brazilian manufacturing remains regionally, though not globally, competitive. It is therefore part of a strategy of softening the impact of globalization on industry. Government policies 'serve as a "wall" between the domestic economy and the international one' (Keohane and Milner 1996: 21). Brazil's economy is around two and a half times greater than that of Argentina, its nearest rival within MERCOSUR (Bouzas 1996); MERCOSUR therefore assures Brazil of a regional market to make up for Brazil's unsuccessful insertion in the global economy. It allows Brazil, and to a lesser extent Argentina, to increase exports within the Southern Cone, and thereby to reduce dependency on the US market, without fully adjusting to international competition. Trade between the members has increased from 8 per cent in 1990, to 14 per cent in 1992 and to over 19 per cent by 1994 of the total volume of external trade of the four members.

Brazilian exports to Argentina in particular experienced a rapid expansion, encouraged in part by the rate of exchange which made Brazilian goods particularly competitive in the Argentine market. In 1990, Brazilian exports to the MERCOSUR countries were worth US$1,320 million; by 1993 this had grown to US$5,395 million. As a result, Argentina has become Brazil's second largest market, after the US. Exports to the two smaller economies of the pact, Uruguay and Paraguay, have also increased. Paraguay represents over 2 per cent of Brazilian trade – though if contraband trade were included, the amount would be considerably higher – and Uruguay 2 per cent. This is more than the value of Brazilian exports to either France or Spain, for example. Over the same period, MERCOSUR's total exports to the US, however, have declined, from 21 per cent of total exports in 1992 to just over 15 per cent in 1994, while imports from the US have remained stable at 21 per cent. This has created fears that MERCOSUR may be trade-diverting rather than trade-creating. However, it is just as likely that MERCOSUR itself is not responsible for the fall in exports to the US; rather this may represent the continuation of an established decline, caused by the increased competitiveness of the Asian economies *vis-à-vis* LAC and their growing tendency to attract TNC investment.

In spite of the creation of the CET and the abolition of internal tariffs within the pact, trade has not been completely liberalized between the member states. There is a list of exceptions of goods that are exempt both from the common external tariff and from internal trade. Again, these benefit principally Brazil and to a lesser extent Argentina. Sugar and automobiles are excluded from free trade within MERCOSUR – automobiles until the year 2000 and sugar until at least 2005. Both Brazil and Argentina have substantial domestic car manufacturing and sugar industries. As the smaller economies, Uruguay and Paraguay are entitled to a greater degree of tariff protection than either of the 'big two', although they have both agreed to eliminate duties in the long term. However, Brazilian protectionism, in particular, which is overwhelmingly through exemptions to free trade or through the use of non-tariff barriers, is more institutionally embedded than the tariff protectionism of Uruguay and Paraguay and will prove difficult to eliminate.

By creating a regional free trade area which it dominates, Brazil hopes to increase its authority to 'speak' for LAC globally. MERCOSUR signifies more than a way of expanding Brazilian exports within LAC. Brazilian elites have traditionally sought an independent place for Brazil (and by extension LAC) in the international system, even in the period of automatic alignment when the relationship with the US was construed as a way of promoting Brazilian interests, rather than as a recognition of US domination over international alignments in return for US backing for elite-dominated government inside LAC, the typical pattern of Cold War US–LAC relations (Nef 1994). MERCOSUR has, therefore, become a way of putting the Southern Cone on the international map. At their most ambitious, MERCOSUR officials talk of it as a fourth bloc, after the North American Free Trade Area (NAFTA), the European Union (EU) and Asia-Pacific Economic Cooperation (APEC). In this, it is assisted by MERCOSUR's developing relationship with the EU, which has been quick to see the advantages of an alternative regional bloc in the Americas favourable to promoting inter-bloc trade with Europe. As a result, the EU and MERCOSUR expect to sign a free trade deal in 1999 and trade between MERCOSUR and the EU is in a period of clear expansion. In 1996, trade between the two blocs was worth US$40 billion, more than US–MERCOSUR trade. Deepening trade ties between the EU and MERCOSUR are built on the foundations of policies of political cooperation, European policies in support of democratization and an expanding European budget for development cooperation aimed at LAC and the Southern Cone from the 1980s onwards.

The Brazilian government under Cardoso has been explicit in its championing of MERCOSUR as an alternative model to integration within the Americas. Indeed, it has frequently been presented explicitly as a challenge to NAFTA. Basically, there are three main differences between the two models of integration. First, in MERCOSUR, there is no developed state around which all the other members of the pact revolve. Brazil is by the far more powerful economy within MERCOSUR, but it cannot play the dominant role that the US does within NAFTA. As a result, the politics of MERCOSUR are qualitatively different from those within NAFTA. Second, MERCOSUR represents an attempt at forging an economic unity out of a pre-established cultural space. Unlike NAFTA, which does not attempt political or cultural integration – and the obstacles to this kind of integration would be enormous – MERCOSUR breathes life into the idea that the 'old' divisions within the Americas, between the rich Anglo North and the undeveloped Latin South, remain valid. Culture, language and history constitute the foundations of integration in MERCOSUR. And third, whereas NAFTA is about trade and investment, MERCOSUR, as we have seen, explicitly encompasses a double process of economic integration and political cooperation. It builds on economic integration as way to expand political autonomy.

Hence MERCOSUR challenges the dominant hub and spoke mode of region-building in the Americas, with the US at the core. At the very least, this means that the US may not be able to determine the parameters of the broad free trade agreement across the Americas which Bush and Clinton have claimed to be seeking. Instead of simply extending NAFTA southwards, the Brazilian government put forward the idea in March 1994 that MERCOSUR could constitute the basic unit from which a South American Free Trade Area (SAFTA) might emerge. This idea was taken up by MERCOSUR and the four member states issued a communiqué supporting the establishment of free trade within LAC as a means to support liberalization and global integration. This was formally adopted as MERCOSUR policy in May 1994. As a step towards building SAFTA, MERCOSUR proposed closer links with the Andean Pact countries and has sucked Bolivia in particular under its influence. Chile and Bolivia became associate members of MERCOSUR in 1996, although Chile at least clearly sought association status with MERCOSUR as a commercial, not a political, enterprise. In order to bring Chile in, MERCOSUR had to drop its insistence that Chile accept the CET. President Cardoso himself is credited with unblocking the negotiations, by accepting that broadening MERCOSUR's membership was more important than insisting on tariff protectionism. At the MERCOSUR summit in Fortaleza, Brazil, in December 1996, at which Bolivia signed a free trade agreement with MERCOSUR, Cardoso explicitly referred to the pact as a 'training ground' for the Free Trade Area of the Americas (*Reuters News Service*, 17 December 1996). He was, in the process, laying claim to Brazilian leadership in building the region, and attempting to wrest it from US control.

Conclusion

So far, MERCOSUR has fulfilled two functions for Brazil: the pursuit of economic growth and adjustment to a globalizing world economy through the regionalization of production and markets; and the furthering of a set of long-held political ambitions for leadership in LAC. MERCOSUR has contributed to the growth of the Brazilian economy without forcing it through a complete liberalization in search of global competitiveness. But there is some doubt about how far Brazil will be able to keep MERCOSUR committed to its current heterogeneous policy mix of protectionism and openness. A World Bank report of 1996 was said to be highly critical of its supposed distortion of international trade by favouring its own capital-intensive industries and raising high tariff barriers to external manufacturers, although it was later toned down. And pressures for deeper liberalization are hard to resist. Brazilian state elites have no choice but to be receptive, to some degree at least, to international pressures. Brazil's trade is still overwhelmingly outside of MERCOSUR and the importance of foreign investment to development cannot be overstated. It is the LAC state which receives most foreign investment – over 3 per cent of all US TNC investment, compared to 2 per cent in Mexico. The government remains committed to staggering liberalization to suit the needs of Brazilian industry, but this is not an easy task. On the one side, there are domestic pressures to resist adjustment completely; and on the other, external pressures are building up for a more complete liberalization, which increasingly find an echo inside MERCOSUR itself as Argentina, with a more open economy and desirous of good relations with the US, favours reducing the CET.

There are a number of possible scenarios which could still derail the initiative. What happens to MERCOSUR is not completely within the control of those actors which have created it. First, the resurgence of currency instability in either Argentina or Brazil will bring integration to a halt. Second, MERCOSUR is vulnerable to changes in US policy. It benefited from the stalling of the US EAI plan and region-wide free trade after 1992, but this is by no means completely off the agenda. SAFTA will prove a far less attractive proposition if access to the US market becomes a real possibility for LAC states. And third, it is also possible that Brazil will not be able to contain dissatisfaction within MERCOSUR over continuing protectionism. The Argentine and Brazilian economies have both benefited from cooperation; but this has not eliminated problems between them which may impede the future progress of the pact. According to Ferrer (1996), Brazilian and Argentine governments differ in terms of their perceptions on globalization and development strategies, and the degree of competitiveness within their national economies. These differences may mean that moving on to second-stage integration – harmonization of exchange rates and macroeconomic policy – will be difficult.

Despite these problems, MERCOSUR is important to Brazilian state elites and to industrialists, who continue to see some kinds of protection as essential. They are supported by nationalist sectors within the state and the Army as well as a whole range of public employees. Continuing commitment to MERCOSUR requires the survival of the present policy coalition. This is uncertain, however, as the very process of internationalization may itself force some renegotitation between domestic actors, leading to policy change. So there are significant tensions within the Brazilian state over integration which remain unresolved. This of course has implications for integration across LAC. On the one hand, without Brazil, MERCOSUR would hardly have any weight at all in the global economy. And, on the other, if Brazil ultimately accepts liberalization and the CET effectively disappears, there would be no real distinction between LAC-wide open integration (SAFTA) and NAFTA. The future for MERCOSUR is therefore far from clear or assured.

5 The Chilean state and new regionalism: strategic alliances and pragmatic integration

Jean Grugel

In the introduction to this book, it was argued that states and state–society relationships remain a key level of analysis in the global political economy and that regionalism is a states-led project which is a response to the trends towards economic globalization. Consequently, the purpose of this chapter must be to analyse the responses of the Chilean state to the challenges of globalization, to the restructuring of the economic space across the Americas, and to the region-building initiatives of other states. Neo-liberal reforms throughout Latin America and the Caribbean (LAC), a search for new markets and for foreign investment and at least a minimal commitment to liberal democracy on the part of regional elites, as well deepening trade and diplomatic relations with the US, constitute the context in which the new regionalism is embedded. Regionalism is therefore linked to a much wider neo-liberal project in the Americas. But regionalism in Chile is not just simply a reflection of global liberalism. In fact, it repays analysis if we wish to understand in particular the *politics* of the new regionalism and sheds light on the kind of role the state can play in a neo-liberal and regionalized global order.

Chile is unique in LAC in that it is the only serious candidate for membership of the two major sub-regional pacts which emerged in the 1990s, the North American Free Trade Area (NAFTA) and the Common Market of the South (MERCOSUR). Membership is not open to all. If regionalism were simply an attempt by the US to impose 'order' through the Americas and a set of disciplinary economic measures for developing states, then it would have spread far more quickly through the hemisphere. Instead, NAFTA is an exclusive club with restricted membership. Accessing either NAFTA or MERCOSUR is only possible in cases where there is strong domestic support for integration and where other members of the regionalist grouping are persuaded of the benefits of enlargement. In Chile, joining both NAFTA and MERCOSUR has enjoyed elite domestic support. But Chile has so far failed to convince the US Congress of the utility of its inclusion in NAFTA, in sharp contrast with MERCOSUR, in which it was eagerly received.

Chile as semi-periphery

Of the countries in this book, Chile is one of the least economically developed. Its economy is small and is at an intermediate stage of development. This can be seen on two fronts: the economic and the social. Incomes are low, infrastructure is underdeveloped, and the quality of public services, including education, health and social security, is poor. These are obstacles to the development of the internal market and to the democratization of the state. In 1990, per capita income was only US$1,750. Income inequalities increased during the dictatorship of Pinochet (1973–89) and around five million of the thirteen million population lived below the poverty line in 1989. Even by 1996–7, seven years after the start of democratization, the minimum wage was still only 65,500 pesos (US$156) a month (*La Epoca*, 20 March 1997). At least 10 per cent of the economically active population were earning less than that. Most people still work in agricultural production, much of which is temporary, and in the unskilled or semi-skilled sectors of the economy. Unionization is low and the trade union federation, the Central Workers' Union (CUT), represents only around 14 per cent of the workforce.

The economy was transformed after the coup of 1973. It is now market-driven, export-led and open to foreign investment. Exports have diversified, diminishing the traditional dependence on copper, which accounted for 45 per cent of the country's exports in 1990, a significant fall from the early 1970s, when it represented around 80 per cent (Meller 1996: 275). Chile's exports of manufactured and semi-manufactured goods rose by an average of 8 per cent annually between 1980 and 1992, an increase second only to Mexico within LAC (ECLAC 1995: 74). The late 1980s in particular witnessed an increase in the number of firms based in Chile exporting to other countries (national, foreign-owned and joint ventures). Firms exporting more than a million dollars worth of goods rose in number from 235 in 1986 to more than 500 in 1990 (Meller 1996: 275). Domestically owned economic groups moved in to fill the vacuum left by the collapse and privatization of state-owned enterprises. Together with transnational corporations, they have become the agents of the new model of production. Export markets have also diversified. By 1992, Chile's most important trading partner was the European Union (EU), which received 29 per cent of the country's exports, followed by Japan, with 16.9 per cent. The US, which had been Chile's most important trading partner until the 1970s, slipped to third with 16.3 per cent. Sixteen per cent of exports went to LAC; Asian countries received 14.2 per cent and 7.7 per cent went to a mix of other countries (Saez 1995). It had thus become a 'global trader' and, as such, a model for the rest of LAC, where dependence on US markets remains pronounced (ECLAC 1994).

But growth masks dependence. Chile produces primary or at best semi-processed goods. The dynamic export performance of recent years has not altered this; it has merely diversified exports away from traditional goods towards new agricultural products. Ninety per cent of export firms are located in the primary sector (Laban and Meller 1996). They are highly vulnerable to international price fluctuations, to changes in the commercial strategies of Chile's trading partners and to competition from cheaper producers or from producers of higher quality goods. Markets built up in the 1980s in the EU, Japan and the US are fragile and have a ceiling in terms of size which Chile may be close to reaching. Their limitations account in some measure for Chile's interest in regional integration. A range of industrial, semi-industrial and manufactured goods are exported to LAC; Chilean firms are also more streamlined and competitive than many of their regional rivals and they could, therefore, do well as a result of deeper integration.

Contextualizing Chilean regionalism

Chile's regionalist strategy is shaped by the confused and somewhat contradictory process of regionalism in the Americas and by the political economy of the transition to democracy. One response to the uncertainties produced by global change is for states to embed themselves economically in their own geographical area. This has occurred in the Americas, where regionalism has proceeded faster and is deeper than in other areas of the world outside of Europe. Initially the changing fortunes of the US state and US-based economic groups were the driving force behind integration. Facing increased competition from the Pacific economies and even from parts of Europe, externally oriented US companies have successfully sought the support of the US state for their strategy of strengthening their hold on the labour forces and the markets of the Americas (Payne 1996). LAC states generally welcomed the US's reversal of multilateralism and its decision to anchor its economy in its own hemisphere. As a result, the Enterprise for the Americas (EAI) initiative by President Bush in 1990 opened the floodgates to a series of bilateral free trade negotiations within LAC, between LAC states and the US, and even between LAC states and Canada. Joining NAFTA, which was signed by the US, Canada and Mexico in 1994, has become the aim of all LAC states (except Cuba) because of the economic privileges to be gained from contiguity to Washington. Chile, with the healthiest economy in LAC, was always the first candidate for entry. Whether Chile can get into NAFTA, therefore, is a test of US commitment to region-wide integration.

But extending NAFTA southwards has proved difficult. Important domestic groups in the US are oppsed to it. At the same time, doubts have been expressed about the wisdom of removing all forms of protectionism in LAC. As a result, an alternative scheme emerged: MERCOSUR (see Chapter 4). MERCOSUR's common external tariff (CET) came into operation in 1995 and differs significantly from NAFTA because it retains protectionism through the imposition of a common external tariff (CET).

For Chile, there is a clear commercial basis for an interest in MERCOSUR, with up to a fifth of its exports going to the MERCOSUR countries, mainly to Argentina and Brazil. Chile's attractions for MERCOSUR are also clear: its Pacific ports mean potential entry into Asian markets, in addition to Chile's own internal market. Chile's inclusion, uniquely, was seen as central to the success of both projects.

NAFTA and MERCOSUR have transformed the map of the Americas. Chile has had no choice but to respond to these changes within its hemisphere. But Chilean responses have been conditioned by its past, in particular the process of economic liberalization, and by the politics of democratization. Any explanation of Chile's regionalist policies, therefore, must take the transformation of economic and state structures effected by the dictatorship of 1973–89 as its starting point.

Liberalization under Pinochet restructured Chile's capitalist class. This occurred in two stages. Immediately following the coup, 'shock treatment' was used to bring down inflation. By the mid-1970s, the 'Chicago experiment' had begun which brought about a broad liberalization of the economy through the introduction of a uniform tariff of 10 per cent, the withdrawal of state subsidies to industry, labour reform, a programme of privatization covering almost all sectors of the economy except copper, a fixed low exchange rate for the peso, and legislation which eliminated restrictions on foreign investment. Liberalization was rapid because of the disarticulation of the political opposition, the repression of labour and of popular organisations, and the enthusiastic support for the reorganization of the economy on the part of business and finance groups. Economic growth was high by the end of the decade, but the economy crashed in 1981–2 under the combined weight of a high external debt and the effective collapse of the domestic financial system, leading to soaring levels of unemployment and a wave of domestic bankruptcies (Oppenheim 1993).

Recovery only really took off again in 1985. Second-stage liberalization was far less ideological and more pragmatic. The reforms of the 1980s combined liberalization of markets with a judicious role for the state in terms of supporting and encouraging the private sector. Tariffs, which the dictatorship had been forced to raise to 35 per cent in 1984, the highest possible rate compatible with General Agreement on Tariffs and Trade (GATT) membership, came down to 15 per cent by 1988, this time in stages rather than at a stroke, thereby encouraging export expansion (Ffrench-Davis and Saez 1995; Saez 1995). This was accompanied by a reorganization of the Central Bank, the introduction of tax reforms in 1984 and 1988 which meant a lighter tax load for business, pension reforms and a second wave of privatisations. Growth, especially in the agricultural sector, took off once again.

These economic changes have obviously had a profound effect on the capitalist class. Before 1973, Chilean capitalism had been dominated politically by the power of the traditional landed elite (Loveman 1979). Import substitution had failed to generate a self-confident industrial elite and mining was mainly in the hands of US multinational companies. Liberalization restructured the business sector (Montero 1997). Its interests have been fragmented. Furthermore, the composition of the economic elite has been transformed because opening the economy meant prioritizing production for export over domestic production. This has weakened Chile's *latifundistas*, located in the Central Valley, where wine, beef and milk production for domestic consumption dominate. On the one hand, it has prompted agricultural diversification into the intensive cultivation of fruit, wood, paper and new mining interests and the modernization of the wine industry. On the other, it is transforming business culture by rewarding market-oriented values of hard work, risk-taking and merit over the claims of birth (Bartell 1995). These changes have threatened the social dominance and political power of the traditional elite, whose position rests on claims of aristocratic distinction upheld by family networks, kinship and the diffusion of cultural values and symbols which privilege unearned income and family lineage (Zeitlin 1968; Petras 1969). Of course, these changes have not ended aristocratic privilege. The economic elite remains small and social mobility is difficult, with the result that new business retains family ties to old money. The *latifundistas* remain important socially and economically. But newer entrepreneurs have emerged in the export sector alongside the traditional landowners that are models of capitalist innovation and competitiveness compared to the pre-1973 economic elite and indeed to much of the rest of LAC.

Liberalization also restructured the state. After 1985, a variant of the 'competitive state' emerged, as it was 'sucked in . . . to the competitive rat-race of the open world economy' (Cerny 1990: 228). The state was forced to play some role in managing, promoting and directing export growth. Tax and labour policies were shaped in favour of business. Government got involved in the active promotion and improvement of exports, leading to the proliferation of state organizations to promote Chilean products. PROCHILE, which dates from the 1970s and the purpose of which is to promote Chilean products abroad, increased its profile and its autonomy from the Foreign Office, becoming in effect a quango. CORFO, the government-run Production Development Corporation, also initiated a variety of schemes to stimulate the expansion of the private sector, including the creation of a technical assistance fund for quality control over exports and technology transfer to encourage small and medium-sized firms to move into the export market (ECLAC 1995: 119). The Chile Foundation, another quasi-autonomous organisation established with compensation funds from the Compania de Telefonos, a subsidiary of ITT, and state funding, became involved in technology transfer and skills acquisition through setting up innovative and risky businesses, which, if successful, are then passed on to the private sector. In overall charge of these policies were the 'Chicago Boys', a team of professional economists and right-wing 'technocrats'. Although they were to some degree insulated from 'politics' by the absence of any form of democratic accountability, they were not autonomous actors in the sense of the 'developmental state', where policy-making is the preserve of state bureaucrats. Under Pinochet, policy was made by an alliance between the technocrats and key socio-economic groups – businesspeople and agricultural producers within the new export industries (Silva 1993).

By the time of the first democratic general elections in 1989, the democratizing forces in the centre-left Coalition of Parties for Democracy (CD) knew that this presented them with a potentially serious problem. Liberalization had strengthened the weight of capital and the dictatorship had institutionalized its representation within the state. As a result, the governments of Patricio Aylwin (1990–4) and Eduardo Frei (1994–) would have faced obstruction had they attempted to change the economic model they inherited. Additionally, their chances of increasing the productive role of the state in the economy were poor and the scope for increasing the power of government over capital had been reduced by the tax reforms of 1984 and 1988 which significantly shrunk state revenues. According to Meller (1996), revenue from income tax fell by 40 per cent after the 1984 reform. Furthermore, legislation in the dying stages by the dictatorship, in particular the introduction of a form of 'institutional insulation' for the Central Bank in 1989, meant a reduction in the government's room for manoeuvre. It could be said, therefore, that the CD was constrained to pursue neo-liberalism by the weight of policies inherited from 1980s.

So, unlike almost everywhere else in LAC, the transition from authoritarianism was not a result of the failure of the dictatorship to engineer economic growth. Indeed, it occurred despite economic growth, as a result of Chilean society's rejection of military dictatorship and of the human costs of the economic transformation, along with a need to catch up with the global trend to democratization, a mix therefore of internal demands and external encouragement.

The CD, which brought together the Christian Democratic Party (PDC), the Socialist Party (PSCh) and the Popular Democratic Party (PPD), a personalist offshoot from the Socialists, won the presidential elections in 1989 and 1994. Both Aylwin and Frei come from the dominant PDC. The PDC and the PSCh both have a long history in Chilean politics, and were protagonists in the confrontational and conflictual pre-1973 period of the country's history. Some ministers, for example Jorge Arrate, Minister of Labour under Frei, had even belonged to the radical wing of the Socialist Party during the Allende government (1970–3). However, both the PDC and more especially the PSCh underwent ideological and organizational transformations during the dictatorship. In opposition, often in exile and deprived of influence over national politics, many of the intellectuals of the centre and the left experienced a shock of intellectual 'realism' which convinced them of the necessity of moderating their hostility towards domestic economic elites and of working with the pressures generated by the changing international order. At the same time, their dreams of revolutionary change within LAC as a whole faded (Barros 1986; Garreton 1991). As a result, the leadership of both parties now recognizes the need to work with the grain of structural pressures. Politically, this means support for liberal democracy and economically for economic openness and integration. The centre-left has made clear its recognition that the state can only have a limited role in redistributing income and that private sector (domestic and foreign) is central to economic growth.

Once in government, the CD pursued a style of policy-making similar in some ways to the pre-democratic era. Economic and foreign policy-making remains 'technocratic', and is largely in the hands of individuals referred to by Hershberg (1997) as 'technopols', politicians with high levels of training and professional competence. Key positions in the Treasury, the Ministry of the Economy and in Foreign Affairs, under both Aylwin and Frei, have been held by professional economists and academics who had hitherto made their careers in international organisations and think tanks. These include Alejandro Foxley, Minister of the Treasury under Alywin, Carlos Ominami, Minister of the Economy under Aylwin, Eduardo Aninat, Treasury Minister under Frei, and José Miguel Insulza, Foreign Minister under Frei. More junior ministerial posts in the Treasury and the Foreign Office have been filled by Juan Gabriel Valdes (who has been head of the team negotiating with NAFTA and MERCOSUR), Heraldo Munoz, Boris Yopo, Alejandro Jara and Alberto van Klaveren, all of whom held academic positions in the 1980s and who made important contributions to the debate pushing for 'realism' in Chile's foreign and economic policy. Policy is therefore in the hands of individuals who recognise the contemporary constraints on government worldwide, and have a sense that the profound restructuring which was carried out in Chile cannot be undone. Consequently, they have pushed for economic policy to be made in conjunction with the private sector and they have actively sought to involve export-oriented groups in decision-making. Nonetheless, a belief that the state should remain the ultimate site of decisions shapes their perceptions of how the relationship between themselves and new business groups should proceed.

As a result, Aylwin and Frei opted not just to maintain an open economy; they have chosen to deepen its export bias. After a shaky start, these governments have presided over a period of sustained economic growth, averaging over 6 per cent a year, and surpassing the targets set by Aylwin's government of 4.5 per cent. The CD signalled very clearly its intentions of maintaining an open economy before taking office. In part, this was designed to reduce the degree of uncertainty for investors, both domestic and foreign, during the transition (Foxley 1995: 9). In fact, unusually for LAC, the parameters of the debate over the economy during the transition were limited to a technical discussion about economic growth without any of the main electoral contenders questioning the overall orientation of political economy in the country (Vial 1995). As a sign of the commitment to continuing trade liberalization, tariffs came down to 11 per cent in 1991 and Frei is committed to a further reduction, possibly to 6 per cent, before leaving office.

Despite continuity in economic policy overall, the transition from authoritarianism to democracy has nonetheless introduced two significant new dimensions to policy-making. First, the CD tries to combine policies of growth with poverty reduction. Readjustments to the tax system, a move entrepreneurs accepted, expanded revenue by 2 per cent of GDP, the minimum wage has increased and there has been a modest rise in social spending (Pizarro *et al.* 1995). So far, the government has been able to convince business that social spending can be undertaken without increasing the overall burden on the wealthy because it has linked it to economic growth (Consejo Nacional para la Superacion de la Pobreza 1996). Extreme poverty has fallen from 17 per cent of the population to 8 per cent, primarily because of the rise in employment (Consejo Nacional para la Superacion de la Pobreza 1996: 53). But Chile remains a much more unequal society than it was before the dictatorship and the CD recognizes that social reforms will be partial, limited and dependent on continuing economic growth.

The second innovation is an active search for new policies to improve linkages with the international economy. This is central to the strategy of growth through exports. Without abandoning the commitment to multilateral trade and a unilaterally low tariff, exporters and technopols have focused attention on deepening relationships within LAC and across the Americas as a way of furthering global integration. This has added a new dimension to Chile's commercial strategy and a series of preferential trading agreements has been signed within the Americas. The transition to democracy in 1989 created the political space for re-engagement within the Americas, since democracy is a *sine qua non* of the new regionalism in the wake of the collapse of communism.

New state, new business: building an internal consensus

It was almost inevitable that cooperation with NAFTA and MERCOSUR would be of interest to the CD for political and economic reasons. Integration offered a chance to increase Chile's diplomatic profile and contributed to stabilizing the environment around the transition to democracy by strengthening the country's place within a community of democratic states. The question was whether the democratic governments could build a coalition internally around regionalism. As it turned out, regionalist policies emerged quite easily out of an alliance between the technopols located within the state and new business groups. The alliance coalesced around the issue of open development more generally. A new policy coalition therefore emerged, unprecedented in Chile, which links the state with domestic exporters and which shapes the broad contours of macroeconomic and external policies.

The origins of this alliance lie in the cooperation between the technocrats and export-oriented business groups under Pinochet. However, it is now far more of a strategic and pragmatic alliance than in the earlier period. Export-oriented business and CD technopols are not natural allies. Their political loyalties and goals are different. But, at least with regards to economic and trade policy, the state listens to business and business has permeated the policy-making arenas of the state. The result is the pursuit of a pragmatic policy of integration on two fronts: with both NAFTA and MERCOSUR.

State elites have taken advantage of changes in the patterns of political representation since democratization in order to build the policy coalition. The relationship between capitalist groups and the right-wing political parties, as well as between capital and the state, changed fundamentally as a result of the combined effects of economic transformation, the dictatorship and democracy. Before 1973, capitalist elites relied on their economic power to pressurize the state, rather than engaging in cooperation over the formulation of policies. They were loyal to the political party of the right, the National Party, which had not been in power since 1958–64. After 1973, the links with the political right diminished as parties were banned and capital came closer to cooperation with the dictatorship. In the 1989 elections, for the most part, capitalist elites supported Hernan Buchi, ex-Minister of the Economy under Pinochet, partly from ideological conviction and partly because he was regarded as a safe pair of hands with the economy. But since 1989 many within the capitalist elite have accepted the need for cooperation over economic policy. In particular, new business groups have taken a pragmatic approach towards the government. These entrepreneurs now have the confidence to negotiate directly with the state, bypassing the mediation of the post-dictatorship right-wing parties, the National Renovation Party (RN) and the Democratic Independent Union (UDI), which have been weakened in the process. One way of putting this is to say that important sectors of the economic elite are modernizing while the political right is still struggling to catch up with the economic and political changes taking place.

The organization of business groups changed radically under the dictatorship. In principle, the Chilean business sector presents a united front through a number of umbrella associations: the Society of Manufacturers (SFF), the National Society of Mining (SONAMI), the National Society of Agriculture (SNA) and the Confederation of Production and Commerce (CPC). These attempt to present, at least in public, common positions on policy (Montero 1997). In fact, however, there are substantial policy divisions. Business associations cannot agree over a range of economic issues: trade, protectionism and exchange rates, for example. Pressure for maintaining an open trading environment co-exists alongside pressure for protectionism. There are divisions between and within the umbrella groups. This has created opportunities for business–state relations outside of the umbrella groups. Some business sectors have established independent links with representatives of the state. In particular, new businesses, agro-exporters and the manufacturers and suppliers of semi-processed agricultural goods, keen to maintain a favourable economic environment for further expansion, have been prepared to work in conjunction with state elites in preparing and negotiating economic policy.

The splits within the economic elite are particularly clear in agriculture. Formally, the SNA represents all of Chile's farmers. In fact, however, around 80 per cent come from the *latifundista* class, traditionally extremely hostile to the centre and the left. In 1990, the SNA broadened its membership to include new agro-exporters, but so far they represent only 20 per cent of members. This has meant that the fruit producers, for example, a key export sector, have in practice been more active in the Federation of Fruit Producers (FEDEFRUTA) than in the SNA. FEDEFRUTA has been more supportive of the CD's economic strategy – and more influential within it – than the SNA as a whole. SNA policy reflects the preference for protectionism of *latifundistas* and insists on defending traditional agriculture for domestic markets, at the expense of the exporters. The SNA pays a price for this in that it has lost much of its political influence since 1989. Its inability to adjust to an open economy in conjunction with its ideological hostility to the centre-left means that it is outside the coalition. Closely identified with the right-wing parties, the SNA continues to function as in the past, almost as a social club for gentleman farmers rather than as an arena for debating agricultural policy. Officials have few channels, formal or informal, into the government, including even the Ministry of Agriculture. Its relationship with the Ministry of Foreign Affairs is distant ('correct but cold', according to one interviewee[1]). Neither President Frei nor his ministers are to be found visiting SNA headquarters and SNA officials are rarely received by the government.

This contrasts sharply with the position of the SFF. Like the SNA, the SFF, which groups together Chilean manufacturing, had played an important role in Chilean politics since its formation (Cavarozzi 1973). Unlike the SNA, however, the SFF has successfully adapted to the changes in Chile's political economy in the 1970s and 1980s. Despite initial resistance from industries dependent on state subsidies and protected markets, manufacturers supported liberalization and benefited from it and came out of the 1980s strong and confident. So, although there are ideological differences with the CD, the SFF opted to work closely with it, forming a 'pragmatic relationship' with the governments of Aylwin and Frei on a range of economic policies, including international trade, regionalism, some aspects of labour policy and infrastructure modernization. One official from SFF explained that the organization was prepared for problems when the Coalition of Parties for Democracy won the elections in 1989, but these have simply not materialized: 'This does not mean that the SFF is ideologically in sympathy with the CD, but that it does not deny it support and advice . . . a common set of interests has been built up between the government and the SFF.' The relationship flows through personal contacts with individuals within the government. It is not institutionalized. President Frei, as an ex-businessman, is particularly respected by the SFF, who see it as important for the continuity of the relationship to keep the presidency in the hands of the PDC rather than the left in the CD.

The pragmatic approach of associations such as the SFF and FEDE-FRUTA means that policy emerges from a relationship between state elites and social actors. It is not the exclusive preserve of the state. But this is not to say that business dictates the terms of economic policy. The authority of the state elites in charge of economic policy is also stronger and more stable now than during the dictatorship. The legitimacy of the technopols does not rely exclusively on their relationship with business. The government enjoys broad electoral support from a variety of social sectors including labour. The technopols are confident enough to resist sectoral demands from business where they think appropriate. They have consistently refused to consider moving away from a unilateral tariff which would open the government up to intense lobbying from different groups. The CD refuses to accept 'special case' pleading from private business and the role of the tariff is to signify that it is determined to be the final arbiter of decisions. The economic team is willing to listen to business, but it will do so only when arguments centre on how to manage the economic model.

Negotiating regionalism

One of the most innovative areas where cooperation has developed between the CD and new business groups is in the area of regionalism. A clear policy line emerged gradually. Strategies *vis-à-vis* NAFTA and MERCOSUR have gone through important changes. Trade policy has moved from single-track multilateralism to the adoption of more complex options which blend a commitment to liberalization with an interest in regional markets. According to Alejandro Jara, director of PROCHILE, the CD did not have a thought-out regionalist plan on taking office; only a commitment to growth through external trade.[2] Advantage was then taken of a set of external events which have unfolded in the course of the 1990s.

In spite of the political benefits which come from rejoining the Americas, regionalism is treated mainly as an aspect of economic policy-making. The opportunities presented by regionalism have been consistently seen as principally commercial. The technopols pay little attention even to the idea that regionalism might strengthen the common negotiating position of LAC with third countries or within the World Trade Organization (WTO). The go-it-alone culture which developed during the period of diplomatic isolation under Pinochet remains potent and has served commercial interests well. NAFTA and MERCOSUR are seen as sets of trade arrangements and policies are driven by this.

As a result, only superficial attention is paid to regionalism as a mechanism for supporting or deepening democracy, although there is an implicit assumption within NAFTA that members should be democratic, or at least be moving towards democracy, and MERCOSUR has a democratic clause attached to it, which entails that any state in breach of minimal democratic criteria will find its membership suspended. The statement by Alejandro Foxley, then President of the PDC, in support of democratic criteria for membership of regional pacts in August 1996 is interesting precisely because it was almost the first time attention had shifted to the political dimensions of the agreement (*La Época*, 20 August 1996). In fact, it is likely that Foxley was taking advantage of the fact that the right was not in favour of MERCOSUR in order to accuse it of being hostile to democracy as well.

The teams negotiating regionalism have come out of the Ministry of the Treasury (NAFTA) and the Ministry of Foreign Affairs (MERCOSUR). In both cases, the team was staffed with technopols, reporting to 'techno-political' ministers: Juan Gabriel Valdes, who led the negotiations, was first responsible to Eduardo Aninat, the Treasury Minister, over NAFTA and later to José Miguel Insulza, the Foreign Minister, over MERCOSUR. Alliances between state elites and some of the business groups were important in constructing internal support for both NAFTA and MERCOSUR. Business groups were also involved directly in some stages of the negotiations. However, I will show below that the technopols counted on support from slightly different sets of business elites in the case of the NAFTA negotiations than for MERCOSUR.

Negotiating NAFTA[3]

Chile was formally invited to open negotiations in December 1994. By early 1995, it was confidently predicted that Chile would become a member the following year. In March 1995, the then US Secretary of Commerce, Ron Brown, even claimed that the negotiations were in the final stages, after which the deal would be sent to the US Congress for ratification (*El Mercurio*, 28 March 1995). However, in the event, Chile failed to gain accession and, at the time of writing (June 1998), the negotiations are still awaiting fast-track approval by the US Congress.

Access was sought in 1995 because of a combination of direct trade benefits to Chile which it was thought were attached to NAFTA and indirect benefits which would result from the US seal of approval on Chile. The immediate commercial benefits were often exaggerated and initially predictions that exports would increase in the order of 18 per cent were not uncommon. But the potential gains from membership were not just seen in terms of expansion into the US market. First, it was thought that NAFTA would increase the exposure of Chilean businesses involved in manufacturing to international competition and would contribute to shaping them into a small but highly competitive sector. Second, NAFTA was considered likely to lock the liberal economy in Chile into a set of international obligations; indeed, the Director of PROCHILE argued that it was useful because it might deepen domestic commitment to liberalization by promoting a reform of public sector services and government procurement policies. And finally, accession would confer a kind of international 'accreditation', symbolizing the success of the economic reforms. As Felipe Larrain of the Universidad Catolica in Santiago claimed: 'It would differentiate Chile from the rest of the region and perceptions of risk that the country represented would fall as a result' (*El Mercurio*, 23 March 1995). So, apart from commercial benefits, membership of NAFTA was thought to guarantee the liberal order on which export-oriented growth rested, and reward Chile for its early embrace of free trade.

Inside Chile, the Treasury was in charge of coordinating the negotiations. Talks were held between Treasury officials and a number of business groups throughout 1995. However, the CPC and the Chilean–North American Chamber of Commerce (AMCHAM) proved particularly supportive. Together with the official negotiating team, they coordinated policy positions for the negotiations with the US Trade Representatives Office (USTR) and lobbying strategies in Washington (*El Mercurio*, 7 April 1995). The CPC and AMCHAM also gave evidence at the International Trade Commission (ITC) in Washington. Additionally, they shouldered much of the burden and expense of lobbying. AMCHAM, for example, organized a series of high-level dinners in Washington through the first half of 1995, bringing together presidents and directors of US companies with investments in Chile with the US senators and deputies from the US home-states or districts where the companies were based (*El Mercurio*, 7 April 1995).

Yet, as the negotiations dragged on through 1995, it became clear that the Republican-controlled US Congress was unwilling to extend the free trade deal negotiated with Mexico though the rest of Latin America as rapidly as Clinton had expected. The negotiations eventually stalled when it became clear that, lobbying in Washington notwithstanding, the Chilean team was unable to convince the US Congress of the value of allowing Chile to join. US officials who had argued for extending NAFTA admitted that many of the problems with the negotiations were unrelated specifically to Chile, and were due to a rising tide of protectionism inside the US (*El Mercurio*, 6 February 1996). By early 1996, the Foreign Minister, José Miguel Insulza, had no choice but to admit that the government was increasingly sceptical about the chances of joining NAFTA in the immediate future (*El Mercurio*, 24 January 1996).

Since then, the Clinton administration has continued to repeat its intention of broadening NAFTA. Responses in Chile, however, are now more guarded, after the disappointments of 1995–6. There is an awareness that enlargement of NAFTA depends not just on what happens in Chile but also on the internal politics of the US. Insulza is on record remarking that Chile would not enter further discussions until there is Congressional approval for fast-track negotiations (*El Mercurio*, 2 April 1996). For all that, joining NAFTA has become important enough within Chile that, by early 1997, the government was once again preparing negotiating briefs. This time, however, the context of the negotiations is different. In the meanwhile, Chile has become an associate member of MERCOSUR, thereby changing its position within LAC. Also, the expectations about export growth resulting from accession to NAFTA are far more realistic. NAFTA is now expected to have only an incremental impact on Chile's exports in the forthcoming future. Consequently, the Chilean negotiators feel able to make more demands. In particular, they are seeking to change aspects of NAFTA legislation so that it benefits Chilean businesses. 'Chile should make it a condition that the US makes its rules of origin more flexible in order to make membership of NAFTA more attractive,' Valdes claimed in an interview (*La Epoca*, 13 December 1996). In accordance with the demands of private business, the team has ruled out accepting the labour and environmental side-agreements to NAFTA, which are seen as a covert form of protectionism on the part of the US. Chile is also unhappy with aspects of the anti-dumping legislation in its agreements with Canada and would see entry into NAFTA as the opportunity to change this.

In all, then, the negotiating team has become more pro-active in terms of defending national interests. These changes in Chile's negotiating positions have come about as the team has realized it has little to lose from hardening its position. After all, the negotiations failed not because of demands Chile made but because of internal politics in the US. Hardening its position prevents domestic opposition to the reopening of the negotiations because it makes the government look as though it is in control of them. The government thereby retains credibility. The failure to deliver membership in 1995 also strengthened the hand of business groups *vis-à-vis* the technopols in determining the agenda and indicates some temporary shift in power within the policy coalition away from state elites. However, this is unlikely to represent a permanent shift because NAFTA is only one aspect of the overall economic strategy.

Negotiating MERCOSUR

The failure of the NAFTA negotiations led directly to a reappraisal of Chile's relationship with its Southern Cone neighbours grouped together in MERCOSUR. Before any kind of deal could be reached with MERCOSUR, however, a solution had to be found for the tariffs problem. MERCOSUR has a common external tariff while the technopols and exporting groups in Chile reject the use of tariffs as a way of allocating resources and as a device to protect internal producers. In the end, a free trade deal, rather than membership, was agreed in June 1996 and ratified, after some domestic debate, in September of that year.

According to economist Hector Asael from the Economic Commission for Latin America and the Caribbean (ECLAC), the benefits to Chile of associate membership are considerable because Chilean exporters now have access to MERCOSUR's internal market. But Chile, by not becoming a full member of the pact, has also been able to protect its economy from competition from Brazil or Argentina if those countries devalue the currency as a result of economic crisis (*La Epoca*, 27 June 1996). Chilean goods now enter MERCOSUR's market with an average tariff of 6 per cent; access will be tariff-free for most goods by 2003. Goods from MERCOSUR enter Chile under the same conditions, although there is a list of exceptions composed in essence of traditional agricultural products, which will be protected for up to fifteen or eighteen years. Tariff-free access to MERCOSUR markets will undoubtedly benefit a range of Chilean goods, including wine and industrial products. The SFF described the agreement as 'of transcendental importance for the country' because it created low-tariff markets for Chile's finished goods (*El Mercurio*, 7 September 1996). The Minister of the Economy, Alvaro Garcia, claimed rather grandly that the agreement will lead to 150,000 new jobs in Chile (*El Mercurio*, 2 July 1996). Independent analyses were somewhat more sober, suggesting that the increase in exports will be partially offset by a corresponding increase in imports, but pointing out that this will lead to lower consumer prices (Muchnik *et al.* 1996). And finally, associate membership also leaves Chile free to pursue, unilaterally, trade agreements with other countries, including the members of NAFTA.

In contrast to the negotiations over NAFTA, this deal was brokered quickly. The Chilean negotiating team was composed of technopols from the Ministry of Foreign Relations, led by Valdes once again. In this case, they were supported in particular by the SFF and, in a less obvious way, by FEDEFRUTA. In fact, the SFF saw MERCOSUR as a triumph for Chilean manufacturers and one which it had done much to bring about. The SFF was pleased with the outcome of the negotiations and had supplied many of the technical reports used during them. In some cases, its staff were even responsible for drafting parts of the official negotiating documents. The relationship between the government and the SFF during the MERCOSUR negotiations was described by an SFF official as 'one of confidence'. However, government representatives and the SFF separately concurred with the view that the SFF only pushed 'policy options', while the government team made decisions: 'In the end the government decided,' said one SFF representative. Nonetheless, according to officials within the Ministry of Foreign Relations, no step was taken without consulting export groups. There was a deliberate effort on the part of the government to pull some private sector groups into the discussions and to win their support.

However, the deal was rather more controversial inside Chile than NAFTA had promised to be. Despite the benefits for Chilean industry and the support of the SFF, the deal with MERCOSUR was opposed by *latifundistas* and the SNA because it undermined traditional agricultural products (wheat, beef and milk). In fact, the divergence of interests within Chile's agricultural community was evident throughout the negotiations. Along with manufacturers, new agro-export groups are eager to keep trade policy biased towards exports. Like the SFF, they were consulted extensively throughout the negotiations, although their profile during the negotiations was lower. But this did not prevent the SNA from trying to block the deal. The SNA went on the offensive, writing to the Ministry of the Agriculture, taking out pages of advertising in the press and winning the support of some of the right-wing in Congress and some of the ideological freemarketeers who were unhappy with the CD's pragmatic approach to economic policy-making.

The SNA claimed that traditional agriculture would suffer losses of around US$460 million as a result of cheaper products coming onto the Chilean market. Their supporters opposed the deal when it went to Congress in August and demanded compensation for traditional agriculture. In the event, however, the SNA could not count on the total support of the two parties of the right. The RN and UDI, divided between old loyalties to the SNA and a commitment to new capitalist groups, split when it came to voting in Congress and only a handful of representatives finally rejected the agreement (*La Epoca*, 14 August 1996). The RN and the UDI recognized that the damage would be much less than the SNA claimed, something that was even admitted privately in interviews with the SNA.

In the end, therefore, the SNA was unsuccessful, indicating its lack of effective channels into economic policy-making. Ultimately, because of the mediation of the right-wing parties in Congress, coupled with the desire of the CD to build consensus on important matters of policy, a considerable delay was introduced in freeing the market for wheat and other traditional staples. Of course, this *could* be seen as a result of the structural power of the large landowners. But in reality, the mere fact that a deal was struck which was detrimental to traditional farming and favourable to new agro-exports and to industry, and then passed through Congress, points to a fundamental shift in the political economy of the country and to a radical change within state–society relationships. The traditional landowners are now removed from the centres of policy-making. Economic policy-making is firmly in the hands of the CD technopols, who prefer to consult with the dynamic exporting groups that emerged in the economic revolution of the 1980s. In the end, therefore, the significance of the deal with MERCOSUR lies beyond the commercial possibilities it represents. It is also a sign that economic policy is being made between technopols representing the executive, who privilege the interests of export-based economic groups, and those export groups themselves.

Conclusion

Regionalism in Chile, perhaps more explicitly than elsewhere, is part of the overall policy of liberalization. Chile's economic liberalization has been unique in LAC in that it began in the 1970s and survived transitions in regime type (from authoritarianism to democracy) and in governments. Judged within its own terms, liberalization and regionalist policies have been highly successful as a result of the formation of a policy coalition linking state elites with society, thereby guaranteeing a consensual and stable environment for policy-making. Of course, this coalition is also, by its very nature, exclusionary. Not only did it leave out the traditional landowners, who argued for protectionism, it also failed to include labour and groups representing the poor and the unemployed in policy discussions. In fact, labour and the poor appear as objects of the government's social policies and as potential voters for it, but not as agents shaping the trajectory of the CD. Chile's regionalist policies tell us a great deal, in fact, about the style of policy-making in the new democracy.

The approach of state elites to region-building has been pragmatic from the beginning. Once having accepted the model of growth through exports, the logical position for Chile, as a small country with diversified markets, was to negotiate access on as many fronts as possible. It is still likely that Chile will be the first new member to be admitted to NAFTA – as soon as the debate about broadening the agreement is resolved inside the US. But in the meanwhile, the negotiations have been an important learning experience both for the technopols and for the business associations involved. Joining MERCOSUR should prove a way of keeping Southern Cone markets open for Chilean companies and even deepening regional markets. But neither NAFTA nor MERCOSUR indicates the reversal of multilateralism within the commercial strategy overall. Chile continues to seek other trading opportunities. These include the possiblity of deals with Asian countries and seeking new partners such as New Zealand. A deal was also signed in June 1996 with the European Union. The CD's relationship with export business, as well as the political support it enjoys as the agent of transition, guarantees a stable internal environment for these policies, even when they signify costs for some domestic groups and classes.

Notes

1   Some of the material in this section is derived from interviews carried out by the author in Santiago in March and April 1997. The interviewees are not identified and preferred to speak off the record.
2   Again, the material in this section comes overwhelmingly from interviews carried out by the author. Except where mentioned, the interviewees are not named.
3   This and the following sub-section draw extensively on interviews carried out by the author, especially with representatives of the SFF and the SNA, in conjunction with Chilean press sources.

6 Becoming Western: Turkey and the European Union

Mine Eder

'We cannot afford to miss this train of globalization: we either become a part of Europe or we face total isolation and marginalization.' These were the words of the then Prime Minister Tansu Çiller (*Dünya*, 14 April 1995). They were used to justify entry into a Customs Union with the European Union (EU), which was approved in December 1995. This chapter will explain why Turkey's developmental options came to be seen in such stark terms. What was the role of the state in Turkey in shaping the agenda of relations with Europe? Does the Turkish state consider attachment to the EU as a strategy for development? While there is no doubt that globalization has significantly limited the ability of the nation-states to carry out their regulatory, productive and distributive functions (Cerny 1990; Strange 1996), this chapter will argue that the role of the so-called 'residual state' in Turkey was crucial in utilizing and implementing policy options and hence was able to shape the outcome and patterns of regionalist policy interactions with the EU.

I discuss first the changes in the political economy of Turkey and the international setting that Turkey faces, analysing how and why regionalism became an option. Turkey is part of the 'weak' semi-periphery in the world economy. Even though the manufacturing industry has grown rapidly over the last fifteen years and accounts for 25 per cent of GDP, more than 40 per cent of the working population is still employed in the agricultural sector, which only accounts for 15 per cent of the total GDP. While the Turkish textile industry has become sufficiently competitive in world markets to provoke anti-dumping measures by both the EU and the US, most other industries are inefficient in terms of productivity, labour and capital investment. Despite significant trade liberalization and economic reforms since the 1980s, export growth has not been accompanied by the industrialization that occurred in the East Asian countries. Furthermore, the amount of foreign direct investment (FDI) Turkey attracts has remained limited. Although the combination of cheap labour as a result of the wage freezes after the military coup of 1980 and the size of the domestic market worked to draw in some investors, FDI expansion has been constrained by the rise of real wages in the early 1990s and the macroeconomic instabilities of that time. FDI increased eight-fold in the 1980s, but the emergence of cheaper labour sources in Eastern Europe and China, coupled with the political uncertainties associated with the rise of Islamic fundamentalism in Turkey, led to a fall in foreign investment. Hence Turkey remains a developing country. Its GDP is less than the total corporate sales of General Motors. It ranks seventy-fourth in the world in terms of human development indicators and has serious income distribution disparities between rural and urban areas (United Nations Development Programme 1997). Most industrial activity takes place in the west, north-west and the south, while the eastern and south-eastern parts of the country have experienced very limited economic growth.

The second part of this chapter presumes that new regionalism is not an unstoppable trend to which all states are subject, but the result of deliberate policy coordination on the part of states in order to meet the new challenges of international competition. The so-called process of 'deep integration' which is at the heart of new regionalism is driven by the state and its impact largely depends on state effectiveness. The Turkish state has been largely ineffective in terms of protecting national interests through its regionalist policies. While some of this ineffectiveness is embedded in the very ambiguities and uncertainties associated with the post-Cold War era, most have arisen from domestic political power games and the uneasy state–society arrangement, particularly between business and the state. Clearly, in Turkey's case, state capacity does not imply state efficiency (Waldner 1996).

The third section of this chapter looks in more detail at the Customs Union between Turkey and the EU and poses the following questions: Were domestic constituency concerns and various interest group pressures the key to understanding why the Turkish government was unable to bargain effectively *vis-à-vis* the EU? Was the Turkish bureaucracy autonomous from public pressures during the negotiations? And is Turkey a 'predatory state', subject to the undue influences of rent-seekers and interest groups? Rent-seeking, as argued by Krueger (1974), constitutes all activities in which incumbents engage in order to benefit themselves and their supporters. They might distribute state resources directly through subsidies, loans, contracts, services or use their authority through laws to create rents for their own groups. High returns from the state discourage investment in productive sectors, thus creating inefficiency and distortion in the market. Rent-seeking states are 'predatory' and 'have no more regards for their societies than a predator does for its prey' (Evans 1992: 122). They constitute a barrier to development through the market.

The Customs Union will have a profound, though uneven, effect on Turkish industry. In fact, the final agreement reflected the tensions between those who had lobbied for the agreement, such as the textile industry, which demanded the lifting of the quotas and restrictions, and entrenched industrial interests that had long relied on state protection, such as the automotive and white goods industries (home appliances, television sets and other assembly-line industries), which were most important in resisting it. Another long-running conflict in Turkish politics, in which the Customs Union debate became enmeshed, was that between those interests that would lose from the restructuring of the state which will follow from it and those who defended the reforms. For the latter group, the Customs Union was an institutional framework that would 'lock in' the economic reforms and increase the credibility of the government.

But the role of interest groups in the negotiations was actually very limited. Although the issues were discussed in the media, interest groups were not consulted during the negotiations with the EU. Interviews with both the Turkish delegation and the EU representatives carried out by the author in February 1996 confirm this. The negotiations were highly politicized and centred mainly on the following issues: human rights, the Kurdish problem, the threat of Islamic fundamentalism and Cyprus. The government carried the discussion onto this ideological plane precisely in order to avoid any discussion based on economic groups' interests. Furthermore, presenting the debate in terms of secularism, which membership of the EU was thought to guarantee, versus Islam prevented even those groups which would be adversely effected by the Customs Union from disputing the particulars of the agreement. In short, the government adopted a populist and politicized discourse, thereby silencing discussion and diverting the real and potential opposition to the agreement. Although there were objections to the way the negotiations were handled from the opposition parties, the government, particularly the True Path Party (TPP), which badly needed the prestige of signing the agreement with the EU, was able to play on the desires of the Turkish people to join the developed world. Prime Minister Çiller even claimed that 'she was carrying Turkey into the Western civilization' (*Milliyet*, 11 March 1995). Thus I argue that, contrary to conventional wisdom, the degree of autonomy of the Turkish state and the governing parties became a barrier to negotiating effectively with the EU, since satisfying the economic interests of domestic constituencies was not necessary in order to get their policies through. Where the local private sector is as weak as in the Turkish case, interest-based coalitions do not hold. The bureaucracy's and governing parties' lack of 'embeddedness' and the absence of a 'concrete set of ties that bind state and society together and provide institutionalized channels for the continuation of negotiation and renegotiation of goals and policies' (Evans, 1995: 12) leave enormous room for interpretation in policy-making, but do not guarantee that those policies will be made in the broader interests of society.

Turkey's changing political economy

Until recently, Turkey's economic development was largely state-led, so much so that *étatisme* was one of the founding principles of the Republic.

Given the absence of independent capital accumulation in the private sector, it is not surprising that the state has consistently intervened in the economy in the form of creating state economic enterprises as well as providing administrative guidance and privileges for the rising business elite. The fact that expansion of the state preceded the formation of a significant private sector had consequences for the overall pattern of state–society relations and largely explains why the Turkish private sector, despite its growing strength, still remains dependent on the state (Bugra 1994). The agricultural boom in the 1950s was followed by nascent indus-trial growth in the 1960s accompanied by import-substituting industrializa-tion (ISI) policies typical of the period. As a result, a new industrial elite dependent on state protectionism and incentives began to emerge in the 1960s.

A strictly instrumental view of the state is not always applicable in the Turkish context due to the ideological aspects of the statist tradition and the role of the military in political life. Nonetheless, it is still possible to argue that the import-substituting era created a close network of relation-ships between the state, on the one hand, and the new industrial elite, on the other, allowing for industrial concerns to expand into the large conglom-erates of the 1970s (Keyder 1987). But, by the end of this decade, a number of ISI-related problems began to emerge: foreign exchange crises, globally uncompetitive goods and a reluctance to invest in technological upgrading, for example. In fact, such was the economic crisis by 1980 that it was a significant factor provoking the military intervention of that year. In many ways the story of Turkey until the 1980s does not really differ from any late industrializing country, and actually has strong parallels with the Latin American countries.

But Turkey began to diverge significantly from the other late industrial-izers with the experience of export-led growth and economic liberaliza-tion. Initially, the Turkish government saw exports and economic liberal-ization as the only way out of the foreign exchange crisis. Backed by the iron fist of a military government between 1980 and 1983, Turkey launched what appeared to be a standard 'neo-liberal' economic reform programme. Even though the military expressed unease about the restructuring of the state, the economic team led by Turgut Özal launched an ambitious package of reforms that included the elimination of price controls, foreign exchange rate reforms, the liberalization of trade and FDI and the privatization of state economic enterprises. *Étatisme*, the new regime argued, was at an end (Nas and Odekon 1992; Önis and Webb 1994; Krueger 1995). The policy mission statements of the Motherland Party (MP), which won the first post-intervention elections in 1983, indicated a determination to apply IMF-style stabilization policies (Önis 1995). The entrenched interests of the import substitution era, argued Özal, who was now Prime Minister, were being pushed aside and replaced with an export-led growth strategy.

However, as Bugra (1994: 264) points out:

These attempts at the restructuring of the economy did not lead to the retreat of the state, an objective which was stressed as a major component of the official ideology of the state. There was a reorganization of the state apparatus, which brought about a centralization of decision-making by enlarging the powers of the executive branch and of the Prime Minister in particular. The legislative as well as the legal and bureaucratic institutions were undermined throughout the process, but this did not imply in any way a decline in the significance of the state for business activity. The state remained – perhaps more significantly than in any other period in the Republican era – the central focus of the Turkish businessmen concerns.

Waterbury (1992: 46) suggests that

> the Özal government favour[ed] turning the economy over to the private sector *and* reinforcing the state. It . . . promoted deregulation and liberalization in the name of efficiency *and* increased the scope of discretionary allocations in the economy. It . . . promoted the survival of the fittest in the export sector *and* entitlements elsewhere.

Thus the liberal reforms did not change the state-governed economic structures. Public investment remained high. The constitution of 1983 actually increased the powers of the Prime Minister and his/her control over the bureaucracy by the creation of the extra-budget funds, such as Mass Housing and Public Transportation Funds, under the direct control of the Prime Minister. State-budget funds totalled between US$3.5 and 5.7 billion in 1987–8. By 1988, the Mass Housing and the Public Transportation Funds alone were estimated to have reached US$2.2 billion (Waterbury 1992: 52). The centralization of authority in the hands of the Prime Minister also increased policy uncertainty, which, in the end, was inimical to the creation of a free market economy.

In short, economic liberalization and export-led growth in the 1980s failed to restructure state–business ties. Some of the industrial conglomerates shifted towards exports largely thanks to the political conditions created by the coup. Mostly, however, a new rent-seeking elite of exporters began to emerge, creating yet another cleavage among the business community between big industrialists and exporters (Arat 1991). Businesses continued to rely on state patronage and 'side payments' from the state (Waldner 1996). Indeed, side payments, such as subsidies to agriculture and certain import tariffs, were crucial to Özal's electoral coalition. Democratic pressures and electoral concerns ironically increased the need for more side payments and extended state patronage (Waterbury 1992). The institutional setting and the nature of bureaucracy remained statist, despite Özal's attempt to create an alternative technocratic elite, and personalized, highly politicized distribution of state patronage continued unreformed.

It is not surprising that, in circumstances such as these, the privatization programme was also slow. Less than 10 per cent of the programme had been implemented by the mid-1990s. In 1996 the World Bank put Turkey among the worst three performers in terms of privatizing state assets. The total revenue from privatization did not exceed US$3 billion in 1987–97. Additionally, the (incomplete) reform programme failed to address fundamental developmental problems such as regional discrepancies, wages and skewed taxation. Both the centre-right coalitions of the Özal governments since 1983 and Suleyman Demirel's and later Tansu Çiller's coalition with the Social Democrats have ignored these issues in order to continue granting side payments to their own constituencies. In the case of Çiller's TPP, these include the farmers, which explains how agricultural prices came to be above world market prices in the 1990s while the presence of the Republican People's Party, with an urban worker electorate, guaranteed wage increases. In sum, the attempts that started in the 1980s to compete through economic liberalization have brought about a rapid increase in exports and economic growth, but left unresolved the problems of inflation and macroeconomic instabilities.

The reform programme had, not surprisingly, also failed to address Turkey's trade problem. Although exports steadily increased in the 1980s, no major growth surges have been observed in recent years. Furthermore, annual exports between 1990 and 1995 were in the order of US$16 billion, while imports averaged around US$25 billion dollars, creating a US$9 billion trade deficit every year. The export/import coverage ratio dropped from 78 per cent in 1994 to 54 per cent in the first half of 1996. One reason behind Turkey's declining trade competitiveness is that it has been rather unsuccessful in terms of diversifying exports. Textiles, for instance, accounted for more than 38 per cent of total exports; agriculture for 11 per cent; iron and steel for 10 per cent; food for 9 per cent; and only the remaining 32 per cent for industrial goods. Overall raw materials constitute more than 25 per cent of exports, consumer goods 58 per cent and investment goods only 16.3 per cent. Out of this 16.3 per cent, 8.9 per cent is constituted by construction goods, which, with textiles, is the only globally competitive sector. A second reason is that Turkey has become less competitive as its advantages as a source of cheap labour have been eroded. Real wages have slowly but steadily increased since 1991. The hourly wage in 1995 was approximately the equivalent of 35 US cents in the private sector and 52 US cents in the public sector. Low by world standards, they are high compared to South East Asia and China. The fact that the main export item of these countries is also textiles creates significant problems for the Turkish textile industry. Meanwhile, Eastern European economies also began to compete with Turkey in textile and manufacturing industry exports in the EU market.

In short, Turkey's problems with restructuring its economy in the 1980s were intensified by the impact of increased globalization and the emergence of new regional growth areas. In particular, the pace of integration within the newly created EU in the aftermath of the Maastricht treaty and the 1992 Internal Market began to raise concerns about being left behind. Turkey's unsuccessful – and somewhat unexpected – membership application to the European Community (EC) in 1987 reflected growing anxiety over marginalization. The application faltered in December 1989, when it was rejected by the European Commission, endorsed by the Council of Ministers. The reasons included Turkey's low level of economic development by EC standards, its high population growth, high long-term foreign debt (approximately US$38 billion), low tax revenue and high state expenditure (twice the EC average), as well as fears of an influx of Turkish labour (Lesser 1993: 105). Nevertheless, Turkey continued to seek attachment to the EC/EU. By the mid-1990s, now facing even tougher global challenges, the second-best option of a Customs Union was tried.

Turkey's regional options and the decision to opt for the Customs Union

The reordering of the international system after the Cold War changed Turkey's geopolitical status significantly. First, the collapse of the Soviet Union undermined the strategic role of Turkey within the Western bloc and NATO. The initial decline of the role of NATO in European security, coupled with the granting of only associate status at the Western European Union (WEU), appeared to point to a weakening of the security and political links between Turkey and the West. This was tempered, however, by the effects of the Gulf War, on the one hand, during which Turkey came to be seen as the key to Middle East stability and which strengthened the strategic ties between Turkey and the US (Önis 1995: 50), and the developments within the former Yugoslavia, on the other. So, and this is the second significant change, Turkey became an important independent actor within the Balkans, as it adopted a clear anti-Russian and anti-Orthodox stance and expressed support for the Muslim population in Bosnia, independence for Macedonia and for the Albanians in Kosovo.

The importance of Turkey as a regional actor is still shaped by its membership of NATO. With over 630,000 troops, Turkey maintains the second largest army within NATO after the US and is an important partner at the Southern flank of the organization. But NATO can no longer be Turkey's only source of authority in the area. Intense disagreements with Greece over the militarization of its Aegean islands, and conflicts over Cyprus and over air and nautical boundaries make it a problematic partner (Fuller and Lesser 1993: 178). Also, as the threat from Russia diminished for the West with the collapse of the Soviet Union, so it became clear that Turkey would now have to deal with any problems in its relationship with Russia largely on its own. Turkey's emerging economic and strategic interests in Central Asia and the Caucasus have to take into account the persisting Russian influence over these republics and its diplomatic support for Azerbaijan during the dispute over Nogorno-Karabakh region had to be tempered by concerns over inciting a Russian response.

The result has been that a number of new regionalist scenarios have had to be considered by the Turkish state. One was the Black Sea Economic Cooperation (BSEC), which aimed to create a loose trading area between Turkey and Albania, Armenia, Azerbaijan, Bulgaria, Georgia, Greece, Moldavia, Russia and the Ukraine. Founded in 1990, the BSEC initially promised to create a market of 330 million consumers. Turkey was also attracted by the possible access to Russia's energy supplies. Although BSEC suffers from financial limitations and the often contradictory views of its members, it has certainly opened up new markets and opportunities for Turkey (Önis 1995: 59). By 1994, total exports in the area were US$89 billion and imports US$95 billion. In the long term, the BSEC aims to create a free trade zone. This would have the advantage of integrating the informal trade between Turkey and the former Soviet Republics into the formal economy. Turkey also hopes to play a liaison role in the area, thereby increasing EU and US investment in Turkey from companies looking for a bridgehead in Central Asia. But internal rivalries within the BSEC, Russian concerns over Turkish influence in the region, coupled with a region-wide absence of capital and technology means that BSEC, though helpful, will not turn Turkey into a core economy. Hence the attractiveness of the BSEC is limited. Another option was increased cooperation with Turkey's Middle East partners and the expansion of ties with the moderate regimes of the area. In fact, a free trade agreement has been signed with Israel and trade talks are underway with Jordan and Egypt (Carkoglu *et al.*, 1997), although trade flows are actually quite limited in volume and the differences among the regime types and the tensions between the Israel and the Arab world constitute real barriers to the future development of cooperation within the Middle East.

All of this means that the option of the Customs Union with the EU has merited most attention, even though Turkey cannot compete with the EU on equal terms. The hope, as a former director of the State Planning Institute argues, was that Turkey's commitment to liberal markets, regardless of how it was actually implemented, would help persuade the EC/EU that Turkey was ready for association status, despite the problems with the 1987 application. The transition to democracy was also partly carried out with an eye on Europe. One reason Turkey aimed to complete the Customs Union with the EU was because it went beyond a simple liberalization of trade. The agreement was seen as the first step towards 'deep integration' with the EU. Indeed, the Turkish government saw it as part of the global trend towards 'new' regionalism, which it took to mean not just mutual trade liberalization but a 'harmonization and possibly coordination of economic policies and domestic law and institutions' (Lawrence 1995). The economic attractions for Turkey, then, were not just, or even principally, couched in terms of the opportunities presented by tariff reduction and the possible increase of trade in goods, services and capital. Rather, it appeared as a way to participate in the European regional production system through the elimination of barriers to investment as well as trade.

Certainly, the deal as it finally emerged between Turkey and the EU contained elements of the kind of concerns inherent in new regionalism. According to De Melo *et al.* (1993: 176),

> almost by definition, any regional arrangement worth its name entailed the imposition of some common rules of conduct on the countries entering the arrangement and a set of reciprocal commitments and obligations. Regional integration thereby enforced a certain degree of arbitrage among national institutions, just as it brings about arbitrage in markets for goods and services.

The agreement went well beyond trade, aiming at the coordination of policy on various issues such as intellectual property rights, competition policies as well as investment incentives. The sixty-three articles in the agreement include a series of measures to harmonize Turkish commercial policy *vis-à-vis* the EU as well as third parties. Turkey received some concessions with regards to countries with which it enjoys special trade status, and was granted five years to bring its trade policy in line with the EU with regard to third parties. The agreement so far has reduced the 10.22 per cent nominal rate of protection that Turkey had with the EU countries to 1.4 per cent and brought down the overall rate against third parties to 6.92 per cent. The preliminary assessments on the prospective loss of revenue is estimated at around US$3 billion by 2002.

The Customs Union with the EU has a number of political and economic consequences. Politically, the main effect will be to restrict and reshape the state. As a result of harmonizing Turkish commercial law with that of the EU, along with competition regulations, the law on intellectual property rights, export incentives, consumer rights and so on, some of the policy tools that were available to the Turkish state will gradually be removed. For instance, the Mass Housing Fund, which was largely used for infrastructural investments, was immediately eliminated in the aftermath of the Customs Union. Harmonizing the industrial incentive mechanisms with the EU also suggests that Turkey might find itself at a major disadvantage in terms of its industrial cost structure. The price of input goods, particularly that of electricity, has been systematically high in Turkey (almost six times higher than the European average) largely due to inefficient state economic enterprises and lack of investment. Some of these cost disadvantages were compensated through incentive mechanisms, which will no longer be available.

It will also affect the state by making institutional reform easier to undertake. As Rodrik (1995: 110) points out,

The harmonization in domestic laws and institutions entailed by deep integration presents an opportunity for reformist governments in developing countries to 'lock in' their reforms and render them irreversible. It is no secret that Carlos Salinas wanted NAFTA at least as badly for its potential role in cementing Mexico's institutional reforms since 1986 as for its market-access provisions. Arguably, the EU's greatest contribution to the long-run prosperity and stability of Spain, Portugal and Greece resides in its having made a return to the military rule in these countries virtually impossible.

Similarly, it may affect perceptions of the state. Regional cooperation can increase the credibility of commitments. Entering into a formal arrangement with the EU might alleviate the credibility gap that plagues Turkey, like other developing countries, by signalling to the private sectors that 'the rules of the game are now changing for good' (Rodrik 1995: 111).

But economically, Turkey's position within the EU is weakened by the fact that it is the first country to enter into the EU without full membership. This means that Turkey will not be able to benefit to any significant extent from the social and regional funds designed to ease the costs of adjustments, especially during the first stages of joining. An aid package of 375 million ECUs was promised in March 1995, spread over five years, to ease Turkey's entry, but was suspended by the European Parliament on human rights grounds. As a result, to date, only 53 million ECUs of this fund have been released. Similarly, aid Turkey should have received as a part of the European Mediterranean Development Programme was also suspended. In terms of GDP, Turkey represents only approximately one-seventeenth of the German economy, the strongest economy within the EU. Yet, in population terms, Turkey represents 17 per cent of the combined population of the EU and Turkey. The economy is also highly dependent on trade with one member of the EU, Germany. Almost a third of imports from the EU come from Germany; half of its exports to the EU go to Germany. And finally, for all that, EU exports to Turkey constitute barely 3 per cent of the total volume of intra-EU trade. It should be clear that, in economic terms the Customs Union represents a tough challenge to the Turkish economy.

One of the main expectations of the Customs Union within Turkey was that FDI would increase. However, no sudden jump has been observed as yet. FDI in Turkey has risen steadily, from US$200 million in the early 1980s to approximately US$1 billion in 1995, but this is not a globally significant figure (*YASED*, Annual Report 1995) since annual average US–Japan and EU investment flows easily exceeded US$100 billion in 1990–2 (Stallings 1995: 79). In fact, FDI in Turkey appears to have actually declined with the onset of the Customs Union. In 1995, out of the US$2.938 billion worth of FDI permits that were granted, US$1.1 billion were realized. In the first half of 1996, FDI permits were granted for only US$751 million

(TUSIAD 1996: 102). Where FDI has entered Turkey, it has contributed to an ongoing denationalization of Turkish industry. The number of firms in joint ventures with a foreign firm increased from 20 per cent of the total manufacturing sector to 29 per cent in 1996. While this makes know-how and technology available, it also means that the national industry is less able than ever to meet European competition on its own.

Indeed, if Turkish industry *is* going to compete within the EU, a radical overhaul is urgently necessary. Turkish industry has been granted twenty-two years to complete the transitional period but, given its backwardness, it was recognized that it would be important to begin this process as soon as possible. Indeed, the government spoke of the necessity to undertake reform before the Customs Union became effective in 1996. What is surprising, therefore, is that the government–industry dialogue, which would have to be the first stage in effective industrial reform, was extremely limited before the agreement was signed and there are no clear signs that this is currently being undertaken either. Subcommittees were formed under the State Planning Department to begin the process when negotiations opened, but the private sector appears unconvinced that integration with the EU will actually be carried through. Meanwhile, Turkey's trade deficit deteriorated even further as the effects of the Customs Union began to be felt in the first months of 1996, increasing 27 per cent in the first eight months and reaching US$27.3 billion. In 1995, the current account deficit of Turkey reached US$2.3 billion; it reached that figure in the first half of 1996 alone (TUSIAD 1996: 8).

Negotiating the Customs Union: 'too much autonomy' of the state?

In the short run, at least, the Customs Union is bad news for Turkish industry. It can only compete in the EU through reforms, of which, so far, there is little indication. How, therefore, can we explain Turkey's decision to push for the Customs Union? As we pointed out at the beginning of the chapter, Turkish state elites were not primarily pursuing economic growth through the Customs Union. On the contrary, the agreement with the EU has been used as a political–populist strategy, symbolized by vague but emotive government language such as 'bridging East and West'. It did not emerge as a result of technocratic negotiations, which would have required constant contact between government and industry and business associations. Instead, its purpose was to try to deal a blow to Islamic fundamentalism and it represented a way of negotiating with the EU over human rights. This was only possible because of the weakness of interest representation, especially business groups, and the strength of the Turkish state which allowed entry to the Customs Union to be linked to such broad political concerns.

Islamic fundamentalism and human rights are highly divisive issues in Turkish politics. Policy on both issues is usually defined along party lines.

While the centre-left parties and centre-right parties differ significantly on how to address the Kurdish problem, the division between the secularists and the Islamists creates a significant cleavage between the Welfare Party (WP), with an Islamic agenda, and the rest of the parties. Indeed the WP was considered as an 'anti-system' party – even though the TPP later formed a coalition government with it. It is interesting, therefore, that at the time of negotiations in 1995, the governing parties, and especially the TPP, chose to formulate the issue along cultural and political lines rather than in terms of economic interests. Only when the issue was formulated in this way could the government build mass appeal into the deal. By associating the Customs Union with secularism, the government was able to present the Customs Union in an attractive light to a large number of voters. Meanwhile, the coalition's centre-left minor partner chose to play up the idea that the EU would guarantee the survival of Turkey's weak democracy in order to appeal to its own constituencies. The Customs Union was therefore associated with overwhelmingly political ends, rather than economic consequences. So effective was the government's strategy that even the business community began to formulate their own positions in terms of becoming part of the West rather than calculating the effects of trade liberalization, for example.

Secularism and Westernization became slogans used to defeat the opposition to the Customs Union. Furthermore, the opposition was institutionally weak and divided. Opposition and reservations came from some political parties, and factions of parties, and from business groups. Moderate opposition to the deal was expressed by the main opposition party on the right, the MP, the party of late President Özal which had formally initiated the application. The MP is generally in favour of the Customs Union but argued, mainly for party political purposes, that the negotiations were being badly handled. Support for this kind of opposition came from the import substituting coalition, which included a faction of the ruling TPP, including ex-President Suleyman Demirel, and some industrialists who recognized that they would face fierce competition from Europe. There is some evidence that an 'old boys network' between the entrenched ISI interests in Turkey and President Suleyman Demirel, who had introduced many of these policies, might have been in operation during the negotiations. But it is just as likely that the hostility between Demirel and Çiller was at least as much responsible for his opposition in view of the general trend for personalized, non-institutionalized structures to determine political alliances.

The most radical opposition, couched in both ideological and economic grounds, came from the WP, which argued that joining Europe was not only incompatible with the country's national interest and its religious/cultural heritage but also a direct threat to the livelihood of much of its own electoral constituency. Indeed, the small to medium enterprises of the newly emerging Anatolian industrial towns formed the economic basis of the WP and are part of a rising Islamic elite. Small businesses have long supported the Islamic parties in Turkey. Also, Islamic business activity took off in the 1980s, assisted by the national policy shift to neo-liberalism, which helped consolidate the financial basis of the party. As Önis (1997: 45) explains:

> The transformation of the Welfare Party from a marginal force to a significant political movement is a parallel phenomenon to and a reflection of the growing power of Islamic business in the Turkish economy and society in the context of the 1990s. More specifically, the rise of the Welfare Party reflects, in part, the growing aspirations of the rising Islamic bourgeoisie to consolidate its positions in society, to achieve elite status, and also in purely economic terms, to obtain greater share of public resources, both at the central and local levels, in competition with other segments of private business in Turkey.

It is precisely these small to medium enterprises, with neither economies of scale, technological know-how nor expertise, that will be most adversely affected by increasing competition from Europe. This explains why the main association of the Islamic businessmen in Turkey, MUSIAD (The Independent Association of Industrialists and Businessmen), vehemently opposed the Customs Union agreement. The organization's policy positions indicate an admiration for a semi-authoritarian and communitarian, East Asian style of capitalism and encourage increasing ties with the Islamic world, particularly in Asia, further distancing it from TUSIAD (The Turkish Industrialists and Businessmen's Association), which essentially represents the interests of large conglomerates in Turkey, reflecting one of the fundamental cleavages within the country's business community. TUSIAD, secular and Western in orientation, by and large supported the Customs Union. But there was some ambiguity even among TUSIAD members. The automotive industry, representing some of the largest conglomerates in Turkey such as the Koc Group, was initially rather lukewarm, fuelled in particular by the fear that the Turkish market would be opened to European used cars. The industry, which has long epitomized the ISI period, largely restructured in the 1980s and increased its partnerships with European and Japanese multinationals such as Renault, Fiat and Toyota. Ironically, it was these European partners who also opposed the complete liberalization of the auto market. Finally, a twenty-year exemption period for used cars was granted, thereby silencing much of their opposition.

Interestingly, labour was silent throughout the debate. The Turkish labour movement, which had expanded during the import substitution period, suffered a severe blow as a result of the broad post-coup consensus around neo-liberalism. Not only were most union rights suspended but wages were also frozen. Turk-is, the largest labour organization, became totally dependent on the state for its survival. Meanwhile, state policy was to deactivate, de-radicalize and de-politicize the labour movement throughout the 1980s.

Even though labour activism took off again in the 1990s with the reopening of some of earlier unions such as Disk and Hak-is, the level of unionization is still very low. Those working in the public sector, one of the most important segments of society in terms of its ability to articulate and coordinate opposition, are banned from union activity. Furthermore, significant ideological differences exist among the unions, which undermines the ability of labour to form a united front. Their lack of influence meant that they were not even consulted about the Customs Union.

In short, therefore, there was no *serious*, and certainly no united, opposition to the agreement from interest groups or from the parties, with the exception of the Welfare Party. The government therefore had the advantage of dominating the debate and tried to maximize its benefits by carrying the discussion onto an ideological plane. Instead of negotiating the terms of trade liberalization, the nature of escape clauses, the products that would be exempt from the Common Customs Tariff, how competition rules and rules on intellectual property rights would be implemented – the whole range of issues which required coordinated and thought-out positions which defended the interests of Turkey's economy, and issues requiring effective bargaining positions – the government shaped the debate within a discourse of 'civilization' and repackaged the entire issue as Turkey's entry to the West. The politicization of the issue made effective bargaining with the EU impossible and, indeed, possibly even made it appear as undesirable, since within the discourse of civilization the EU appeared as coming to the 'rescue' of secularism in Turkey. In other words, the government was not bargaining with the EU on how the quotas on textiles should be removed, for example responding to pressures from the textile lobby, but was using a crude, undifferentiated threat of the rise of Islamic fundamentalism to force the EU to accept Turkey as a partner.

The absence of serious opposition from an independent and uniform private sector and the lack of firm party institutionalization, coupled with the habit of dispensing state patronage whenever necessary, made the politicization of the deal all the easier. The uncertainty of the outcome of the Customs Union, the ambiguity regarding how it really affects the Turkish economy, also explained government success. In effect, its strategy for dealing with the Customs Union allowed it to overcome a major dilemma: only as a result of translating the Customs Union into reality could it gain the prestige and credibility to carry out future reforms, yet if the terms of the deal were to become the centre of the debate, then the government could not rely on economic interest groups to support it. The solution was to link it to broader and more emotive themes such as 'realizing the European dream of a secular Turkey' (*Hurriyet*, 16 March 1996).

The degree of politicization, and the absence of serious detailed discussion, is evident from the process through which the agreement was carried through. The negotiations were largely conducted by the State Planning Organization and the Ministry of Foreign Affairs. Relevant ministries were then invited to the steering committee responsible for the overall negotiations. While the State Planning Organization wanted to rely more on the views of the interest groups and take time for the negotiations, the Ministry of Foreign Affairs, responding to the demands of the governing coalition, chose instead to rush the agreement through. Most of the interest group organizations only found out what was being negotiated after the agreement was approved. The haste with which the talks were conducted reflected the urgent need of the government to legitimize itself (Interview with the State Planning Organization negotiating team, 15 August 1996).

Consequently, it comes as no surprise that Turkish economic interests ended up with a sub-optimal outcome as a result. The government needed to use the negotiations to increase its electoral appeal. To do so, it used the instability of the Turkish political system and the threat of Islamic fundamentalism. However, this negated the need for the government to construct effective bargaining strategies with the EU. In turn, the government's populist strategy was only possible in view of the absence of interest-based pressure groups, industry–state ties and an 'embedded' state (Evans 1995).

Conclusion

Different bargaining options and policy choices exist for countries facing regionalism. Choosing regionalist strategies depends not just on the international and regional context, but also on the kind of state–society arrangements which have developed within the country. Clearly, the kind of bargaining states engage in affects the terms of the regionalism and the effects of joining a regional bloc over the long term. In the case of Turkey, the microeconomic repercussions of the policy choice to pursue a Customs Union with the EU were not subject to close scrutiny. The consequences of the state's choices were overlooked in the hasty negotiations shaped around the themes of Westernization and globalization. Most importantly, the governing coalition phrased the debate in threatening terms: basically, their most effective argument with the EU, and with important segments of the Turkish population, was 'If you do not accept our entry, there is a risk of an Islamic backlash in Turkey'. But the threat of Islam also served to obscure a discussion of the economic consequences of the deal. Arguably, the cost of adjustments which Turkey is now facing could have been mitigated if macroeconomic and institutional changes were put into effect or more funds were made available for adjustment. Neither of these options became available since funds were not negotiated with the EU and the deal served to entrench current state practices.

I conclude with the general implications of the argument I have offered. If states are still major actors and contribute to shaping the patterns of regionalization through region-building, then understanding the 'side-effects' of globalization, particularly for the South, should involve deconstructing political spaces, the state, the party system and party–society links. Contrary to conventional wisdom, an 'embedded' or even a 'predatory' state, influenced by independent interest groups and democratic pressures, rather than an autonomous one like Turkey, might be the best path to deal effectively with the effects of globalization.

7 China: the challenges of reform, region-building and globalization

Shaun Breslin

When the post-Mao leadership initiated the reform of the economic system in 1978, they also set in motion a process of political reform. This did not mean the introduction of a multi-party political system or the end of communist party rule as witnessed in Eastern Europe and the Soviet Union. Rather, it refers to the massive changes in both the processes and functioning of political power within the existing framework of party rule. Economic reform forced the elites to remake the sources of their power in response to political and economic changes that they had themselves initiated. A series of challenges to established state elites thus emerged out of the domestic economic reform process.

In the 1990s, China re-engaged with the global economy and the country's international economic relations expanded. This 'internationalization' of the economy has led to Chinese elites becoming involved in regional economic initiatives. But the complexity of the East Asian regional economy, and its relationship with core markets in the developed world, make global rather than regional frameworks of analysis more appealing to the Chinese. Crucially, China's role in the international economy has been influenced by existing tensions within the Chinese party-state elites, and has also exacerbated those tensions. As such, this chapter focuses on the two-way relationship between state actors and the globalized economy, namely the way in which the state and state actors influence Chinese responses to globalization, and the way that globalization, in turn, influences the role and reconfiguration of the state and state actors. China's view of Asian regionalism will be discussed below, but the chapter starts and ends with the central theme of the transformation of the Chinese state.

The changing state

Despite the partial liberalization of the Chinese economy since 1978, 'insiders' in the form of party-state officials are still the main actors within the state system. This is not to say that the state system of the old days of central planning remains unchanged – far from it. But the *main* consequence has been to redistribute power within the existing party-state elites. In dismantling the state planning system, the post-Mao leadership implemented two forms of decentralization. The first was 'administrative decentralization' or the transference of power previously held by the central party-state admin- istration to lower level tiers of organization (primarily provincial-level bureaucracies). In theory, at least, this process should be a zero-sum game – what the central authorities lost, another level of administration should gain. However, the process of administrative decentralization was compli- cated by liberalization, which is in itself a form of decentralization of the state planning system – 'market decentralization'. As a result, the power to make economic decisions flows outside the previously (relatively) autonomous party-state bureaucracy into the hands of non-state actors (managers, producers and consumers) – from the party-state to markets.

Initially at least, the transference of power from the state-plan to the market was only partial. Whilst the planning structure lost control over elements of the demand side (with significant consequences in terms of inflation and shortages), the supply side of the equation was much less clear-cut. Many of the reforms originally aimed at increasing enterprise management and auton- omy failed to reach their intended destination. Instead, considerable devolved power became lodged in the hands of local-level party-state organizations, newly strengthened by administrative decentralization (Breslin 1996).

New participants in the power game are clearly emerging, most notably China's new entrepreneurs and business interests. However, Goodman (1995: 133) notes that these new non-party economic elites are not pressing for political influence, but are instead almost solely concerned with wealth creation – they lack both the desire and the ability to influence the deci- sion-making process. Furthermore, Goodman and others note that many of the non-party economic elites owe their new positions to the old elites. For example, Wong and Yang's (1995: 39) survey of the growth of township and village enterprises in China found that the new managers and direc- tors had previously served as party officials and state administrators. Even those who do not have these formal structural linkages with the party-state system tend to have good, close and often subservient relations with it.

So, one of the most significant features of the Chinese reform process is the transformation of relationships between existing state actors, and the changing basis of their power. On one level, we can identify the beginning of the transformation of political power into economic power. Particularly at the local level, power holders are switching the prestige, influence and wealth that came from forming part of the political structure for the wealth that comes from being a factory manager, or a member of the board. To be more accurate, they are not so much swapping one source of power for another, but using their political positions to increase their economic potential and bargaining power. In an economy where land, raw materials, transport and finance capital are still in relatively short supply, occupying a gatekeeper role (or knowing somebody who does) has an important economic premium.

On another level, there are growing conflicts of interest between newly powerful local state elites and the central state elites, and between different local state elites. It is important to distinguish between the national state and local states for a useful analysis of the Chinese state structure, although this division is an inherently difficult one to make. To start with, the linkages between the two remain structurally intact. Provincial and other local-level leaders remain part of the central elite through membership of the Chinese Communist Party (CCP) central committee and the National People's Congress. Furthermore, many central leaders cut their teeth in provincial politics. Finally, the central party leadership retains the ability to remove and appoint local leaders. Nevertheless, the reform process in the 1980s and 1990s has facilitated the *ability* of local leaders to pursue their own economic ends, frequently at odds with both competing strategies coming from other provincial elites and with the central government's own national plans and objectives. In terms of China's position within the global economic system, the relationship between the local and the international is now a key determinant of China's international economic position and stance, enhancing the power of local decision-makers. At a time when the need for a coherent framework within which China's international economic activities can function is greater than ever, these developments appear to have decreased the agency of the national central government, thus posing significant questions over whether the state can implement a clear regionalist policy or take a leading role in the establishment of an effective regional bloc of any meaningful kind.

China as semi-periphery

China's re-engagement with the global economy in the 1980s and 1990s marks the end of a long and often violent transition from China's traditional international isolation. For centuries, China's imperial leaders turned their backs on the international community, claiming that China, the centre of all civilization, could gain nothing from contacts with foreign barbarians. Furthermore, the Confucian imperial state adhered to an economic doctrine which saw agriculture as the basis of national wealth. Trade was seen merely as a means of moving wealth from one place to another, and development, in a capitalist sense, had little meaning.

China was eventually brought, kicking and screaming, into the global economy after 1840 through the imposition of unequal treaties after military defeat at the hands of major Western powers. For the best part of a century, economic development in China was shaped by the priorities of foreign colonial powers, with large parts of the country becoming their *de facto* and *de jure* responsibility. Popular antagonism to this forced internationalization and colonialization was a major factor in the collapse of the imperial system and the rise of revolutionary movements in the first half of the twentieth century. For Mao, restoring China to its rightful place of global pre-eminence was at least as important as building a communist state – indeed, for many revolutionaries, communism was more a means of restoring China's strength and independence rather than an end in itself.

Even after the CCP established a new political order after the 1949 revolution, China's position within the global economy remained an extremely minor one. With Mao rejecting contacts with the capitalist world, and the capitalist world following the US-led trade and diplomatic embargo, China was essentially left isolated, with only the Soviet Union as a major economic partner. But even the extent of China's inter-communist world trade remained relatively low. China never joined COMECON, and was fiercely antagonistic to any Soviet attempts to pull China into Moscow's communist division of labour. The Chinese revolution had largely been fought and won as a battle against foreign imperialism, and Mao in particular had no intention of replacing Western and Japanese colonization with a new form of Soviet economic imperialism.

As Sino-Soviet relations deteriorated after the 1950s the Beijing government took on an ever more isolationist economic policy. Self-reliance became the order of the day – not only national self-reliance, but also local self-reliance and self-sufficiency resulting in low levels of both international trade and internal trade between provinces. At the same time, the Sino-Soviet hostility led China to adopt a more conciliatory diplomatic attitude to the international community in the 1970s. China regained its United Nations seat from Taiwan in 1971, and normalized diplomatic relations with Japan in 1972. However, it was not until after the death of Mao (and the replacement of the Maoist successor Hua Guofeng) in 1978 that China really began to integrate itself more fully into the global economy. This process was initially very limited in scope and objective. The West had certain technologies and practices that the Chinese could learn from to aid their development, and might also provide limited markets for Chinese exports. But full-scale integration would damage the Chinese economy, and was highly questionable in terms of China's residual socialist legitimacy. Thus, four Special Economic Zones were established to provide a controlled and limited link between China and the global economy. These zones were to act as a window through which to view the global economy, and would remain under strong control, thus reducing the pernicious spiritual pollution that dealing with the West might bring.

Controlling international economic contacts in this way proved impossible. The growth of the Special Economic Zones spurred the national government to expand the number of 'open' areas, and also sponsored intense provincial lobbying from areas which wanted to share in the fruits of dealing with the capitalist West. Slowly, more and more areas were opened up, although the central authorities retained significant control over approval of projects, and over foreign currency allocations and earnings. By the end of the 1980s, the entire country was essentially open for international business, although the actual amount remained relatively low.

For many investors from East Asia, the attraction of China was as a low-cost production site for export-oriented production. This has typically entailed using China for low-tech, low-skill, labour-intensive production where components produced in other states are assembled for onward transition to other markets. China's entry into the global economy coincided with a period of fragmentation of production in East Asia, and rising production costs within the newly industrializing economies (NIEs). Whereas Taiwan and South Korea had served as the first destination for Japanese producers eager to lower costs of exports, these second-generation East Asian developmental states had subsequently become relatively expensive producers themselves. With the majority of investments in labour-intensive production, the rise in wages (and rents) gradually undermined their attraction for Japanese investors. Furthermore, the appreciation of the new Taiwanese dollar and the Korean won relative to the US dollar reduced the profit margin on exports from the NIEs to the major markets in the developed world (Bernard 1991). So, by the mid-1980s, not only the original Japanese investors, but also new Taiwanese and Korean producers were looking to locate their production in low-cost production sites, with a compliant workforce, limited enforcement (if not regulation) of environmental standards, and a favourable exchange rate with the US. As the 1980s progressed, China increasingly met all of these criteria.

The fragmentation of production in East Asia is key in understanding China's new global and regional economic role. China has become part of a regional division of production driven by foreign direct investment (FDI), with Japan as the core investing economy. Japan is a major trade partner for other Asian states, and is also a significant funder of Asian development through bilateral aid and through contributions to the World Bank and the Asian Development Bank. More significantly, Japan is the major corporate investor in the rest of Asia and also holds a clear and significant advantage in technological innovation and exports. For Bernard and Ravenhill (1995: 172), the combination of FDI and technological superiority and control places the rest of Asia in a position of technological dependence on the Japanese core, a situation which Hatch and Yamamura (1996) argue is 'a structural condition that arises out of the complementary relationship between Japanese developmentalism and Asian "pseudo-developmentalism"'. To put the case more bluntly, they cite the son of the head of the Hyundai *chaebol*, who argues that 'it's not a matter of choice in Asia. That's a very hard fact to recognise. In terms of money and technology, the Japanese have already conquered Asia.'

For much of the post-Mao era, China's major exports were primary commodities such as iron and coal. Textiles have also come high on the list of export commodities, and have also been the cause of considerable Sino-US trade friction as a result of continued state protection for Chinese textile producers. However, particularly after the huge increase in FDI to China after 1992, the structure of China's international trade underwent a rapid and dramatic transformation. As FDI from the rest of Asia soared, China increasingly became a major component production site for other Asian investments. For example, China moved from Japan's fifth to second biggest export destination between 1992 and 1994 as a result of the growth of Japanese components exports to subsidiaries and other dependants now operating within China (JEN, 24 January 1994).[1] The FDI–trade linkage is particularly important here. Chinese trade mushroomed as component imports increased, were screwdriven together in China, and the finished products re-exported. Thus, the transformation of China's trade profile from primary product exporter has not really moved it away from the weak semi-periphery – it has merely increased other forms of weak semi-peripheral activity.

China's position, even within the East Asian region, is relatively lowly. It is on the bottom layer of an East Asian hierarchy of states with Japan at the top as the regional technological and investment core, and Taiwan, South Korea, Singapore and Hong Kong as the intermediate investors. Along with countries like Vietnam and Thailand, and to a lesser extent Indonesia and Malaysia, China is in competition to emphasize low-cost and low-regulation advantages in order to attract and maintain foreign investments. This East Asian division of labour, then, has to be placed in the global context of continuing East Asian dependence on major Western markets (particularly North American) for exports. For while inter-East Asian trade has grown significantly in recent years, much of it is due to the internationalization of production of single commodities – without Western markets for the finished goods this inter-regional component trade fired by inter-regional FDI flows would be unsustainable.

China and APEC

In terms of China's position within the East Asian regional economy, the most significant economic regional organization is the Asia-Pacific Economic Cooperation (APEC), established in 1989. Students of regional organizations in the West (or even in the former Soviet bloc) would not easily recognize APEC's regionalism as the same phenomenon. The notion of any form of closed economic region is anathema to APEC. Originating as an informal discussion group with limited participation, it has evolved along the twin lines of open regionalism and inclusivism. The Bogor Declaration (the APEC Declaration of Common Resolve) of November 1994 established six major objectives (Woods 1995):

- to complete free and open trade and investment by no later than 2020 (by 2010 for industrialized nations);
- to expand and accelerate APEC's trade and investment facilitation programmes;
- to fulfil the General Agreement on Tariffs and Trade (GATT) Uruguay Round commitments ahead of schedule;

- to gain a commitment from each member to unilateral trade and investment liberalization;
- to establish a moratorium on unilateral protectionist policies; and
- to 'reaffirm their [APEC's] strong opposition to the creation of an inward-looking trading bloc that would divert from the pursuit of global free trade and the strengthening of the open multilateral trading system'.

In essence, then, APEC has a free trade and investment agenda with an emphasis on private business and enterprise as the dynamic of regional growth (Higgott and Stubbs 1995) – an agenda, in fact, which sometimes makes the World Trade Organization (WTO) look like an agent of protectionism.

The evolution of APEC into a large inclusionary free trade-oriented organization is a reflection of the complexity of the East Asian regional economy. Regional integration is heavily dependent on the growth of FDI (and particularly Japanese FDI) and on continued access to American markets. APEC is not so much a regional organization where Asian peripheral states are simply tied into their regional core (Japan) as one which also ties East Asian production into North American markets. But the size and diversity of APEC member states are major sources of problems when it comes to building the region. The vast disparities in types of development, levels of development, dominant economic philosophies and political cultures all contribute to the difficulties. Furthermore, there is deep disquiet in some states regarding US objectives for the organization, motivated by the strength of the US economy, its role in East Asia, and its strategic interests and history in the region. This has led to demands for an 'Asian Asia', which does not include Anglo-Saxon states, notably on the part of Malaysian leader Mahathir bin Mohamad.

As far as the Chinese are concerned, the only viable regional organization at present is APEC, which China joined in November 1991. Despite reservations regarding its viability as an effective regional organization, the Chinese government has been drawn in for a number of reasons. First, the evolution of the European Union (EU) and the establishment of the North American Free Trade Association (NAFTA) generated considerable fears in Beijing over the perceived growth of protectionism in the West. Second, although China's preferred solution to reducing the potential threat of protectionism in the developed world is to gain entry to the WTO, playing an active and responsible role on APEC gives the Chinese an opportunity to try to persuade the US that it is committed to free trade principles. And third, since APEC is a reality, but one in a state of flux, state elites argue that it is better at this stage to be inside the organization than out. The official Chinese media have long articulated the leadership's concerns over Japanese and US motives in East Asia (Wang 1997). Japan, it is argued, is trying to build a regional economic network to compete with NAFTA and

Europe, while APEC is seen as Washington's attempt to maintain its regional hegemony by enforcing its economic paradigms on Asia. Crucially, the US is portrayed as 'drawing Japan into its gang to seek joint hegemony' (Zhang 1996) and establishing the US–Japan axis as the key and dominant relationship in the region (Gao 1996). If China turned its back on APEC, then it would be unable to influence the creation of regional frameworks, practices and ideas that will affect China's development into the next century. Far better, then, to place China at the heart of the APEC initiative, and replace the old Sino–US–Soviet military–strategic triangle in East Asia with a new Sino–US–Japan economic triangle.

Despite the Chinese state elite's broad acceptance of APEC's neo-liberal agenda, there remains concern that too rapid liberalization will harm key sectors of the Chinese economy. It threatens the subsidies on agriculture, the help that the national and local state provides to exporters, and the loss-making state-owned industries risk facing potentially fatal market competition. The state elite fears the growth of urban unemployment more than anything else because of the social and political problems that they calculate would follow.

China's attitude to APEC, therefore, is complicated by the way development has taken place and by the nature of the Chinese state. On one level, there is the problem of reciprocity. While China expects open regionalism to guarantee access to other economies, it is reluctant to allow reciprocal open access to its own economy. On another level, there is a dichotomy between President Jiang Zemin and other members of the top party and state elites who participate in intergovernmental negotiations, and those people who are the real driving force behind China's regional economic integration. The real locus of initiative here lies in the provinces, and it is the interaction between the local and the international which is the main determinant of China's position within the regional and global division of labour. As yet the different local elites are too preoccupied with attracting inward investment in competition with each other to be a force for tighter regional cooperation and formal integration. They are too busy and too new to the game to promote regonalism through the central state. State structures, therefore, currently impose severe limitations to China's pursuit of East Asian regionalism.

The Chinese state revisited: globalization and developing states

The Chinese state, then, is in a state of transition. The economic reforms implemented after 1978 have resulted in significant changes in the way that the Chinese economy functions, the redistribution of power within the existing party-state elites, and a partial increase in non-state economic actors. But in many respects, the Chinese political system has yet to develop new structures to reflect or accommodate these changes. In particular, the central state elites are struggling to deal with the many, new and often conflicting demands that economic reform has generated.

Whilst much of this uncertainty and many of the new challenges have emerged from domestic economic reform and restructuring, China's re-engagement with the global economy has not only created a new set of issues for the state elites to deal with, but also compounded existing 'domestic' issues. In the introduction to this book, it was suggested that globalization has four main implications for developing states:

- globalization engenders a strong element of competition between developing countries for investment;
- globalization adds more actors to the policy process and increases the power of 'external' actors over state policy;
- globalization leads to the recomposition and renegotiation of relationships between state actors; and
- globalization leads to a fragmentation of the developing world between those states that can and do respond to restructuring, free trade and liberalization and those that cannot.

With some adaptations, this provides a useful framework for understanding how globalization has influenced the evolution of the Chinese state.

First, then, the notion that globalization engenders competition between developing states. China is not the only nation in East Asia which tries to attract foreign investment as a means of providing investment finance for growth. In one respect, China has a huge advantage over these competitors. For those foreign investors seeking new markets for their produce, the opportunity to sell to 1.2 billion potential Chinese consumers is a great attraction. But for the majority of potential investors, those who are looking for cheap production sites for goods that will be sold in the developed world, the major attraction that China offers is relatively cheap land, a cheap and disciplined labour force, lax environmental legislation (more correctly enforcement) and favourable exchange rates with major markets. In addition, there are a number of national and local tax breaks, rent reductions, and so on, which act as further incentives.

The problem here is that emphasizing low-cost comparative advantages may pull China into a downward spiral of offering ever greater incentives to increase its comparative attraction over other states – to adopt what Palan and Abbott (1996: 140–164) have dubbed a 'downwardly mobile' state strategy. And as we have noted above, international competition is exacerbated by competition between different locations within China itself for investment. Globalization, then, not only increases competition between developing states, but, in the Chinese case at least, engenders competition from different actors within the state itself. In the process, potential foreign investors are able to extract considerable incentives from competing Chinese hosts.

This brings us to the second implication of globalization for developing states – the increase in the number of actors in the policy process and the power of 'external' actors over state policy. If the central state elites are facing problems in staying in control of development in the face of competing provincial development strategies, many of the local state elites are finding that their own local power is often subject to the 'approval' of external actors. For example, in Shenzhen, one of China's original Special Economic Zones, the local leadership tried to restructure the local economy by imposing disincentives for processing industries and component assembly in 1995. While these industries did decline, the planned-for high-tech and finance investments simply did not appear – Shenzhen's priorities did not fit with the priorities of external investors. As a result, the local authority reversed its policy, and reintroduced a number of incentives to lure back the processing and component assembly investments that had found willing hosts elsewhere in China (CNS, 6 December 1995).

The power of foreign investment is also evident in the evolution of China's external trade. Ash and Kueh (1995) and Qi and Howe (1995) have demonstrated that the massive increase in Chinese trade – particularly to North America through Hong Kong – since 1978 has been considerably influenced by exports from Asian investments in China. Indeed, China's presence on American and European markets owes an enormous debt to Taiwanese, Japanese and Hong Kong (including third party) investment decisions. The growth of China's trade dependency has been remarkable, with foreign trade rising from less than 10 per cent of GNP in 1978 to 38 per cent in 1993. This compares to just over 14 per cent in Japan (China's major trading partner) and under 17 per cent in the US (Nogami and Zhu 1994). These trade dependency disparities lend strength to the concern of some officials that China is becoming over-dependent on Japanese and US markets for exports.

China is increasingly reliant on the FDI sector for its international trade, and, crucially, for maintaining a trade surplus with the US. For example, the processing trade (the import–export activities of foreign capital) accounted for 47 per cent of all Chinese trade in 1995 (*CD*, 13 January 1996). Whilst this figure in itself is not that surprising, two points warrant attention. First, the speed of the transformation should be noted, as the processing trade was almost non-existent before 1984. Second, just as FDI is not evenly spread across China, so the foreign trade implications of FDI are also unevenly distributed. In those areas on the coast that have received the lion's share, the importance of re-exports is even greater – as high as 68 per cent in Guangdong Province (CNS, 11 August 1995). Trade from China's main coastal areas is now dominated by imports of components and exports of screwdriver-assembled produce.

The uneven spread of investment has contributed to the Chinese economy taking on something of a dualistic character. On one side, there are the modern, foreign-oriented light industrial sectors, primarily in south and eastern China, where private enterprise and market distribution dominates – the manifestation of the new socialist commodity economy. On the other, there is the stagnating domestic-oriented state-owned sector – the remnants of the old planning system. One of the major challenges to the Chinese leadership is to marry these two sectors together. As components and managerial expertise are frequently imported, technology, know-how and investment do not feed down to the rest of the economy in terms of developing component suppliers or increasing managerial and workplace skills. The overall picture is of a regionalization process, through incorporation into the global economy, which includes parts of China but not all of it. As the bits that are in become ever more part of the regional production network, then the divisions that already exist within China may intensify, exacerbating the real disparities within the country. Large parts of China become peripheral to the coastal areas, which are themselves a periphery of both the intermediary East Asian states and Japan.

The increase in power of external actors also plays a part in the third implication of globalization for developing states, in that it contributes to the recomposition and renegotiation of relationships between state actors. The notion that globalization and international economic contacts reconfigure class formation in developing states is not new. In the Chinese case, the local state elites are primarily providing the bridgehead for foreign investors. As a result, key sections of the Chinese state elites have made considerable fortunes from the expansion of China's international economic relations. The position of Chinese party-state cadres as gatekeepers under the old state planning system has only been partly altered by the introduction of new economic models in the post-Mao era. They retain control over key economic decisions – the allocation of real estate, the allocation of construction contracts and supply and staffing contracts, for example. One result is corruption, which is now endemic within the Chinese ruling elites at virtually all levels.

Marketization is reconfiguring the relationships between local elites and investors as complex webs of relationships are created which link the local state elites to East Asian investors. In large parts of southern China, foreign investors have established joint ventures with Chinese local state agencies to establish new factories. These new factories have poor records in a number of respects, from working conditions to health and safety in the workplace – Chan (1996) refers to such factories in Guangdong Province as 'boot camps'. Workplace accident figures are not easily available, but there is clear evidence that as well as suffering austere working conditions, workers' lives are at risk. There have been a number of major disasters in factories which have been reported in the national press. In one case, for example, workers were forced to stay at the workplace while a fire destroyed parts of the factory and killed workers who were sleeping in the accommodation quarters, which under the law should have been in a separate location.

The official justification for this state-sponsored neglect of workers' rights amounts to the suggestion that it is better to work in these conditions than not to work at all. The average hourly wage rates in the new factories remain comparatively very low – just over two yuan an hour (eight yuan are worth one dollar). However, with overtime, workers can earn around 600–700 yuan a month (US$70–82), and also receive subsidized (or free) accommodation, medical care and food (Chan 1996). By comparison, a university professor in political science in Beijing will earn around 400 yuan a month (US$50) as a basic salary, rising to around 1,000 yuan (US$121) after bonuses are added. More significantly, large sections of the rural population remain both relatively and absolutely poor, making the jobs in the new factories more attractive than they appear at first.

In 1994, around 75 per cent of Chinese still lived in rural areas and had an average income of 1,000 yuan (US$121) a year (Reuters, 21 September 1995). Even with a marked increase in rural incomes resulting from record harvests, the average farmer still only earned 1,900 yuan (US$229) in 1996. These figures are somewhat skewed, however, by the disparities in income between the coastal regions and the interior. Incomes are higher in the developed coastal regions and as much as 40 per cent of rural incomes come from non-agricultural activity. In those areas where rural incomes are predominantly agriculturally based, average incomes are much lower – for example, farmers in Shanghai earn three and half times more than those in the southern province of Guizhou (*CND*, 27 January 1997).

As these figures indicate, development policies have benefited the local peasantry in those areas where investment and growth have taken place, thereby assuring the state of some support from these sectors at least. The local peasantry has no need to work in the new factories because it has benefited from selling or renting the leases on the land to the investors. It therefore constitutes a part of the new rich class in the foreign enclaves which, like the local state elites, is a major beneficiary from policies of internationalization. The vast majority of the workers in these East Asian investments are migrant workers from the rural hinterland, usually with no contacts in local political structures. They are often young women (70 per cent in Chan's [1996] study) and are typically from the poorest regions. Whilst China has gone a long way in eliminating poverty, the official *Workers' Daily* reports that around 6 per cent of Chinese households live below a poverty line defined as earnings of less than 530 yuan (US$64) per person per year, and half of these people have annual incomes below 300 yuan (*GRRB*, 26 January 1997). This means that up to seventy million Chinese live in official poverty, and it is these poorest segments of society which are most attracted by wages and conditions that many urban Chinese would shun.

The 'informal' migration which has characterized employment in the investment zones is now becoming formal government policy. With the aid of World Bank poverty alleviation funds, the central government has embarked on a wide-scale investigation into rural poverty. Research groups have been established from China's leading academic institutions and from late January 1997 were dispatched to different parts of China to assess the causes and solutions of poverty. From interviews conducted in Beijing and Shanghai in January 1997, it is clear that the favoured solution is to further facilitate the transfer of workers from rural areas to the coastal development zones in the hope that the money that they send home will be the road from poverty. Of course, the wisdom and implications of such an approach must be at least questionable in developmental terms – can these policies be said to address the root causes of poverty in these regions? But in the shorter term, they ensure a ready supply of cheap labour for the foreign investors at a time when some are beginning to consider transferring their production sites to even lower cost sites (particularly Vietnam) and disrupt mainly the political disenfranchised. However, it also places the Chinese developmental process more firmly at the whim of the foreign investors – or, perhaps more correctly, at the fate of globalizing forces – than ever before.

The fourth and final implication of globalization under discussion here is the fragmentation of the developing world between those states that can and do respond to restructuring, free trade and liberalization and those that cannot. Again, in the Chinese case at least, this concept holds for comparisons within different parts of the Chinese state, and not just for comparisons between states. Chinese policies throughout the 1990s have pointed to the determination of the leadership to liberalize the economy. But economic reform has generated, or at least exacerbated, a series of political problems inside the country and poses a number of developmental dilemmas for the leadership. These relate to China's place within the East Asian region and to the role and function of the state. In some ways, China provides an illustration of the costs which are involved in adapting to the global agenda of free trade, open regionalism and liberalization.

This chapter has concentrated on the dynamics and implications of China's continuing integration into the global economy and the consequences of this for its relationships with the East Asian region. This has involved first discussing what the 'East Asian regional economy' is and where China fits within it. Despite the formal opening of the whole of China for international economic contacts, large parts of China remain relatively unaffected by international contacts and are not yet tied into international trade and investment networks. This suggests that the East Asian regional economy is not shaped, confined or contingent on the borders of national state borders. The most pertinent question therefore is not whether China is part of the East Asian regional economy, and the implications of this for the Chinese state, but rather which parts of China are in, which are not and what is the significance for the state of this partial incorporation of the country into the East Asian region.

Research along these lines has led to the formulation of concepts such as 'the region state' and 'growth triangles' as a result of the presumption that the central state can no longer determine the politics and development of provinces/cities which are incorporated in production terms into the global/regional economy. The linkages between Hong Kong and the Pearl River Delta and between Fujian and Taiwan appear to be very much examples of rapid development and incorporation without any firm leadership from the central states. Moreover, China is not unique in East Asia in that foreign investment drives development and the FDI sector is insulated from the host economy (Bernard and Ravenhill 1995: 197). This suggests an East Asian economy which has little to do with national boundaries, and much to do with investment and trade networks built in part around a regional division of labour.

Following this line of argument, Kenichi Ohmae (1995) has argued that maps actually get in the way of understanding regional development – we are too constrained by cartography. Yet in his own vision of region states, he remains cartographically bound – his regions may transcend political boundaries, but are still based on geographic proximity. The alternative is to follow Bernard's (1996: 654) suggestion and deploy a network-centred approach which, drawing us even further away from the map, conceptualizes a more complex structure built on buyer commodity-driven chains of decentralised production networks (Gereffi 1996). This approach focuses our attention away from the simple bilateral relationship of FDI from country A to country B and emphasizes the forward (markets) and backward (technology supplies or brand naming, etc.) linkages.

Whatever the theoretical model we chose to describe China's (partial and uneven) links with the international and the regional economy, it is important to look at the implications of this for the Chinese state and for the composition of its complex state structures. In particular, the key question is how can the central party-state reconcile the conflicting demands and requirements of those parts of China participating in the international economy with those that are not? These conflicts, which pit one region inside China against another, or, more accurately, the state elites which control development in one province against local elites from another area, are cross-cut with conflicts between the needs of the state sector with those of the new market-oriented sectors. While the private sector is the centre of growth, the ailing state-owned sector is facing severe problems.

The consensus in Beijing is that, on economic grounds at least, reform of the state-owned sector is an essential prerequisite for further economic advances, for two main reasons. First, as Zhou Shulian, a research fellow with the Chinese Academy of Social Science, puts it: 'With the majority of state enterprises staying out of market competition, it is difficult to redistribute resources for better efficiency' (*CD*, 10 March 1996). On one level, the 'top slicing' of scarce raw material, and particularly energy, resources to the state sector denies more efficient producers of resources. On another, the quality and reliability of supplies from the state sector is so low that the World Bank estimates that 17 per cent of China's GDP consists of 'unsaleable' goods produced in state-owned enterprises (*CBR*, March-April 1997). The second, more pressing, concern is that money is simply draining away from many state-owned enterprises. In addition to leaning on the state for supplies and markets, many also rely on the state to underwrite their losses. For example, the Chinese government's State Statistical Bureau reported in 1986 that around half of state-owned enterprises were running at a loss, and that unpaid loans to various levels of government by these enterprises accounted for around 10 per cent of Chinese GNP.

Notwithstanding the economic case for reform, the party leadership is quite simply not prepared (perhaps not able) to cope with the projected impact on employment in Chinese cities, and the social consequences that they fear this unemployment might bring. It is difficult to overestimate the importance of employment considerations for the central party-state leadership. The number of officially unemployed urban workers in China was reported as twenty-seven million in May 1997. Furthermore, of the current 450 million people employed in rural areas, 130 million are designated 'surplus' labour. By the end of the century, the rural surplus labour is expected to rise to 214 million, and of those, it is predicted that 137 million will be unable to find new sources of employment. As around eighty million of these 120 million rural workers have moved to the cities in search of employment, the issue of rural unemployment is also becoming an urban issue (*CND*, 1 December 1995 and 28 May 1997).

The central state leadership is caught between an economic logic and a social–political logic which is manifested in policy vacillation. For example, a policy of 'streamlining' the state-owned sector was adopted in 1996. However, the keynote front-page editorial on the New Year's Day edition of *People's Daily* (*RMRB*, 1 January 1997) stated that social and political stability was now the main priority, and streamlining state companies would lead to social instability as workers lost their jobs and associated welfare benefits. But by September 1997, the emphasis had moved back from social to economic priorities, when State President and party leader Jiang Zemin announced a policy of privatization of the state sector.

These policy vacillations are a consequence of the regime's strategy of retaining political control in an era of rapid economic change. With Marxist ideology relegated to an irrelevant side-show, the party elites needed to build new pillars of legitimacy in the post-Mao era. To an extent, they have been aided here by the collapse of political and economic certainties in the former Soviet Union – stable authoritarianism is perhaps more attractive than chaotic political freedom. Perhaps more correctly, stable authoritarianism and rapid economic gains are more attractive than chaotic political freedom and poverty. The Chinese elites have clearly placed an emphasis on attaining popular legitimacy (or political acquiescence) through generating rapid economic improvements. But it has also inoculated key sectors of the Chinese population from suffering the negative impact of participating in competitive domestic and international economies. It has, in effect, implemented a system of 'safety-net socialism' whereby the jobs and interests of the workers in the traditional state-owned enterprises in the cities are protected by the party. The communist party has ironically evolved to protect the interests of the Chinese state-owned working class from the vagaries of a liberalized economic system that the party itself has introduced.

China is by no means unique in defending its domestic sectors and interests whilst promoting its internationalized sectors, mainly as a result of pressures from domestic actors who would otherwise lose out. However, there are two key considerations in the Chinese case. The first relates to the extent of the subsidies. The central government spends over a third of its overall budget on subsidies of one kind or another to maintain social stability – to inoculate key sectors from the negative impacts of marketization and internationalization (subsidies to state-owned industries, to maintain urban purchasing power, to guarantee rural procurement, etc.). Despite the dramatic growth in the post-Mao era, the central authorities have not received enough of the extra money generated to cover its subsidy burdens. For example, at the start of the reform process in 1978, state planning agencies and financial authorities controlled 76 per cent of internal national investment capital. After the introduction of decentralization reforms (particularly the 1984–5 banking reforms), this proportion fell to just over 33 per cent in 1986 (Zhu 1987). Despite the introduction of new income tax and other fiscal reforms in 1994, the central state has been unable significantly to claw back funds, and has largely funded spending through budget deficits. It is perhaps pushing the point too much to say that there is local and private responsibility for profits and national (and state) responsibility for losses, but it is only partly an exaggeration. Of course, this raises questions over how far it is possible for the central state to continue to subsidize in the future.

A second consideration is how far China's growing internationalization is creating a set of obligations to external actors to reduce subsidies anyway. In pushing for liberalization, the key external actors are the WTO, APEC and the US. Chinese state elites are pushing vigorously for entry into the WTO primarily to sideline tensions with the US from its development and trade strategies, and to retain access to American and European markets. But membership depends on China liberalizing and convincing the US and the EU to let it in. Thus, China has embarked on a series of reforms to open its markets, including the reduction of import tariffs from 35 per cent to 23 per cent in April 1996, and the gradual (and as yet incomplete) liberalization of exchange rates.

Basically, the Chinese state is facing external pressure to abandon what Amsden (1989) suggests is the defining role of the 'developmental state', namely that of subsidizing industrialization. Largely because of the potential and sheer size of the Chinese economy (not to mention China's existing US$39.5 billion trade surplus with the US), it is being pressured to downsize, if not abolish, subsidies to the domestic industrial sector at a much earlier stage in the developmental process than other states in East Asia did.

If it accedes to these pressures, then its domestic economy, and through this domestic political stability, may be undermined. If it does not, then it may face international trade conflicts resulting in the relocation of FDI to other low-cost production sites.

These conflicting tendencies are reflected in (and compounded by) the different interests within the Chinese state elites themselves. The pressure from the new entrepreneurs and from those local elites tied in to foreign investment may be to comply with these international influences. Furthermore, it appears that those top officials charged with negotiating China's international economic relations are more in favour of further economic liberalization than many of their colleagues. But despite the fact that more sceptical colleagues have been encouraged to accompany these officials on international missions, and the argument that the state sector can only survive by responding to international competition and market disciplines, many state elites in the interior provinces, in the subsidized state sectors, and in related central ministries and agencies remain unconvinced.

Conclusion

It is difficult to disentangle the impact of the internationalization of the Chinese economy from the consequences of domestic reforms. It would certainly be wrong to explain all the structural changes in China in terms of globalization forces. Nevertheless, the internationalization of the Chinese economy has at least compounded those internal domestic changes, and is in some cases the dominant dynamic of change. It is important here to draw together the consequences of these changes for the state and for the position of China within the East Asian region.

As a major recipient of investment from the rest of East Asia, and as a regional economic force in absolute (if not yet per capita) terms, regional affairs are clearly important for the Chinese leadership. In addition to playing an active role in APEC – not least to use it as a stepping stone to WTO entry – Chinese leaders are trying to engage with ASEAN and leaders of ASEAN states. This in part reflects the recognition that China, like many East Asian states, is too dependent on Western markets for its exports, and that expanding 'Asian East Asia' as a market for itself would make sense for everyone in the region. But it is also partly a diplomatic charm offensive designed to allay the fears in some parts of East Asia that a strong China is not a good thing for the region. These fears not only arise from the prospect of competition from an economically strong China, but have been fuelled by Chinese territorial claims over the Spratly Islands in the South China Sea, by missile tests in the Taiwan Straits, by the naval build-up off southern China, and by Chinese influence over Myanmar (Burma). Indeed, while the Chinese are concerned over Japanese and American influence in Asian regional organizations, China itself remains a focus of concern for other regional states.

However, the key conclusion from this chapter is that the formal initiatives, policies and strategies of the central state elites are at best constrained by the redistribution of power within the party-state elites in the post-Mao era. The relationship between local elites and international economic actors is not only a key determinant of how China interacts with the regional and global economy, but is also an increasingly important determinant of how different parts of China interact with each other. And if dealing with the often conflicting demands from different domestic and sectoral interests was not enough, the central state elites are also facing demands to change from external actors like the WTO and the US.

So, while globalization has increased the importance of regional perspectives for the Chinese elites, it has also created more pressing concerns. On a domestic level, it has contributed to a fragmentation of power within the party-state elites. On an international level, the Chinese state elites are currently more preoccupied with finding global rather than regional solutions. While it is true that the share of East Asian exports flowing to the US fell from 34 per cent to 24 per cent between 1986 and 1992, we should be wary of assuming a corresponding decline in access to US markets for East Asian states (Calder 1995: 155). The growth of East Asian FDI into other East Asian states has fuelled a growth in inter-Asian trade in components. But this component trade in itself remains largely dependent on access to the US and other major markets. For the Chinese state elites, as indeed for many of their East Asian counterparts, regime legitimacy and political and social stability are predicated on continued economic growth. To greater or lesser extents, continued economic growth is itself dependent on the markets of the developed world remaining open to East Asian exports. As such, whilst APEC is important for Chinese state elites, the most important task is to negotiate entry into the WTO – or, more correctly, to try to strike a deal which allows China access to US and other major markets, whilst protecting domestic producers and interests from the full rigours of participating in a competitive global economy.

Note

1   The following newspapers/news services have been used in this chapter: *China Business Review* (CBR); *China Daily* (CD); *China News Digest* (CND); China News Service (CNS); *Gongen Riao* (GRRB); Japan Economic Newswire (JEN); and *Renmen Ribao* (RMRB). Dates are cited in the text.

Part III
Reconfiguring regions

8 Regional integration in South East Asia

Chris Dixon

The growth of regionalization that has characterized the global economy since the late 1970s reflects two distinct but related processes (Cook and Kirkpatrick 1997). First, there is informal, natural or open regionalization, where a group of countries develop more intense trade and other cross-border arrangements as a result of complementarity and limited restrictions on the movements of goods, services and finance (Lorenz 1991). This type of development has been promoted by the activities of transnational corporations (TNCs) which have increasingly organized their production and investment on a regional basis. For semi-peripheral and peripheral countries, this form of regional integration has been assisted by the liberalization of trade and financial regimes through the implementation of structural adjustment programmes (SAPs) and related policies principally at the behest of the International Monetary Fund (IMF) and World Bank. The international and regional development agencies have also supported the development of a variety of cross-border arrangements as a means of promoting economic growth and structural change. Overall, the development orthodoxy that has emerged since around 1980 is one that seeks to minimize both the restrictions on the movement of trade and finance and the economic role of the state. This has been conducive to the development of informal regionalization and has given TNCs the major role in its promotion (Dicken 1993: 102). Second, formal regionalization, or regionalism as it is referred to in this book, has proceeded through a variety of arrangements ranging from preferential trading agreements to economic union (International Monetary Fund 1993). This reflects the view that the global economy is moving towards a series of highly managed trading blocs.

It is the intention of this chapter to explore the processes of regionalization and regionalism in South East Asia (Figure 8.1) and its linkages to the wider Pacific Asian region. The Association of South East Asian Nations (ASEAN) is frequently cited as one of the world's most effective and long-lasting regional associations. In addition, South East Asia has emerged as one of the most dynamic groupings in the global economy with high rates of economic growth and structural change. These developments are depicted as spreading from Singapore into the 'new' newly industrializing

Figure 8.1 South East Asia

economies (NIEs), Indonesia, Malaysia and Thailand, and the re-engaging socialist economy of Vietnam.

Regionalism in South East Asia

South East Asia has a comparatively long history of attempts to establish formal regionalization. From the 1950s onwards there was a recognition of the need for some form of regional organization, at least on the part of Malaysia and the Philippines, Singapore and Thailand (Thanat 1992: xvii). However, the initial impetus came from outside the region with the establishment of the South East Asian Treaty Organization (SEATO) in 1954. The Organization could be 'described as part of the world-wide US-led system of anti-Communist military alliances, or security arrangement' (Palmer 1991: 160), rather than a true South East Asian regional body. Only two regional powers, Thailand and the Philippines, signed the South

East Asian Collective Defence Treaty. This reflected the Philippines' 'camp follower' status *vis-à-vis* the US (Lyon 1991: 25) and Thailand's increasing concern over the spread of 'communist subversion' from North Vietnam and its rapidly developing links with the US. In the event, SEATO was never an effective security organization and was losing effectiveness and support by the early 1960s. Despite this it survived until 1977.

In 1961 there was a more regional-based attempt to establish a formal structure. This was the Association of South East Asia (ASA) and involved Malaysia, Thailand and the Philippines. The need for such an organization rested heavily on strategic considerations, particularly the recognition of the need for regional states to protect themselves amidst rivalry by the major powers and the necessity of making themselves heard and effective in the international arena (Thanat 1992: xvii). However, ASA proved ineffective in the major territorial dispute over North Borneo (Sabah), which involved Indonesia, Malaysia and the Philippines. Thus the organization effectively collapsed within a matter of months of its founding. In 1966 another more broadly based organization was established, the Asian and Pacific Council (ASPAC), initially involving Japan, South Korea, Taiwan, Australia and New Zealand as well as the South East Asian states of Malaysia, the Philippines, Thailand and South Vietnam. But the organization was rendered ineffective following the admission of the People's Republic of China (PRC) and the eviction of Taiwan. It lingered on in a shadowy form until 1975 (Thanat 1992: xviii).

Changed regional and national circumstances during the mid- and late 1960s produced conditions more conducive to regional organization. These included the re-engagement of Indonesia in the international system and the installation of an anti-communist regime there, the expelling of Singapore from the Federation of Malaysia, the Chinese Cultural Revolution, the escalation of the Vietnam War, increasing insurgency movements, the ending of a British strategic presence 'east of Suez', and the emergence of an American view that South East Asia should take increasing responsibility for its own security (Hagiwara 1973: 445). With these developments as a backdrop, ASEAN was established in 1967.

The 1967 Bangkok Declaration briefly set out the aims and purpose of ASEAN. These were primarily social, cultural and, above all, economic. Nowhere was it stated that ASEAN members would cooperate in political, strategic or military areas. The founder members appear to have believed that regional economic cooperation would contribute to their own economic growth (Khaw Guat Hoon 1984: 225). Despite this, no commitments to economic integration or the establishment of a free trade area were made. However, at least for some of the promoters, there was a clear recognition of the desirability of some form of integration along the lines of the European Economic Community (EEC) (Thanat 1992: xix). Despite the content of the Bangkok Declaration, a number of commentators have stressed the role of the US in the establishment of ASEAN and the significance of political and strategic considerations (Caldwell 1978: 14). Indeed, the communist bloc was never to be convinced that ASEAN was anything more than a Western-inspired military alliance directed against China and the Indo-Chinese states. In addition, many regional security specialists concluded that a *de facto* regional pact existed (Jeshuruan 1992: 368). Leifer (1978) suggests that ASEAN should be regarded as a regional security organization without the structure associated with such an alliance. Much of the strategic, political and military activity that involved cooperation between all or some of the member states has tended to take place outside ASEAN's formal structures. Indeed, it was clearly stated in the Declaration of ASEAN Concord of 1976 and reiterated in the 1987 Manila Declaration that member states would be responsible for their own security and cooperation would take place on a 'non-ASEAN basis' (Abad 1996: 239–240)

Whatever the original intention of the founder members, it became rapidly apparent that the progress of economic cooperation would be seriously inhibited by security issues and political tension. Indeed, the resilience of the new organization was almost immediately tested by major disputes between Malaysia and the Philippines (once again essentially over Sabah) and between Indonesia and Singapore. Both were eventually settled through negotiations which involved the other member states, and the normalization of relations between the disputing states was announced through ASEAN. The disputes indicated the ongoing potential for intra-regional conflict among the member states. But the manner of their resolution suggested that the members also saw a very clear need for the organization to continue. In this the changing regional and global circumstances already alluded to were clearly of major importance.

During the early 1970s, ASEAN members began to coordinate negotiating positions with countries and organizations outside of the region, notably with the EEC through the establishment of a Special Co-ordinating Committee of ASEAN Nations (SCAN) in 1973, with General Agreement on Tariffs and Trade (GATT) through the ASEAN Geneva Committee established in 1973; with Japan during 1973–4 over synthetic rubber production; and with Australia over the provision of aid to ASEAN as a corporate entity (Leifer 1975: 8–9). There were also some signs of interest in political cooperation, including the 1971 Kuala Lumpur Declaration calling for the establishment of a Zone of Peace, Freedom and Neutrality (ZOPFAN) in the region. Furthermore, meetings were held during 1972 and 1973 to discuss policy towards Vietnam, the second of these promoted by the Paris Peace treaty (Irvine 1982: 28). However, it should be stressed that discussions of ZOPFAN and Vietnam all took place at informal ministerial meetings outside the formal ASEAN structure (Khaw Guat Hoon 1984: 231).

In 1975, communist victories in Cambodia, Laos and Vietnam dramatically sharpened the divide in South East Asia between ASEAN and non-ASEAN members. This resulted in the rapid formation of a consensus amongst ASEAN members that the organization must be seen as purposeful, serious about regional cooperation and able to deliver concrete achievements (Khaw Guat Hoon 1984: 233). This renewed impetus for formal regionalism was codified in February 1976 at the Bali Summit meeting. From this meeting there emerged the provision for an ASEAN Secretariat, the Treaty of Amity and Cooperation and the Declaration of ASEAN Concord.

The stimulus to regional cooperation given by the events of 1975 continued with the reunification of Vietnam in 1976, the persisting and, in some cases, worsening internal security problems for most of the member states, the Vietnamese invasion of Cambodia and the general economic down-turn that was affecting the entire region. It was, however, the 'Cambodia problem' that was seen both as the major barrier to the establishment of ZOPFAN and as a major imperative for the establishment of effective regional cooperation (Luhulima 1989). In some ways the ongoing Cambodian issue inhibited many aspects of regional cooperation from the late 1970s until the early 1990s because it led to a 'let's fix Cambodia first' attitude (Philippine Foreign Minister Raul Manglapus cited by Antolik 1992: 144). Nevertheless, the long-term negotiations over Cambodia, which brought about the Vietnamese withdrawal in 1989, and the 1991 Paris Peace Agreement served to develop ASEAN's ability to negotiate both regionally and internationally as a unified group. Perhaps more significantly, during these negotiations ASEAN came to occupy a prominent position on the world stage and became recognized as a significant player in international affairs.

The Paris Agreement has also to be seen in the context of the ending of the Cold War, the virtual removal of any regional presence on the part of the Great Powers and the internal reforms in the former Indo-Chinese states, in particular their opening to trade and investment and the establishment of cordial relations with the PRC. Throughout most of the Cold War period, the PRC had been viewed as a major security threat by the pro-Western states of South East Asia. However, following the Vietnamese invasion of Cambodia in 1978 and the break with the PRC, there were moves on the part of Thailand to establish cordial relations with Beijing. This initially generated friction with the other members of ASEAN, notably Indonesia. But with the ending of the Cold War and the opening of the PRC to international trade and investment, relations improved. Most significant was the establishment of diplomatic relations with Indonesia, for the first time since 1967, and with Vietnam. The new relationship with the PRC is reflected in the fact that ASEAN meetings were held in Beijing in 1997. A certain wariness still governs ASEAN–PRC relations, however. There is the potential for disputes over, for example, offshore oil and gas, fishing and the ownership of the Spratly Islands, and their resolution has not been eased by the PRC's preference for bilateral negotiations and refusal to accede to ASEAN's Treaty of Amity and Cooperation, which would provide a mechanism for settlement (Abad 1996: 247)

Following the 1991 Paris Agreement, there was also a rapid improvement in relations between ASEAN and its South East Asian neighbours. This was driven by the progress of reforms, particularly in Laos and Vietnam, and the attraction of these countries as markets, sources of raw material and cheap labour. In July 1992 Laos and Vietnam became signatories to the Treaty of Amity and Cooperation, obtained observer status at ASEAN meetings and attended subsequent ASEAN Ministerial Meetings (AMM). Both countries expressed their interest in joining ASEAN, and during 1994 Cambodia indicated that it would also like to sign the Treaty of Amity and Cooperation and attend meetings as an observer. In 1995 Vietnam became a full member of ASEAN and Cambodia, Laos and Myanmar were scheduled to join in July 1997. In the event Cambodia's admission has been delayed by a coup d'état.

The incorporation of Cambodia, Laos, Myanmar and Vietnam may well further the integration and prestige of ASEAN. But it is important to remember that the organization's regionalism was shaped by the Cold War and the Cambodian issue (Hoang Anh Tuan 1993: 287). The dissolution of these problems has necessitated the development of a new region-building logic in which economic cooperation might be expected to be paramount. However, in contrast to the achievements on the diplomatic and strategic fronts, progress on economic integration and cooperation has been limited. This is in spite of the regular reiteration of the importance of these areas and the emergence of a number of initiatives.

Formal economic integration

Proposals for economic cooperation go back to the very early years of ASEAN. In 1969, a United Nations study advocated a programme of trade liberalization, the establishment of complementary industrial specialization and the construction of a number of large industrial projects aimed at the regional market. In 1976, a programme of action was adopted by the member nations. This emphasized the need for cooperation in the supply of basic goods, particularly food and energy, the importance of the establishment of large industrial concerns utilizing local raw materials and serving the regional market, trade cooperation aimed at producing preferential agreements in the long term, and joint efforts to improve markets outside of ASEAN and coordinate approaches on international trading matters. Yet economic integration within ASEAN is limited (see Table 8.1). While the volume of intra-regional trade has risen and all the members have become more trade-dependent, particularly since the mid-1980s, there has been little sign of intra-regional trade becoming significantly more important.

Of the five major joint industrial projects agreed in 1976 only two urea plants, one in Malaysia and one in Indonesia, have been constructed. It is likely that that these would have been constructed anyway and in any case they serve only national markets. Similarly, the achievements of the industrial complementarity schemes have been negligible. The industries where there was most scope for these programmes, such as motor vehicle

Table 8.1 Intra-regional trade as a percentage of the total value of trade

	1970	1975	1980	1985	1990	1995
Brunei	83.2	9.7	3.1	21.6	29.0	44.8
Malaysia	25.4	22.2	30.3	23.9	22.7	23.3
Indonesia	21.0	8.9	6.5	7.8	9.3	8.3
Philippines	1.2	3.2	7.3	8.2	9.1	11.2
Thailand	15.0	17.2	14.7	15.8	12.1	15.2
Singapore	27.1	20.8	24.3	21.1	18.6	24.8
Vietnam	—	—	—	—	17.6	21.4
Total	21.5	14.8	22.7	17.1	16.5	19.6

Source: IMF, *Direction of Trade Year Book*, Washington, various issues.

manufacture, had all received considerable government support and protection. The rationalization that the complementarity programmes would have involved proved unacceptable to the member states (Rieger 1987: 10). At the same time, Singapore has been reluctant to participate because that would mean 'sourcing' from high-cost ASEAN producers instead of cheaper international suppliers. Trade liberalization has also been limited. Ten years after it was signed, the 1977 Preferential Trade Agreement covered some 12,000 items, of which 95 per cent were not normally traded (Abad 1996: 247). From the early 1980s there was a general fall in the level of tariff protection, principally as a result of structural adjustment policies, but these still left very high tariff and non-tariff protection of key import substitution areas. As may be seen from Table 8.1, the reduction in average tariff levels has had little impact on intra-regional trade.

The limited progress of regional economic integration reflects the lack of complementarity between the states. The pro-Western states have followed broadly similar patterns of development from the 1950s, emphasizing the urban-industrial sector and progressing from import substituting to export-oriented strategies. The detail of development policies, general views of development (Rigg 1997a: 46–50) and, more especially, the form of the states differ strikingly (Crouch 1984; Appelbaum and Henderson 1992; Hewison *et al.* 1993) but the broad similarities, together with their location and resource endowments, have engendered a high degree of competition between all of them except Singapore. Policies are broadly similar in a range of areas, including foreign investment, TNCs, labour, wages and welfare. Dragsbaek-Schmidt (1997) has depicted the move towards increasing labour and welfare restrictions as 'competitive austerity' as well as a major source of political tension and conflict at the national level.

In Singapore, support for regional economic integration has been evident since the mid-1970s. There have been few signs of internal opposition to integration, in part because of the form of the state. However, given the long-standing open nature of the Singapore economy, there are few interests that would be disadvantaged by economic integration with the rest of South East Asia (Rodan 1987: 154). This is far from being the case elsewhere in the region. Although generally authoritarian in nature, most governments are to varying degrees obliged to take account of pressure from below as well as from various, often conflicting, elite groups. So, although there are interests that would be served by greater regional integration, these have been generally outweighed by those who would be disadvantaged.

Even in Singapore, the government's enthusiasm for regional integration is tempered by other aspects of policy, in particular the tendency of the People's Action Party (PAP) to raise the spectre of external threats, which strain relations with neighbouring states. This serves to justify security expenditure and social and political control and to encourage the maximum participation in 'Team Singapore' and support for the 'Head Coach', Goh Chok Tong. It can be seen most clearly in periodic public statements on Malaysia, Vietnam and the PRC (see, for example, *Singapore Bulletin* 25, No. 7: 18–20), but is also present in comments on, and treatment of, migrant labour and the banning or restrictions of publications from other Pacific Asian countries.

Outside Singapore, the entrenched import substitution sectors, often closely allied to bureaucratic and military interests, particularly in Indonesia and Thailand, have used their influence to oppose trade liberalization. Thailand illustrates this well. Between 1980 and 1986, the government proved unwilling or unable to reduce tariff levels, import controls and subsidies when these were key elements in structural adjustment 'conditionalities' (Dixon 1993, 1995). The failure to implement adjustment and open the economy more fully to regional and global trade reflected the weakness of successive coalition governments in the face of opposition from entrenched interests. Similarly, in Indonesia moves to open the economy since the early 1980s had been countered, until the resignation of Suharto in May 1998, by the increased protection of the interests of, in particular, those closely connected to Suharto's family (*Far Eastern Economic Review*, 22 May 1996: 52).

The rapid expansion of export-oriented manufacturing since the early 1980s has increased the influence of groups that might be expected to favour increased freedom of trade. In Thailand, for example, many domestic concerns reoriented their products towards the export market, particularly in the textile, food processing and electronic assembly sectors (Dixon in press). A small number of domestic companies have also turned themselves into regionally based TNCS. However, few of these have any major interest in freer regional trade. In general their interests have been better served by the liberalization of foreign investment and exchange controls. The way these companies develop is illustrated by the Thai-based Charoen Pokphand group, which diversified from a producer of seeds and animal foodstuffs for the domestic market into the export of frozen chickens, marine products and other processed food. It subsequently went transnational and entered the PRC to establish feedmills, motor cycle assembly, chemical and brewing. By 1996, Charoen Pokphand had 130 ventures in the PRC and was believed to be the largest single foreign investor (*Far Eastern Economic Review*, 20 September 1996). Further diversification into telecommunications and chemicals has resulted in Thailand, Indonesia and Cambodia.

Generally, in all the countries except Singapore, the import substitution sectors remain extremely influential. Similarly, there are elements within organized labour that are against freeing trade because of its possible impact on employment. There are also considerable potential conflicts of interest over the trade in agricultural produce. Thailand and Vietnam, as the region's two major food exporters, are clearly in favour of freer trade. This is not in the interests of the protected and subsidized Indonesian and Malaysian rice sectors, although lower cost food does appeal to consumers and employers. For both Indonesia and Malaysia, the promotion of the rice sectors to provide national self-sufficiency and raise rural incomes has been an important developmental goal. Free trade in rice would bring in significantly cheaper Vietnamese and Thai rice and would pose major political problems. In Malaysia, protecting the agricultural sector has been part of a defence of the predominantly rural Malay population and it is difficult to envisage that being undermined.

Since the early 1980s, there has been increasing socio-economic differentiation and class formation within the ASEAN states. There is considerable debate as to whether the changing class structures will lead to the emergence of less authoritarian forms of government. There are signs that governments have become more responsive to pressures from below, particularly in the Philippines and Thailand, especially from the increasingly wealthy, vocal and organised middle class. In addition, economic growth and structural change have generally increased the influence of the business communities. Business groups might favour regional integration, but they appear to be as yet insufficient in number or resources to speed the process. The only significant exception to this is Myanmar and the former Indo-Chinese states. Here interests in the exploitation of markets, raw materials and cheap labour have clearly influenced the rapid development of cordial relations and integration into ASEAN, discussed below. Similar influences have also been important in the establishment of relations with the PRC.

Overall, then, by the early 1990s little real progress had been made in the establishment of formal regional economic integration. However, in October 1992, member states decided to adopt a proposal for the formation of the ASEAN Free Trade Area (AFTA). This established a fifteen-year programme (subsequently reduced to ten) of tariff reduction (Rigoberto 1992: 50). But the prospects of substantial economic gain from AFTA appear limited. In addition there is little likelihood of AFTA proving an attraction to foreign investment and TNC activity in the way that the European Union (EU) did as a result of the Internal Market programme. The initial enthusiasm for AFTA must be seen as a response to the establishment of the European Internal Market and North American Free Trade Agreement (NAFTA). However, given the structure of the ASEAN economies, whether further trade liberalization will result in increased intra-regional trade flows is in doubt (Rieger 1987), and since AFTA was signed there have been few signs that the ASEAN countries are committed to freeing regional trade (Vatikiotis 1993: 48). In Thailand, for example, fears have been expressed that freer trade may adversely affect the still poorly developed basic manu-facturing sector.

But as enthusiasm for AFTA waned, interest in wider Pacific cooperation increased. An interest in the idea of broad Pacific cooperation began in the late 1970s. In 1980, following a lead given by Japan and Australia, the Pacific Economic Cooperation Conference (PECC) was established. Representatives of the US, Japan, Canada, Australia, New Zealand, South Korea and the members of ASEAN attended. By 1991 membership had been extended to include Brunei, China, Mexico, Taiwan, Hong Kong, Peru and Chile. In addition, the Soviet Union sent observers and lobbied for membership. PECC was essentially an advisory non-govenmental organization. But it provided an important forum for discussion and was the launching pad for the establishment of the inter-governmental Asia-Pacific Economic Cooperation (APEC) in 1989. Malaysia has been a particular advocate of the kind of wider economic cooperation between ASEAN and East Asia envisaged within APEC. More recently Thailand has also appeared to favour this development. For, while the prospects for gains from cooperation within ASEAN appear very limited for the majority of the members, there are increasingly important investment and trade links with East Asia. Hence it would appear that broader Pacific Asian integration is being led by economic linkages rather than formal regional structures.

Singapore's role in regional economic integration

Singapore, long established as a regional entrepôt, with relatively developed industrial and financial sectors, dominates intra-ASEAN trade (Table 8.2). Although there have been no overall increases in the proportion of regional trade involving Singapore, the composition of that trade has changed signif-icantly since the early 1980s. The share of primary products such as oil has declined while trade in manufactured goods, components and capital goods has increased, particularly with respect to trade with Malaysia and Thailand.

Like the other Asian NIEs, Singapore was beginning to lose its compar-ative advantage in labour-intensive manufacturing in the late 1970s. However, rising relative costs and labour shortages were compounded by official policy (McCue 1978; Rodan 1987: 157). This prompted the rapid development of higher value-added production and financial services. The inflow of foreign labour (principally from Malaysia) was curtailed and a

Table 8.2 Trade with Singapore as a percentage of total regional trade

	1970	1975	1980	1985	1990	1995
Brunei	1.2	17.5	12.9	30.6	45.9	71.2
Indonesia	73.8	84.3	80.0	78.2	72.0	42.2
Malaysia	84.4	82.4	80.0	78.2	72.0	42.2
Philippines	58.0	68.9	30.1	31.6	38.9	39.3
Thailand	46.7	39.5	46.3	55.1	61.2	60.5
Vietnam	—	—	—	—	83.4	64.5

Source: IMF, *Direction of Trade Year Book*, Washington, various issues.

'wage correction' policy implemented. In essence, this was aimed at forcing low-value, labour-intensive activities to either upgrade or cease operations (Rodan 1987: 159). Consequently, since the early 1980s, a great deal of manufacturing activity has relocated from Singapore to lower cost locations in South East Asia. Frequently this has involved retaining skill and capital-intensive activities in Singapore and the desegregation of the internal processes of the firm at the regional level (Van Grunsven and Verkoren 1993). In general, industrial concerns have adopted a 'decanting' approach, transferring increasingly sophisticated segments of their operations out of Singapore in the face of declining profits. This is giving rise to the development of a very clean regional division of labour between Singapore and the lower cost South East Asian locations, particularly Thailand and Malaysia, and more recently Vietnam. It is particularly evident in the electronics sector. Indeed, the trade in integrated circuits and related components between Singapore, Thailand and Malaysia reflects complex organizations which take advantage of markedly different labour costs and the availability of skilled labour (Dixon in press).

The development of a Singapore-centred regional division of labour has been accentuated by the pivotal position that the city-state occupies within South East Asia. In effect the regional entrepôt function established during the colonial period has been extended to manufacturing and finance. A combination of location, infrastructure, virtually free movement of goods and capital, and government policy has made Singapore a favourite location for the headquarters of TNCs operating in South East Asia. As a result, much of the region's investment is channelled through Singapore (Okposen 1993). Singapore has attempted to capitalize further on these developments by becoming a 'total business centre' for TNCs based in South East Asia through the Operational Headquarters Scheme (Dicken and Kirkpatrick 1991). The government promotes Singapore as the economic hub of South East Asia (for an example, see *Far Eastern Economic Review*, 18 August 1989: 77). Nevertheless, other South East Asian states do not necessarily share Singapore's vision of its regional role or attach the same significance to economic integration (Crouch 1984).

The emergence of Singapore as the centre of a South East Asian regional division of labour was accompanied in the early 1980s by the development of a more localized production structure involving the adjacent Malaysian state of Johore and the Indonesian islands of the Riau group (Perry 1991; Yeoh *et al.* 1992; Okposen 1993; Van Grunsven and Verkoren 1993). This 'inner triangle' or SiJoRi triangle (Figure 8.2), as it is often known, has developed through the relocation of labour-intensive activities from Singapore. Although labour costs in Johore are substantially lower than in

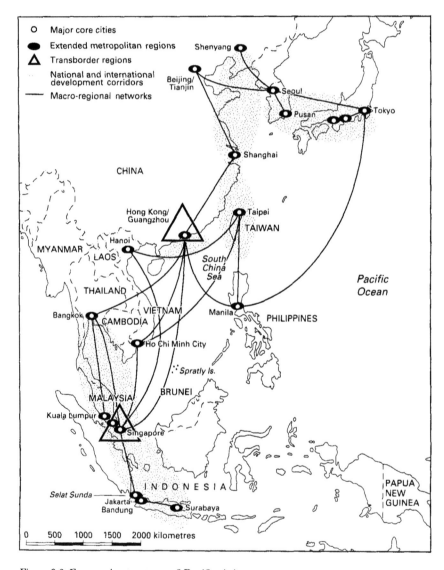

Figure 8.2 Economic structure of Pacific Asia

Singapore, they are the next highest in the region. Nevertheless, the loss of cost advantages appears to be more than offset by the advantage of close proximity to Singapore. In addition to the relocation and disaggregation of production at the sub-regional scale of Singapore-based activities, there has also been an influx of branch plants, particularly from Japan, Hong Kong, South Korea and Taiwan. Many of these concerns have no activities in Singapore but see the higher costs of Johore offset by the advantages of location adjacent to a comparatively sophisticated industrial and service complex (Van Grunsven and Verkoren 1993: 18). Singapore's policy is to promote the further development of the inner triangle. However, as Acharya (1995) concludes, such sub-regional development may well exacerbate inter-ethnic and political tensions between the participating states as well as fostering inter-state suspicions over the uneven distribution of economic benefits.

Thailand and the integration of the mainland sub-region

Thai ambitions are for Bangkok to become the focus of a major sub-regional economic zone in mainland South East Asia and Thailand has taken a lead in establishing trade and investment links with Myanmar and the former Indo-Chinese states, reflecting the then Prime Minister Chatchai Choonhaven's often quoted comment on the need to change 'Indo-China from a battlefield to a market place' (cited in *Far Eastern Economic Review*, 21 April 1990). Although Thailand's bridgehead function into Vietnam was rapidly eclipsed by Japan and the NIEs, it remains the most important trading partner for Cambodia, Laos and Myanmar. The desire to use Thailand's more developed manufacturing and financial sectors to exploit the resources and markets of its immediate neighbours is the motive behind the country's strong support for extending ASEAN membership to Cambodia, Laos and Myanmar. However, an Indo-Chinese federal structure centred on Vietnam remains a possibility and this has to be set against Thai ambitions (see Ky Coo 1994: 401).

A new set of relations are developing between Thailand and its immediate neighbours based on access to resources, driven in part by the depletion of Thailand's resource base and reinforced by the imposition of political limitations on their further exploitation. Timber and water resources are particularly affected. Evidence of widespread environmental damage combined with the emergence of increasingly effective environmental pressure groups resulted in the imposition of a national logging ban in 1989. In 1988, a combination of urban-based middle-class environmentalists and rural community organizations successfully halted the Nam Choam dam, placing a question mark over similar developments elsewhere in the country. Since then, successive Thai governments have negotiated directly with Cambodia, Laos, Myanmar and Vietnam over the exploitation of fishery, mineral, timber and water resources. This 'resource diplomacy' has given rise to a certain amount of international friction (Innes-Brown and Valencia 1993). Logging and gem mining in Cambodia has been seen as giving financial support to the Khmer Rouge, for example. In addition, Thailand has become embroiled in the domestic politics of Myanmar and the former Indo-Chinese states (see, for example, *Far Eastern Economic Review*, 28 January 1993: 21; 25 February 1993: 4).

The largely unexploited water resources of Laos and Myanmar in particular have attracted increasing attention from the Electricity Generating Authority of Thailand (EGAT) and the Royal Irrigation Department (RID). Proposals have been advanced for a major power generation project in Myanmar on the Salween river and a series of projects involving Laos have centred on the exploitation of the waters of the Mekong and its tributaries. The latter is part of the reactivation of the multilateral Mekong Scheme of the early 1970s. Increasingly ambitious proposals are being advanced to transfer very large amounts of water from the Mekong system into depleted Thai rivers and dams in order to increase power generation and irrigation capacity. These proposed developments appear to benefit Thailand disproportionately while imposing considerable environmental cost on its neighbouring states (Hirsch 1993:11). Also, there is mounting evidence of environmental damage from the largely uncontrolled exploitation of other resources (Hirsch 1993: 10–13). Indeed, despite official attempts to control the situation, unstable resource exploitation regimes are already appearing in the neighbouring states, heralding a repetition of the Thai situation (Hirsch 1993: 10). As a result, the development plans are generating friction at both the regional and international levels.

In trade terms also, Laos and Cambodia have became closely tied to Thailand. Overall, particularly with respect to Laos, Thailand is creating a dependency structure (Rigg 1995, 1997b). Laos' principal sources of foreign exchange are the sales of logs and electricity to Thailand. It would seem that Thailand wishes to develop a similar relationship of dependency with respect to Cambodia and Myanmar, and, in view of Thailand's industrial development and the poverty of neighbouring states, this is by no means an impossible project. Thai ambitions to exploit the resources of Vietnam, however, are unlikely to be realized. The absence of a common border, the Vietnamese emphasis on developing an industrial economy and insistence on the processing of raw materials should block this move. Indeed, while the resource-rich economies of Cambodia, Laos and Myanmar complement Thai development, Vietnam is rapidly becoming a competitor for foreign investment and the production of labour-intensive manufactured goods.

South East Asia in the Pacific Asian context

The development of a degree of regional and sub-regional integration in South East Asia should be seen in a broader Pacific Asian context

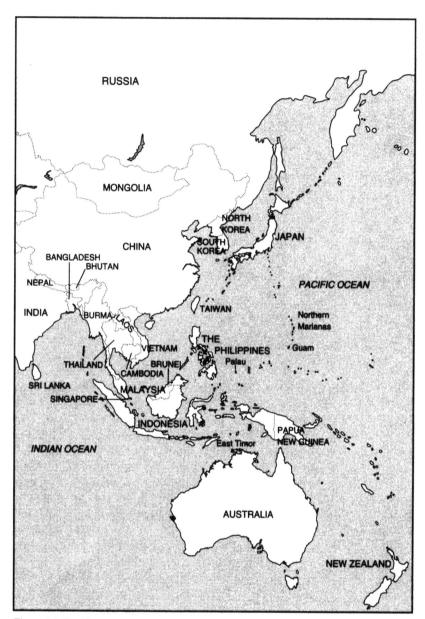

Figure 8.3 Pacific Asia

(Figure 8.3) as the region is coming to comprise an increasingly integrated third core of the world economy centred on Japan (Dicken 1991; Dixon and Drakakis-Smith 1995). Between 1980 and 1993, the Pacific Asian grouping increased its share of the global product from 15.2 per cent to

Table 8.3 Pacific Asian regional trade as a percentage of the value of total trade

	1980	1993	Change 1980–93
Japan	24.0	40.5	+16.5
Hong Kong	45.1	67.9	+22.8
South Korea	31.4	60.1	+28.7
Singapore	45.4	60.1	+14.7
Taiwan	31.1	46.7	+15.6
Total NIEs	38.5	46.7	+8.2
Indonesia	61.4	59.4	−2.0
Malaysia	51.9	61.2	+9.3
Philippines	38.2	51.7	+13.5
Thailand	35.8	46.7	+10.9
PRC	42.0	76.2	+34.2
Vietnam	39.0	79.9	+40.9
Total re-engaging Socialist [a]	41.9	76.7	+34.8
Total Pacific Asia	33.5	53.6	+20.1

Sources: IMF *Direction of Trade Year Book*, Washington, various issues; *Industry of Free China*, Taipei, various issues.
Note: [a] Includes Cambodia, Laos and Myanmar

22.3 per cent and its share of global exports from 14.5 per cent to 26.4 per cent. During the same period intra-regional trade as a percentage of total trade increased from 33.5 per cent to 53.6. As Table 8.3 shows, between 1980 and 1993 there was a substantial increase in the importance of regional trade for every country except Indonesia. The figures for the ASEAN states are particularly significant in the light of the limited expansion of South East Asian regional trade (Table 8.1). Particularly for Malaysia, Thailand and the Philippines the increase in Pacific Asian trade reflects deepening links with Hong Kong, Japan, Taiwan and South Korea. For a number of writers the Pacific Asian region has not only become a dynamic new global 'core'; it is one that is increasingly able to generate growth internally contrary to trends elsewhere in the global economy (Kwan 1994).

For the South East Asian states, the development of Pacific Asian integration rests on the relocation, particularly since the early 1980s, of manufacturing activities from Hong Kong, South Korea and Taiwan, reinforced by a further cycle of decanting by Japanese industry. This resulted from rising costs and the loss of comparative advantage. It was reinforced by growing concern over environmental issues, leading to the export of a variety of highly polluting processes (Hesselberg 1992). Thus, large numbers of Japanese and East Asian NIE-based manufacturing concerns have 'gone transnational' regionally. As in Singapore, this pattern of regional production is

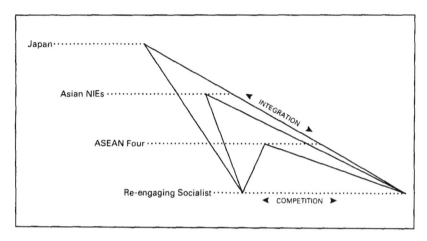

Figure 8.4 Nested regional divisions of labour in Pacific Asia

most apparent in the electronics sector (Henderson 1989), but is also emerging in other areas, notably textiles and garments (Finnery 1991; Hill 1991). Overall, the development of broad Pacific Asian divisions of labour have been reinforced by Western-based TNCs which increasingly organize their Pacific Asian activities on a regional basis (Henderson 1989; Van Grunsven and Verkoren 1993).

The relocation of NIE manufacturing activity from the early 1980s initially emphasized Thailand and Malaysia, subsequently spreading into Indonesia, Vietnam and the PRC. This reflected the relative costs involved as well as the views of business on political stability, liberalization and economic reform. As a result, a succession of rapidly growing economies, heavily driven by Pacific Asian-based foreign investment, have emerged in Thailand, Malaysia, the PRC and Vietnam (Dixon and Drakakis-Smith 1993, 1995; Dixon 1995). Pacific Asia is now depicted as a region in which integration is progressing rapidly through a process of 'informal regionalization' involving trade and investment flows (International Labour Office 1992: 48). This rests on a series of regional divisions of labour (Figure 8.4), principally reflecting differential labour costs. However, integration is taking place between a group of economies in which there is considerable competition (Dixon and Drakakis-Smith 1995: 82).

Conclusion

The ASEAN grouping has emerged since the mid-1980s as a significant force in regional and global affairs. This has been driven by the organization's apparent success in establishing political, strategic and diplomatic cooperation, contributing to the maintenance of regional stability. ASEAN has also proved itself capable of negotiating with wider regional and international institutions. In addition, with the exception of the Philippines, the member states are experiencing rapid and consistent rates of growth and structural change. However, ASEAN itself has played virtually no role in the member states' economic growth. Furthermore, despite the evident long-term success of ASEAN, it is apparent that the relations between the long-standing members are far from easy. Comparatively minor issues can speedily flare up into major diplomatic incidents. This gives weight to the view that the more serious disputes over, for example, off-shore oil and gas, fisheries and territory could rapidly escalate into major rifts between the member states. To these prospects for discord should be added the still high levels of military expenditure and the upgrading of facilities which are taking place (Acharya 1994; Sukhumbhand 1994: 249–50; Nagara 1995). The critical question is whether ASEAN will be able to manage disputes between members under circumstances very different to those in which it was created.

In terms of recent economic growth, the critical linkages for Thailand, Malaysia, Indonesia, the Philippines and, more recently, Vietnam are with Japan and the Asian NIEs. While at the South East Asian regional level there are significant trade and investment linkages with Singapore, these can be seen as part of wider links with the NIEs. With the exception of Singapore, the more recently established links between Thailand, Laos and Cambodia, and between Malaysia and Vietnam, the economic integration of the rest of the South East Asian economies remains of a very low order.

This chapter has stressed the lack of complementarity between the economies of Indonesia, Malaysia, the Philippines and Thailand. Indeed, they are increasingly in competition for investment, TNC operations and markets. This will not only mitigate against the success of the proposed development of AFTA but also encourage individual states to negotiate unilaterally rather than collectively. The integration of Myanmar and the former Indo-Chinese states may well exacerbate this situation. Already Vietnam is attracting domestic and, more especially, foreign investment away from Indonesia, Malaysia, the Philippines and Thailand. The further opening of Vietnam, together with China, Laos and Myanmar, is likely to intensify this type of competition. In addition, it seems likely that Indonesia, Malaysia, the Philippines and Thailand will increasingly compete for access to the markets, resources and cheaper labour of China, Laos, Myanmar and Vietnam. Indonesia, Malaysia, the Philippines and Thailand compete with one another for investment and branch plant activity from the NIEs and Japan. It is the prospects for the intensification of competition within the present and prospective sub-groups of ASEAN that appear most likely to undermine the successful establishment of AFTA and hence the continuation of ASEAN as a political and diplomatic force.

A final consideration is that regional cohesion in South East Asia may also be adversely affected by the internal affairs of states. Faltering growth and domestic political instability are very clear possibilities in many of the countries. The concentration of recent economic growth in the extended metropolitan regions of Bangkok, Manila, Jakarta, Hanoi and Ho Chi Minh City are giving rise to serious tensions between these areas and the rest of the countries. These strains may well rekindle the ethnic, cultural and linguistic differences which characterize the region. Another source of instability within states is the limited development of civil societies and the fragile nature of political structures and processes. There are real concerns over the inability of institutions in a number of states to produce orderly leadership transitions. In Thailand, for example, the 1991 coup d'état and the May 1992 democracy movement reflect the continuing weakness of democratic structures. The military will almost certainly continue to undermine Thai democratic development and a major force for stability and consensus will disappear when the present King dies. This may well produce a period of intense political instability. It is not that in Thailand, or any of the other South East Asian states, the combinations of economic and political instability will result in the collapse of any individual state, but that such events may seriously weaken the development of regional unity and integration, especially in an atmosphere of increasing economic competition amongst the member states and the linkages to a wider Pacific Asian regional grouping.

9 Unequal partnership: Europe, the Maghreb and the new regionalism

David Seddon

The Maghreb today comprises five states – Mauritania, Morocco, Algeria, Tunisia and Libya – and one disputed territory – the Western Sahara. The constantly changing economic and political relations between these states and their struggle over the direction of national and regional development provide crucial elements of the 'internal' definition of the contemporary Maghreb as a region. The Maghreb is both the western extension of the Arab world and a part of north-west Africa; it is a region shaped in part by its 'external' relations with the Middle East and with Africa. But the Maghreb is, and most significantly, a region whose economic and political development has for over 500 years been dominated by its relationship with Europe and, particularly during the colonial period, by direct European intervention. This may be seen positively as part of the (still unfinished) process whereby societies in Africa, Asia and Latin America have, over the centuries, been integrated into a global capitalist political economy, and thereby modernized (Warren 1980). Alternatively, it can be conceptualized as an integral part of European imperialism which has persistently undermined any local initiatives to constitute distinctive and alternative modes of development, including most recently the construction of alternative regional economic and political groupings.

Over the last fifty years, the Maghreb has struggled first to emancipate itself from colonialism and then to achieve a degree of autonomous development (Walton and Seddon 1994: 175–182). Promoting greater regional cooperation and integration was a part of that struggle. During the late 1970s and early 1980s, the project of independent development for the Maghreb was increasingly compromised by mounting debt and growing pressures for economic reform, which led during the 1980s and 1990s to structural adjustment and liberalization. This, in turn, while promising access to the 'benefits' of globalization and the 'free market', effectively undermined still further the possibilities for independent development and increased the vulnerability of the Maghreb economies to exploitation as part of the periphery of a new region constituted by a hegemonic Europe.

The two most recent regional initiatives affecting the Maghreb – the establishment of the Union of the Arab Maghreb (UAM) by the governments of the five Maghreb states in 1989 and the initiation by the European Union in 1995 of the Euro-Mediterranean Partnership (EMP) – both in their different ways highlight the crucial significance for the contemporary Maghreb of its relationship with Europe. Some see these two initiatives as complementary; others argue that they represent different and conflicting forms of regionalism. This chapter will take the latter view.

Europe and the 'independent' Maghreb

Following Independence, the economies of the newly independent Maghreb states found it difficult to achieve the growth and stability that had been hoped for – largely because of the flight of (European) capital and the diffi- culties of restructuring economies built in the interests of the metropolitan powers. Amin (1970: 225) emphasizes the extent to which 'between 1955 and 1965 production remained stagnant . . . investments fell . . . and exports, with the exception of oil, were in decline'. Furthermore, despite their efforts to build links with the Middle East and with Africa and to reduce the degree of economic and even political dependency on the former metropolitan powers, the Maghreb states remained critically dependent on the dynamics of the European political economy, and on France in particular, in such a way that the concept of 'imperialism without colonies' (Magdoff 1972) is not inappropriate.

They also faced an emerging European Economic Community (EEC) concerned to maintain a degree of control over its former colonies. The Treaty of Rome was signed in March 1957, just over a year after Moroccan and Tunisian independence. The Final Act contained a declaration of intent on the association of the independent countries of the franc area with the EEC which formally expressed the readiness of the six member states to open negotiations with the countries in question with a view to con- cluding conventions for economic association with the Community. The ostensible purpose of such conventions was 'to maintain and intensify the traditional trade flows between the member states of the EEC and these independent countries and to contribute to the economic and social dev- elopment of the latter'. The foundations for the so-called 'new' regionalism were established, as far as 'the European region' is concerned, by the Treaty of Rome.

The Mediterranean countries that now constituted the southern periphery of the new EEC were in general highly dependent economically on it; an average of more than 50 per cent of all Mediterranean exports went to the EEC, and the figures were higher for the Maghreb and Cyprus. In the Maghreb, exports (mainly minerals and agricultural produce) to Europe accounted for almost 30 per cent of GDP by the end of the 1960s (Tsoukalis 1977: 426). During the 1960s, the export of labour from the Maghreb to Europe also became a crucial structural feature of the economies of the region, serving the double function of providing employment for the rapidly growing numbers entering the labour market (population growth rates were high) and generating foreign exchange through the remittances sent home by migrant workers abroad. By 1973, official remittances were 23 per cent of total exports for Morocco and 22 per cent for Tunisia, amounting to US$211 million and US$91 million respectively. The value to the Moroccan economy of remittances from migrant workers (mainly in Europe) was to increase through the 1970s to reach US$100 million by 1980 (Richards and Waterbury 1990: 390). Algerian migrants, mainly in France, were also responsible for a substantial inflow of foreign exchange during the same period, despite efforts by the Algerian government to limit emigration, precisely because of the dangers of dependency.

Between 1961 and 1971, the EEC concluded a series of agreements with twelve of the seventeen Mediterranean countries. The most comprehensive agreements were those signed with Greece and Turkey in 1961 and 1963 respectively; but these were not repeated. Most such agreements were of limited value. In 1969 the EEC signed two five-year Association agreements on trade with Morocco and Tunisia; for Morocco the agreement conferred 'partial association'. The early 1970s saw the establishment of further preferential trade agreements, with Spain and Israel (in 1970), Malta (in 1971) and Portugal, Egypt and Lebanon (in 1972). But in 1972, the European Council declared that the EEC would from now onwards develop a more coherent and comprehensive (rather than a piece-meal) Mediterranean policy. The aim was not only to consolidate long-standing economic relations but also to create, eventually, a free trade zone in industrial goods encompassing the Community and the entire Mediterranean area. The Community promised to eliminate tariffs by 1977. Almost full reciprocity would be demanded from the more developed countries of the northern Mediterranean, but for a small number of sensitive products the timetable for the free trade area would be extended to 1985; and for the Maghreb the timetable would be extended even further (Tsoukalis 1977: 429).

This policy resulted in a further series of cooperation agreements with non-EEC eastern Mediterranean countries over the next few years. Agreements with Morocco, Algeria and Tunisia were all signed in April 1976. These envisaged free access to the EEC market for all industrial goods, with the exception of a few so-called 'sensitive' products, namely refined textiles, petroleum products and cork products from the Maghreb. A reduction on customs duties into the EEC was offered for Mediterranean agricultural exports, but quotas applied for olive oil, citrus fruits and wine exports. These concessions were always on condition that the rules applying to the organization of the EEC market were respected, and were subject to safeguard clauses. On the other hand, no reciprocity was demanded at least for an initial period of five years. A specified amount of financial assistance was offered to each individual country, while separate clauses provided for the treatment of immigrant workers from the Maghreb in the Community.

Whatever good intentions the European signatories of these agreements may have had, the application of the agreements was constrained by the sharply deteriorating economic climate in Europe during the second half of the 1970s and the early 1980s, and by the increased protection afforded to the (now) European Community (EC) agricultural sector by the strengthening of the Common Agricultural Policy. One of the consequences was a rapid deflation of the rhetoric regarding the 'global Mediterranean policy'. At the same time, the EC began to move towards the strategic incorporation of the southern European states. From 1975 (when the Greek application was lodged) until 1985 (when the treaty providing for the accession of Spain and Portugal to the EC was signed), the focus of the Community was on 'the second enlargement', to the exclusion of the non-EC Mediterranean countries. The implications were serious for the Maghreb. Tsoukalis pointed out as early as 1981 that, in view of 'the increase in the Community's self-sufficiency in all Mediterranean products', it was 'almost inevitable that relations with Mediterranean non-member countries will become even more difficult in the future' (Tsoukalis 1981: 228).

Conflict and cooperation: the UAM

While the EC was engaged in the strategic enlargement and internal consolidation of the early 1980s, leading to the further 'peripheralization' of the non-EC Mediterranean countries, the Maghreb experienced the profound trauma of economic liberalization and structural adjustment. The effects of the global recession on the Maghreb economies, Libya excepted, included deepening economic crisis in the second half of the 1970s and into the 1980s, associated with a deteriorating balance of payments and growing foreign debt. This led to pressures, both from within and from external agencies (notably the International Monetary Fund [IMF] and the World Bank, but also Western European governments and private banks), for the implementation of economic reforms directed towards stabilization, structural adjustment and liberalization. Morocco and Tunisia experienced these pressures first; Mauritania and Algeria somewhat later. Only Libya, with its growing oil revenues, appeared to benefit initially from global adjustment (Walton and Seddon 1994).

There is not the space here to deal with the complex legacy of the economic crisis of the 1970s and 1980s. Nonetheless, it is important to stress the degree to which the crisis both created opportunities for and constrained the new regionalism, the origins of which can be traced to this period. As the Maghreb struggled with economic reform and political crises, the EC once again began to reconsider its relationship with the countries on its southern periphery. This was prompted in part by the new security agenda of the 1980s resulting from US involvement in Libya and the rising tension between Israel and the Palestinians. The enlargement of the EC in 1986 to include Spain and Portugal was preceded by an announcement in 1985 reiterating the importance attached by the EC, despite a period of abeyance in fact of nearly a decade, to the idea of 'a global Mediterranean policy' – an importance which, the Maghreb was assured, was not diminished by the accession of Spain and Portugal to the Community. Talks concerning the precise implications of this policy continued through 1986 and 1987.

In the Maghreb, the prospect of a renewed thrust by the EC to define relations with its periphery prompted new efforts to develop closer regional links. In 1986, Libya proposed a union with Algeria. Algeria responded with little enthusiasm but subsequently suggested that a framework for a new Algerian–Libyan relationship already existed in the Maghreb Fraternity and Cooperation Treaty of 1983, between Algeria, Mauritania and Tunisia. Economic links between Libya and Algeria expanded and in 1987 the two governments agreed in principle on a treaty of political union; but opposition to this within Algeria led to a proposal that Libya should sign the Maghreb Fraternity and Cooperation Treaty. In February 1988 the three heads of state of Algeria, Tunisia and Libya held discussions concerning a proposed regional accord, following which the border between Libya and Tunisia was reopened. In March 1988, Libya and Algeria signed two agreements relating to industrial development, and the following month, Libya and Tunisia signed a cooperation pact encompassing political, economic, cultural and foreign relations.

During the latter part of the 1980s, despite the continuing disagreement over the future of the Western Sahara, as the economic and political situation in Algeria deteriorated and the government reduced the level of its support for the Polisario, the resistance movement fighting for the independence of the Western Sahara against Morocco, the balance of forces in the war in the desert swung increasingly towards Morocco. At the same time, the prospect of continuing economic liberalization in the face of an enlarged and even more dominant EC prompted a reappraisal of regional economic cooperation. Cautiously, the two major regional powers moved slowly towards a closer relationship; in May 1988, diplomatic relations were renewed between Morocco and Algeria.

In June 1988, after the Arab summit in Algiers, the five heads of state met to discuss prospects for 'a Maghreb without frontiers'. Shortly afterwards, rail links between Morocco and Algeria were re-established, the electricity grids joined and a framework agreed for the further development of transport and comunications links. Algeria and Libya discussed the basis for a federation of the two states within a Great Arab Maghreb. All of the Maghreb states agreed to send their most senior representatives to regular meetings of the newly established Maghreb Commission. Despite continuing disagreement between Morocco and Algeria over the Western Sahara, both countries affirmed their commitment to 'a just and final solution' to the conflict based on a regular and free referendum for self-determination.

In July 1988 the Maghreb Commission met for the first time in Algiers and announced the creation of working parties to consider integration in various areas, including finance and economics, regional security and education. In August, the Tunisian President, Ben Ali, visited Libya, signed a series of cooperation agreements and established a technical commission to accelerate the process of integration. A second meeting of Maghreb heads of state was held in February 1989 at which the participants concluded a Treaty proclaiming the formation of a Union of the Arab Maghreb (UAM) involving the five countries of the Maghreb – Mauritania, Morocco, Algeria, Tunisia and Libya – in an association designed to promote and orchestrate improved economic relations within the area. The objective was to promote the eventual free movement of capital, goods and services, and labour throughout the region.

A heads-of-state council and foreign ministers' council were set up. Plans were also made for a fifty-member parliamentary consultative council; this was doubled in size in January 1990. Similar plans were also proposed for common juridical and financial institutions. At the second summit meeting of the UAM, held in Algiers in July 1990, it was agreed that Libya would hold the annual presidency in 1991. Even common security issues were discussed in November 1990 at a conference in Algiers as the crisis in the Gulf deepened and plans were drawn up in December 1990 for a staged programme of integration – a free trade zone by 1992, a customs union by 1995 and a full common market by the year 2000.

The UAM and the Gulf crisis: political cooperation

If the Gulf crisis was to divert European attention away from economic issues to those of security in the Mediterranean and the Middle East, it provided the UAM with a major test of its capacity to develop, and sustain, a broadly unified position on a crucial, yet divisive, political issue.

When the Arab League met in Cairo, immediately after the Iraqi invasion of Kuwait, Egypt pushed through a resolution condemning the invasion and supporting the sending of Western and Arab forces to the Gulf. This was opposed by Libya. Mauritania expressed reservations; Algeria abstained; and Tunisia boycotted the meeting altogether. Only Morocco supported a military response, promising some 1,500 troops to the multinational force. Even then, King Hassan of Morocco emphasized the fact that the gesture was purely symbolic and claimed that, despite opposing the Iraqi invasion, he recognized the reasons for it and criticized 'the greed of our Kuwaiti friends' (cited in Seddon 1991: 6). At the beginning of September, the foreign ministers of the UAM produced a working document setting out a common position, to be submitted to the member heads of state 'as a contribution to the search for a solution to the Gulf crisis'. There was, then, an effort to develop a coherent approach in favour of a negotiated settlement, the key elements of which included the withdrawal of Iraqi forces from Kuwait, the withdrawal of foreign troops from the Gulf and 'an Arab solution' to the crisis.

In October, despite protests from the Maghreb states (including Morocco), the Arab League headquarters was transferred from Tunis to Cairo. The Arab League, now deeply divided, was moving its 'centre' eastwards and away from the Maghreb; at the same time, the growing commitment of the US and its regional allies to a military build-up and possible war in the Gulf alarmed the governments of the Maghreb. The Tunisian President, Ben Ali, declared the intentions of his country to redouble its diplomatic efforts and Morocco revised its initial support for the multinational force in the Gulf. King Hassan's call in November for an extraordinary Arab summit to provide 'a new and last chance' for a peaceful solution was supported by the other Maghreb states, including Algeria. President Mitterrand welcomed the Moroccan proposal and Saddam Hussein sent his second-in-command, Taha Yassin Ramdane, to Rabat to discuss it, while another envoy from Baghdad visited Tunis and Tripoli.

But the Arab summit never took place. In the meanwhile, Mauritania had adopted a more positively pro-Iraq stance, at odds with the rest of the Maghreb states. The governments of the Maghreb all continued, however, to favour 'an Arab solution' to the crisis and to press for mediation and compromise; and President Chadli of Algeria embarked in mid-December on a tour of Middle Eastern states with a view to taking negotiations further. During the first two weeks of January 1991, the initiative moved away from the Maghreb, and indeed from the Arab world altogether; but the Maghreb states continued to call for 'an Arab solution' right up to the actual assault on Kuwait and Iraq on 17 January 1991. Indeed, even after the war had started, the governments of the Maghreb sent a joint proposal to the United Nations for a ceasefire. But prospects for a diplomatic breakthrough faded and the ground offensive started on 23 February.

In the aftermath of the Gulf War, the divisions within the Arab world were greater than ever. But the Maghreb states had shown a capacity for coordinated diplomatic and political activity during the Gulf crisis. Could they maintain that impetus and develop the basis for lasting economic and political cooperation through the UAM?

The UAM fails to deliver

During 1991 a number of initiatives within the UAM were launched. Detailed proposals included the setting up of a Maghreb Bank for Foreign Investment and Trade to handle external financial transactions and of a Maghreb International Bank to deal with internal UAM financing. The latter was to be a cooperative venture based in Europe, involving the Maghreb states, the African Development Bank, the International Finance Corporation and the European Investment Bank. Tariff reductions were signed in March 1991, and plans to move towards standardized exchange rates and the free movement of capital and goods through the UAM were initiated.

However, there were also problems. The UAM heads of state were supposed to meet once every six months with each taking the chair in turn. By 1993, however, only three such summit meetings had been held and a special summit called in June 1991 was cancelled at short notice because of the internal political crisis in Algeria. This special summit had been scheduled after the planned March summit was postponed because of disagreements over the UAM's attitude towards US proposals for a Middle East peace conference. In addition, differences over the Western Sahara issue led King Hassan to refuse to attend. The next summit, in Casablanca in September 1991, was not attended by Colonel Qaddafi, who was then engaged in an attempt to develop a closer relationship with Egypt. Despite this, the Casablanca meeting agreed that the UAM secretariat was to be located in Morocco, the secretary-general was to be a Tunisian; the consultative council was to be located in Algeria, the UAM court in Mauritania, the new financial institutions in Tunisia and the UAM academy of sciences in Libya.

But UAM activities faltered during 1992. Libya effectively withdrew from the organization in reaction to UAM compliance with UN sanctions against Libya following the Lockerbie bombing; Algeria, preoccupied with the deterioration of its internal security situation, had little time for UAM affairs; Mauritania, the weakest of the Maghreb economies, embarked on a new tough programme of structural adjustment under the auspices of the IMF and the World Bank; and Morocco and Tunisia began to concentrate on developing new bilateral relations with the (now) European Union (EU) following its proposals for 'new regionalism' and new free trade arrangements.

UAM was meant to offer 'an alternative economic forum for growth' (Joffe 1993: 205). Ultimately, it has failed in this crucial regard. All of the Maghreb governments continue formally to subscribe to the UAM's objectives. But it has been eclipsed, in part by efforts to secure advantageous bilateral relations with the EC/EU and in part by the growing preoccupation of all member governments with domestic economic and political concerns. These problems led to an intensification of conflict on the domestic front for a number of Maghreb states, which, in turn, promoted a renewal of European interest in the region.

The Maghreb states shared a growing popular challenge to the legitimacy not only of government economic policies but of the regimes themselves by the beginning of the 1990s. The rise of Islamic militantism is one of the most striking expressions of popular disaffection. It is one aspect of a more general determination on the part of the people of the region to express their anger and outrage at what is widely seen as a failure of governments to provide economic policies which safeguard security and welfare and more broadly as a failure to provide the framework for social justice and development. It has emerged out of the groundswell of popular opposition to the austerity measures which accompanied the economic reforms of the 1980s, but become increasingly more orchestrated and more ideologically defined (Walton and Seddon 1994: 211–214). Not confined to the Maghreb, with Egypt, the Gulf states, Jordan and Turkey also significantly affected, Islamism has proved of major importance in Algeria and Tunisia, where the struggles between the state security forces and the more militant sections of the Islamic movement have been particularly bitter and bloody.

In Morocco, the government pushed ahead in the late 1980s and early 1990s with economic liberalization and privatization measures, despite growing concern at the social effects of drastic reductions in public expenditure, at rising unemployment and growing inequality. The government was able to limit overt opposition to economic reforms and suppress – with effective use of the state security forces – any potential social or political unrest. This gave rise to growing concern in Europe and elsewhere regarding the human rights situation in Morocco. Nevertheless, and despite a burgeoning debt, international credit continued to flow into the country. Morocco's international creditors and indeed the EC/EU, continue to support wholesale economic reform and further liberalization.

In Tunisia, as in Morocco, continuing economic reform gave rise to serious social hardship and many, the urban poor in particular, suffered from serious deprivation and a decline in living standards. With increasing restrictions on immigrant workers in Europe, employment opportunities abroad as well as remittances from migrant workers in Europe – a major source of foreign exchange since the mid-1960s – fell significantly in Tunisia as in Morocco. Towards the end of the 1980s and particularly after the Gulf War, Islamic opposition movements began to gain ground in Tunisia; but the government has maintained control, largely through heavy state repression of the Islamists (whose organizations remained illegal despite a degree of political liberalization in the immediate aftermath of the Gulf War). The human rights situation in Tunisia, although less well known than that of Morocco or of Algeria, has significantly deteriorated and international organizations such as Amnesty International now express growing concern.

In Algeria, a degree of political liberalization followed the bloody clashes of 1988. The Islamic Salvation Front (FIS), which had rapidly gathered strength in the preceding years, was officially recognized in September 1989, and in June 1990 it swept to power in Algeria's first contested municipal elections since Independence, wresting control of all major metropolitan areas. The FIS's arrival as a major political force was confirmed when it proved successful in the first round of the legislative election at the end of 1991. Fearful of the FIS coming to power through the ballot box, the elections were nullified by the government in January 1992; within a month the FIS was outlawed and thousands of known or suspected supporters arrested and jailed. A state of emergency was declared and since then a virtual civil war has torn Algeria apart, with estimates of anything up to 60,000 dead.

In sum, increased internal conflict in Algeria during the first half of the 1990s, and a growing human rights problem throughout the Maghreb, combined with the continuing political uncertainties of the Middle East in the aftermath of the Gulf War, heightened perceptions in Europe of the entire region as a major 'security risk'. This, in turn, led to renewed efforts by the EC to extend its influence and even control in the Mediterranean.

The Maghreb and Europe in the 1990s

At the rhetorical level, the EC welcomed the formation of the UAM. Almost immediately after the announcement of its establishment, the EC Commissioner for Mediterranean Policy, Abel Matutes, congratulated the member states on the progress achieved towards regional integration. He attempted to calm fears of the possible detrimental effect on EC–UAM trading relations of the creation of an Internal European Market in 1992, arguing that the new regional grouping would facilitate cooperation between the EC and the Maghreb.

In December 1989, the European Commission reaffirmed its concern to strengthen ties with all the countries of the Mediterranean. One of the Commission's first initiatives in the context of what Jacques Delors called the Community's 'proximity policy' was to present the main points of a 'revised Mediterranean policy'. This was to go beyond the framework established at the beginning of the 1970s, which was considered 'no longer appropriate for the needs of the 1990s'. The Commission emphasized the importance to Europe of the stability and prosperity of the Mediterranean countries – indeed, it was argued that the Mediterranean area was 'a key element in the stability, prosperity and security' of the Community itself (*Europa*, December 1989).

A financial aid programme was announced by the EC in 1991 which would provide a total of US$5.8 billion for eight Mediterranean countries – of which 50 per cent would be in the form of concessionary loans. Morocco would receive US$543 million, making it the largest beneficiary. However, despite assurances from Commissioner Matutes and promises of a rethink of EC economic policy towards the Maghreb,

> the proposals put forward . . . showed little novelty. In essence, they sustained the traditional policies of limited aid but did not offer . . . economic cooperation. . . . Although additional aid was promised, particularly to smooth the path of economic restructuring, there was no bold initiative on economic development or migration, nor, even, on foreign debt.
>
> (Joffe 1993: 206)

The Fourth Protocol, as it was known, was designed to provide the framework for the EC's relationship with the Maghreb between 1992 and 1996. It led to agreements with Morocco, Tunisia and Algeria. It included a 36 per cent rise in assistance (46 per cent more for Algeria, 31.5 per cent for

Morocco and 27 per cent for Tunisia), but the total sum involved remained small. Even when the additional structural adjustment aid is added, the total is still small – less than US$1 billion annually. The agreement with Morocco was also delayed by nine months as a result of a protest by the European Parliament against human rights abuses. Morocco, in return, initially rejected it, until the offer of free trade was added. Additionally, it should be noted that the Protocol excluded Mauritania and Libya, despite vehement protests from Tripoli.

Nonetheless, since 1992, the EC/EU has continued to develop closer economic relations with the Maghreb states, but on an individual (bilateral) rather than a collective basis. This process has been primarily and explicitly associated with efforts to promote economic liberalization in these states. Furthermore, and very significantly given the fact that the UAM includes all of the five Maghreb states, these relations have privileged Morocco and Tunisia and to some extent Algeria; Mauritania remains effectively marginalized and Libya entirely excluded.

In the case of Mauritania, which falls outside the scope of the new European interest in 'the Mediterranean', the EC has supported efforts at continued structural adjustment on a bilateral basis, and initiated specific agreements under Lomé IV. The Programme of Consolidation and Renewal (PCR) which followed the Programme for Economic and Financial Adjustment (PREF) continued the emphasis on the promotion of the private sector, but was adversely affected by a succession of years of low rainfall, a decline in the price of iron ore, a serious reduction in the fishing catch, and the Gulf crisis. In 1990, the Mauritanian GNP declined by 1.5 per cent, inflation increased and the external debt mushroomed to 227 per cent of GNP. Negotiations for a second structural adjustment programme, begun in late 1988, were halted at the end of 1990 in the light of the Mauritanian government's policy of 'active neutrality' in favour of Iraq. Arab capital from the Gulf withdrew and other external sources of finance dried up.

Political reforms in 1991 opened up the way for improved international relations; and an outline agreement was concluded in 1991 with the EC under Lomé IV for the period 1992–4, based on 'a very clear and precise programme of economic reform' (*The Courier*, No 137, January–February 1993). Talks with the IMF also began again at the end of 1991. The objectives of the new structural adjustment programme, endorsed by the IMF and the World Bank, were to reduce the country's external debt and improve its balance of payments by devaluation (40 per cent against the franc and 28 per cent against the dollar) and liberalization. Food prices rose by 40 per cent and there were riots, leading the government to impose a two-week dusk-to-dawn curfew in the capital, Nouakchott.

External 'donors', however, approved the austerity measures. The IMF agreed a loan in December 1992 to support the economic and financial reform programme from October 1992 to September 1995. By 1993 external debt had risen to US$2.2 billion, but in May 1994 a meeting of donor states promised to support the economic reform programme up to the end of 1996. In January 1995, the IMF approved a series of loans to run from 1995 through to 1997, again to help reduce the budget deficit through spending controls and increased revenues, and to privatize public sector enterprises. In the same month, a 25 per cent increase in bread prices again provoked serious rioting and clashes between protesters and security forces in Nouakchott, the imposition of a night-time curfew and the banning of all demonstrations until further notice. Early in 1996, the French government also concluded an agreement to provide support for the Mauritanian government's efforts to reduce the balance of payments problem and to promote structural reform. Mauritania has not, however, been included in any of the EC's efforts to promote the closer integration of 'the Maghreb' into the new expanded Euro-Mediterranean Partnership.

Neither has Libya, which throughout the last two or more decades has been regarded as a virtual pariah state by virtue of its distinctive political stance on what have been seen as key security issues in the region. The Lockerbie affair is only the latest of a series of 'incidents' for which Libya has been blamed and isolated. As Jon Marks (1996: 1) observes, Libya 'has been reduced by political problems to becoming a white void on the European Commission's increasingly complex map of relations with the so-called Mediterranean Non-Community (MNC) countries'.

This means, effectively, that the EC/EU has redefined the Maghreb as Morocco, Tunisia and perhaps Algeria. This, in turn, has contributed to weakening Maghreb unity. Despite a number of bilateral economic links and projects, and a broad commitment to economic integration of the Maghreb economies, the UAM has not managed to divert the priorities of the governments of the Maghreb states from their individual relationships with Europe towards a common project of economic and political cooperation. Intra-Maghreb trade remains low – less than 5 per cent on average – despite an increase in agricultural trade between Morocco and Algeria and an initial spurt in trade between Libya and Tunisia following the opening of borders between the two countries in 1991.

One reason for this failure to develop systematically a greater flow of investment and trade between the economies of the UAM is the fact that the national economies of the Maghreb states have continued to undergo economic reforms designed to further liberalize and 'open up' their economies, and to reduce the role of the state. This has tended to weaken their capacity for collective action. Although some would argue that there is no intrinsic reason why economic liberalization should not result in increasing intra-Maghreb capital, commodity and labour flows, there is little evidence elsewhere that local regional groupings can alter the dominant 'North–South' direction of such flows without very considerable state and supra-state orchestration. Economic liberalization is inherently inimical to such state intervention.

More significantly still, it could be argued, the failure of the UAM to develop economic relations between Maghreb states could be explained by precisely the series of initiatives taken by the EC/EU over the past decade or more to 'carve up' the area – thereby directly undermining the UAM – and to integrate the favoured Maghreb states (Morocco, Tunisia and Algeria) individually rather than collectively into a regional partly free trade nexus in which the enlarged Community maintains its dominance. Indeed, the evidence suggests that the programme of the UAM for greater *horizontal* cooperation within the Maghreb has effectively conflicted with the European policy of *vertical* integration of the Maghreb states into a Europe-dominated regional association. In the first, Maghrebi solidarity in the face of the prospect of an integrated European common market is emphasized; in the second, the links being developed are essentially between the EU and individual Maghreb states. The suggestion of complementarity between the EU's strategy and the development of closer economic integration within the UAM is not borne out by the evidence.

In fact, the advent of the Internal European Market after 1992 meant that Maghreb industrial exports increasingly faced serious non-tariff barriers particularly as regards standards and quality restrictions. Even more strikingly, new controls on the immigration of labour were introduced as a result of the Schengen and Trevi Agreements and of the national policies that have been systematically developed by governments in France, Britain, Spain and Italy. These informal mechanisms of economic protection and formal controls on immigration have led to the construction of what some refer to as a 'Fortress Europe', to which access by Mediterranean exporters and migrant workers is carefully circumscribed but from which investment and exports and tourists may flow freely into the 'structurally adjusted' economies of the Maghreb and other Mediterranean states.

As Joffe (1993: 205) observed, 'the most acute problem [for the UAM] will be over employment, for the implication of EC policy over migrants will be that Europe will no longer offer a convenient alternative labour market as it has done for the past thirty years'. The EC legally employed well over 1 million Algerians, 950,000 Moroccans and around 300,000 Tunisians – and probably employed a further 500,000 illegally – in the early 1990s. There are now some 2.3 million Maghrebi migrants in Europe – representing 8–10 per cent of the region's labour force. But restrictions imposed on immigrants and on those seeking asylum by member states during the last few years have tightened access to employment and residence in Europe; the 'free market' does not extend to Maghreb labour. The rate of demographic increase in the Maghreb is such that Algeria needs to create 90,000 jobs a year to keep pace with demand, while Morocco needs over 70,000 and Tunisia 40,000. Prospects for growth are not good, and the social and political implications are very serious. Unemployment is likely to rise in view of the absence of any major expansion of employment opportunities within the region through growth in the productivity, output and exports of key sectors of the Maghreb states' economies.

Popular unrest, as was noted earlier, has fuelled Islamic militancy. The rise of militant Islam in the countries of the southern and eastern Mediterranean littoral during the early part of the 1990s was increasingly seen in Europe as posing a distinct and powerful threat to European security. This, linked to the growing concern regarding immigration from this region, provides a political basis for a renewed effort by the EC, now the EU, to develop a coherent policy towards the region.

The EMP: theory and practice

Joffe argued in 1993 that 'unless there are bold EC initiatives to help the UAM, this initiative for regional economic integration and development will wither on the vine. Instead, member states will have to deal with their problems separately and will become ever more dependent on an unsympathetic Europe' (Joffe 1993: 206). As if in response, in June 1994 the EU summit at Corfu called for 'a new policy' towards eastern Europe and the Mediterranean.

One of the key documents produced subsequently proposed that the objective should be to work towards a Euro-Mediterranean Partnership, starting with the progressive establishment of free trade alongside substantial financial aid. It was envisaged that closer political and economic cooperation would follow. In November 1995, twenty-seven foreign ministers representing the member states of the EU and twelve Mediterranean 'partners' (including Morocco, Algeria and Tunisia in the Maghreb) unanimously adopted the Barcelona Declaration establishing a Euro-Mediterranean Partnership (EMP) (Barbe 1996).

The EMP emphasizes mainly economic objectives, chiefly the creation of a Free Trade Area linking the Mediterranean countries on Europe's southern periphery with the Internal European Market by 2010 (Galal and Hoekman 1997). In fact, it has three dimensions: a political and security partnership; an economic and financial partnership; and a partnership in social, cultural and human affairs. Each is to be implemented in two separate but complementary ways: via bilateral agreements and regionally. Priority, however, appears in practice to be accorded to the economic dimension.

As far as the Maghreb is concerned, the new emphasis on the Mediterranean means the incorporation of selective Maghreb states into 'partnership' with the EU continues. In the first instance, the 'partnership' has focused on two of the Maghreb economies (Tunisia and Morocco), although Egypt and Jordan are likely to be involved in the near future; it is not clear when Algeria is to be included. Tunisia and Morocco have both recently signed comprehensive 'integration' agreements with the EU (the first in July 1995 with Tunisia and the second with Morocco in November). One reason given for this prioritization of 'the Maghreb economies' was their strong dependence on Europe.

It is certainly true that Algerian, Moroccan and Tunisian trade remains heavily focused on Europe. Algerian trade relations are still dominated by France and Italy – over a third of Algeria's imports come from those two countries and between a third and a quarter of Algerian exports go to them also. In 1992, Algeria imported goods worth roughly US$5.4 billion from the EC countries out of a total of US$8.6 billion, and in 1994, US$5.2 billion out of US$9.6 billion. Only US$221 million (in 1992) and US$259 million (in 1994) came from two of Algeria's partners in the UAM – Tunisia and Morocco. As regards exports, in 1992, Algeria exported US$8 billion to countries of the EU, out of a total of US$11.1 billion; in 1994, the figure was US$5.9 billion out of US$8.6 billion. Only $215 million and $214 million went to Tunisia and Morocco, in 1992 and 1994, respectively.

Moroccan international trade is similarly dominated by the EU, with France overwhelmingly its largest trading partner, accounting for roughly a quarter (23 per cent) of imports and roughly a third (33.2 per cent) of exports in 1993. Capital goods comprise about a third of French exports, while consumer goods account for more than half of the imports from Morocco. Spain and then Italy are the two next most important sources of imports and markets for exports. In the first half of the 1990s, approximately half of Morocco's imports came from EU countries, and roughly three-quarters of Morocco's exports went to the EU. Morocco's trade is likely to remain crucially dependent on Europe, as the EU takes more than 50 per cent of exports and provides more than 40 per cent of imports. In 1993, less than 5 per cent of Morocco's imports came from its Maghreb neighbours (mainly Algeria and Libya); about 7 per cent of Moroccan exports went to the three other members of the UAM.

A very similar picture obtains in the case of Tunisia, whose international trade is again dominated by France, which accounts for about a third of imports and a quarter of exports – with Germany and Italy as the next most important trading partners. In 1992, Tunisia imported goods worth US$4.5 billion from countries of the EU, out of a total of US$6.4 billion, and in 1994, US$4.4 billion out of US$6.5 billion. As regards exports, in 1992, Tunisia exported goods worth US$3.1 billion out of a total of US$4 billion to countries of the EC, and in 1994, US$3.6 billion out of US$4.6 billion. Between 4 and 5 per cent of Tunisia's imports come from other countries within the UAM (mainly from Algeria, but also from Libya and Morocco), while between 6 and 7 per cent of Tunisian exports go to countries within the UAM.

The EMP – a raw deal for the Maghreb

The agreements of the EU with Tunisia and Morocco consist of two essential elements – increased aid flows and technical assistance in return for reductions in trade barriers and other impediments to the flow of goods and investment into the Maghreb economies over a period of twelve years. Nearly half of the proposed assistance to the region from the EU's expanded aid programme is directed at preparation for free trade, including expertise for modernization, restructuring, venture capital and training. Lawrence (1995) argues that the types of agreements being concluded between the EU and the Mediterranean countries, while having the potential to be (or to become) 'deep integration' arrangements, are perhaps better characterized as simple traditional trade arrangements with an element of support for restructuring and liberalization, but not involving flows of investment, services and labour as well as of commodities.

The terms of the 'partnership' are therefore limited and highly inequitable. The contrast between the emphasis on 'free trade' into the Maghreb and the growing restrictions on the 'free flow of labour' into Europe are very striking. But there is also little sign of a flow of investment into the Maghreb, while the comparative advantage of the Maghreb with respect to certain agricultural and fish products has been effectively countered by the inclusion of Greece, Spain and Portugal within the Community in the early 1980s.

As regards comparative advantage in a more liberal trading environment, analysts from the World Bank (Page and Underwood 1997: 115) conclude that for the economy in aggregate, neither Morocco nor Tunisia reaches the long-run total factor productivity (TFP) growth rates of any European economy, and both countries have declining comparative advantage relative to potential trading partners in Europe. Industry-specific estimates tell much the same story. TFP growth rates for Moroccan industry were close to zero between 1985 and 1990, contrasted with rates in the range 1–2 per cent in major European economies. Morocco is lagging Europe least in textiles, clothing and footwear, and basic metals, but on the whole Moroccan industries are failing to move closer to European best-practice technologies; dynamic comparative advantage is also deteriorating at the industry level.

Analysis of Morocco and Tunisia's trade patterns suggests a comparative advantage in agriculture and fisheries, the inclusion of the Southern European states into the EC in the 1980s notwithstanding, but recent agreements regarding access to the European market in agricultural and processed agricultural exports tend to be restrictive (although both allow some scope for expanded agro-industrial exports, according to Page and Underwood 1997: 111). Furthermore, the end of the transition period during which Spain and Portugal adjusted to EU membership ended in 1996, severely affecting Moroccan and Tunisian agricultural exports. Page and Underwood (1997) conclude that substantial benefits are unlikely to accrue to either of the two Maghreb countries without additional policies to promote export production and global trade; they also argue, interestingly, for the need to promote greater inter-Maghreb trade.

Analysis of the Tunisian agreement in particular (Brown *et al.* 1997), suggests that Tunisia may not have a great deal to gain either. The agreement amounts essentially to Tunisia eliminating its bilateral tariffs *vis-à-vis* the EU, since Tunisia already has had duty-free access to the EU except in some agricultural products and certain types of clothing exports. The trade-diverting effects of such a discriminatory tariff reduction are likely to be harmful, especially in the short run. Furthermore, the agreement does not in itself appear likely to generate an inflow of capital into Tunisia. Brown *et al.* (1997) conclude that Tunisia will gain little or nothing from the agreement, in the short run at least, and could experience significant adjustment problems stemming from labour and capital movement. Moreover, in the absence of complementary policy actions, no large inflow of foreign direct investment is expected. They suggest that Tunisia would do better to diversify its international economic relations and liberalize its trade barriers and foreign investment policies multilaterally.

It has also been suggested that, for both Morocco and Tunisia, 'the gains to universal liberalization of trade are approximately 50 per cent higher than those from liberalization with respect to Europe alone' (Page and Underwood 1997: 121). It may be that 'the existing "hub and spoke" nature of the EU agreements provides no strategic motivation for investors to locate in either economy to serve both markets, nor does it facilitate production sharing arrangements' (Page and Underwood 1997: 122). Writing for the World Bank, Page and Underwood are clearly unprepared to argue that the proposed arrangements with the EU are entirely disadvantageous to the two Maghreb economies involved. They suggest instead the need for 'a parallel agreement which liberalizes trade between the two countries within the overall EU framework' (Page and Underwood 1997: 121–122) and recommend 'both Morocco and Tunisia should begin negotiations for a free trade agreement between themselves'. This is ironically precisely what was envisaged by the UAM on its formation, although it was to occur on a Maghreb-wide scale rather than between individual states on a bilateral basis. Such moves towards the development of a Maghreb-wide economic union have, however, already been systematically undermined by the EU and the EMP, which is no real partnership but rather a structure which will increase the dependency of the weaker economies and serve the interests of the hegemonic European economies.

Page and Underwood (1997) go on to suggest that the disadvantages to the two Maghreb economies of the arrangements under the EMP could be reduced by technological upgrading, which depends in turn primarily on foreign direct investment and expansion of exports. In fact, they recommend an 'export push' strategy combined with policies to attract foreign direct investment in non-traditional exports for the global market. Policies of this kind, adopted by the governments of the Maghreb states, they suggest, could increase the chances of agreements recently reached with the EU under the EMP fulfilling their promise. But the 'hub and spoke' nature of the agreements reflects the asymmetrical power relationship between Europe and its Mediterranean periphery and is, I would argue, a crucial feature of the EU strategy. It thereby effectively precludes the adoption of such 'complementary' measures by Maghreb governments.

The EMP initiative, of which these agreements form a major part, is undoubtedly one element of a broader European strategy – a 'new' regionalism which differs little as far as the Maghreb is concerned from the 'neo-colonialism' of the previous forty years except in the degree and extent to which it is now coordinated and orchestrated. The EU forges trade alliances with the 'liberalized' and weakened economies on Europe's periphery on terms favourable essentially to itself. Its benefits to the Mediterranean and Maghreb countries involved are debatable, to say the least; it is my contention that they will prove negligible. Worse still, the new arrangements will further inhibit any effective national or regional development, let alone the establishment of a significant regional 'bloc' capable of restoring a degree of balance in what is now a very unequal 'partnership'.

10   Regionalism versus regional integration: the emergence of a new paradigm in Africa

Daniel C. Bach

In sub-Saharan Africa, formal regionalism (institutional forms of coopera-tion or integration) has been increasingly challenged by the development of strong trans-state flows ('informal' or 'network' integration or regionaliza-tion) (Amselle and Grégoire 1988). Despite being closely interrelated, the two forms of regionalism appear to be mutually exclusive because of their different impact on state institutions, territorial legitimacy and adjustment capabilities. Formal regionalism postulates the aggregation and fusion into broader units of existing territories or fields of intervention. Network regionalism (regionalization) is a result of the exploitation of dysfunctions and disparities generated by existing boundaries, with debilitating effects on state territorial control.

The need for regional integration has been emphasized by African leaders ever since Independence; yet nearly forty years later, the results achieved by existing arrangements are only marginally significant. Attempts to promote market integration through sub-regional trade liberalization have achieved little. But the assumption that frontiers, due to their colonial origins, are arbitrary and costly impediments to market circulation ignores the crucial importance of survival and accumulation strategies associated with the management of frontier disparities. Borders are important economically. Large groups of the population – at times whole states – owe their survival to the semi-official, and often clandestine, flows which go across boundaries in Africa. One of the reasons for the failure of trade liberalization schemes has been the fact that they do not address this issue.

Regionalism through global integration via outward-oriented adjustment policies assumes that external trade liberalization and the regional liberal-ization of factor markets are complementary. Accordingly, trans-state regional flows are often reduced to the status of being convenient indica-tors of imperfect trade liberalization and monetary adjustments. They are conceived as a *de facto* contribution to the dismantling of protection and a contribution to the pursuit of outward-oriented policies. The main prob-lem with this approach is that it fails to identify the corrosive effects of 'informal' regional flows, which tend to undermine the territorial control and legitimacy of the states involved. Policy initiatives designed to improve

Africa's insertion in the world market therefore have the unwanted effect of encouraging disintegrative pressures.

The co-existence of two conflicting integration patterns

Formal integration as a strategic ambition

Formal regionalism is the outcome of state policies involving the transfer of national state powers to a supra-national body (global or sectoral integration) or a hegemonic state. Formal regionalism can also result from the more modest desire to coordinate sectoral policies through an inter-governmental body (regional cooperation). In sub-Saharan Africa, the impact of formal regionalism on inter-state relations remains only marginally important, except in the case of the African Financial Community (CFA) zone and the South African Customs Union (SACU). Despite the long-standing political emphasis that the states have placed on panafricanism and regional integration, the contribution of some 250 organizations has only been significant in the fields of thematic and sectoral cooperation (Coussy and Hugon 1989; Mansor 1990–1; Lancaster 1992).

If the scope and intensity of the commitments involved are used as criteria to classify types of formal regionalism, we can discern three ideal-typical approaches: thematic or sectoral cooperation; sectoral integration; global and multisectoral integration. Most frequently, formal regionalism has resulted from thematic or sectoral cooperation at the regional or even the continental level. A common characteristic of African regional institutional arrangements is inter-governmental coordination, as opposed to the surrender of state sovereignty, which would be the result of a policy of integration. Regional institutions include the Permanent Inter-State Committee for the Battle against Drought in the Sahel (CILSS), the former Southern African Development Coordination Conference (SADCC), the Organization for the Sharing of the River Senegal (OMVS), the Kagera Basin Organization (KBO) or, more modestly, the Agency for the Safety of Shipping in Africa and Madagascar (ASECNA), the African and Malagasian Council for Higher Education (CAMES) and the African Postal Union (AFP). The inter-governmental, technocratic and explicitly outward-looking nature of these organizations has often been the very basis of their success. The limited commitments required for the schemes appeal far more to member states and external donors than the open-ended integration projects launched within broader institutions. Sectoral cooperation has proved most effective when it has led to regionally focused coordination by the different regional actors, as exemplified by CILSS and the ex-SADCC.

The promotion of formal regionalism through sectoral or global integration is a far more ambitious objective. Sectoral integration may be built by establishing a customs union, a common currency or even the integrated management of production and service activities. A number of institutions have emerged with the ambition of achieving this objective, but none of the schemes have led to the establishment of common policies on a supranational basis. This failure has been compounded by the trend towards the dismantling of colonial integration schemes (Hazlewood 1967), which have survived in only three cases: the Nigerian federation, discussed later in this chapter, the SACU and the CFA zone. They offer the only examples of effective institutional integration currently observable south of the Sahara.

SACU has a common external tariff, a mechanism for the redistribution of customs and excise revenues, and makes possible the free movement of goods and services (though not of labour) between South Africa and the BLS states (Botswana, Lesotho, Swaziland; BLSN after Namibia's independence in 1990). The implementation of SACU's redistribution formula is tied to the use of the South African rand as a common currency. SACU's arrangements can be traced back to 1889 and were renegotiated in 1969 to account for the independence of the BLS states. Monetary integration within the CFA zone is also the result of the adaptation of institutional arrangements which existed between France and its colonies before Independence. The fourteen member states of the zone are grouped within two monetary unions, the West African Economic and Monetary Union (UEMOA) and the Economic and Monetary Community of Central Africa (CEMAC) which together form the world's largest 'complete' monetary union (Medhora 1997). The member states share a fully convertible currency issued by a supranational bank, which also oversees the operations of an external reserve pool (*compte d'opération*) maintained with the French Treasury in Paris. The arrangements depend on a fixed parity of the CFA to the French franc and the CFA's free (until 2 August 1993) and unlimited convertibility. The deal is stabilized and dominated, though not fully controlled, by France.

As they currently stand, the CFA zone and SACU offer unparalleled examples of integration; this is, however, the result of the continuation of colonial arrangements through an incomplete transfer of sovereignty at the time of Independence. Furthermore, specific national state powers have been entrusted not to a supranational body but to a core state. Integration did not involve a qualitative jump therefore, nor did it result from the '*communautarisation*' of pre-existing national policies. It remains externally driven and controlled by France, in one case, and by South Africa, in the other. France's leading role within the CFA zone is the counterpart of the Treasury's guarantee to the CFA. Since the early 1990s, a number of projects have been launched with the intention of dynamizing the adjustment policies of the CFA states, while deepening the level of integration (Lelart 1993). For the first time since their independence, the West and Central African member states of the franc zone have been requested to organize the sectoral transfer of sovereignty towards common sub-regional institutions. Motivated partly by a desire to avoid adjustment, devaluation of the CFA franc in January 1994 indicated, however, that the results of this would be limited.

In sharp contrast with France's relations with the CFA zone, South Africa exercises tight control over tariff policy and the redistribution of customs revenues within SACU. Indeed, the management of SACU takes place outside any specific institutional framework, as part of the activities of the South African administration. A 'secret memorandum of understanding' attached to the 1969 agreement provides the legal basis for the relationship. It stipulated that the BLS states would receive compensation for the price raises that were to result from South African tariffs and other import restrictions, and that they would accept a loss of fiscal powers as a consequence of their acceptance of South Africa's tariffs and excise duty codes and provisions.

Over the last thirty years, the colonial origins of the CFA zone arrangements and, in the case of SACU, the region's dependency on a 'pariah' state often elicited strong external criticism. It has also been argued that the CFA arrangements were incompatible with the establishment of a larger community, aiming at global and multisectoral integration. All too often, assessments of the global and multisectoral integration schemes moved beyond the rhetoric of institution-building. This is not to deny that progress may have been achieved in the field of functional cooperation by such West African institutions as the ex-Community of West African States (CEAO), the Mano River Union (MRU) or the Economic Community of West African States (ECOWAS); by the Economic Community of the Great Lakes Countries (CEPGL), the ex-Customs Union of the Central African States (UDEAC) or the Economic Community of Central African States (ECCAS) in Central Africa; or by the Preferential Trade Area (PTA), Common Market of East and South African States (COMESA) and Southern Africa Development Community (SADC, established in 1992) in Southern/Eastern Africa. But there are no obvious spill-over effects resulting from sectoral cooperation.

Trans-state integration as a de facto process

Trans-state regionalism relates to a cluster of practices which, depending on authors and circumstances, are described as 'informal' or 'unrecorded' trade; as the 'underground', 'second' or even, in extreme cases, the 'real' economy; as 'smuggling' or 're-exportation'; and as 'popular' or 'bottom-up' regionalism (Constantin 1983; Portes *et al.* 1989; Turnham *et al.* 1990). This proliferation of concepts mirrors the different interpretations of trans-state regionalism. Not surprisingly, the phenomenon itself is the source of conflicting perceptions and interpretations: depending on circumstances and location, it is argued that trans-state circuits should be fought against or should be officially condoned by state policies. This semi-official acceptance of the operation of trans-state networks may result in decriminalizing certain sectors of trans-state activity; yet states cannot publicly endorse it since profits are realized at the expense of the state(s) on the other side of the border. What a rent-taking government must avoid at all costs is a strict enforcement of its neighbour's border-line. It must also avoid its tacit acceptance of trans-state transactions prompting counter-moves by adversely affected states. Not surprisingly, quantitative assessments of trans-state flows are unable to pin down changes in their composition, status, circuits and end-destination.

The development of trans-state flows may be understood as a corollary of the range of opportunities generated by frontier lines; these are in turn exploited through chains of social relations which are autonomous, though not disconnected, from institutional or corporate procedures. Trans-state regionalism may therefore involve trade and financial flows and may follow economic, political and even religious patterns of interaction and mobilization. The strongest incentive to trans-state regionalism is the co-existence of areas with convertible and non-convertible or partly convertible currencies. In West and Central Africa, the franc zone has become a focal point for the development of trans-state flows (Vallée 1989; MacGaffey *et al.* 1991; Igué and Soulé 1992), just as, in Southern Africa, the SACU/MMA area has had a strong polarizing effect on trans-state flows. This trend is not new (Sriber 1958; Thill 1959), but access to foreign currency has become an essential component of trans-state regional patterns under the combined pressure of the states' deepening financial difficulties and the lack of regionally coordinated structural adjustment policies. Curtailing the costs incurred by trans-state flows between Nigeria, Ghana and ex-Zaïre (now the Democratic Republic of the Congo) and the franc zone was an essential component of the decision to suspend the convertibility of CFA banknotes circulating outside the franc zone banking network in August 1993.

But the convertibility of currencies is not all that counts. In those parts of Africa where there are no convertible currencies, sophisticated trans-state regional integration patterns still develop, despite what some authors have argued with respect to Southern Africa (Meagher 1996). Throughout the African continent, trans-state flows involve commodities like gold, gem stones, diamonds, ivory, spices and, increasingly, narcotics (*Politique Africaine* 1983; Maliyamkono and Bagachwa 1990; Meagher 1990; Fottorino 1991; Labrousse and Wallon 1993). These provide highly lucrative access to the world markets. Trans-state regional flows may equally well develop, though usually on a lesser scale, on the basis of differences of tariffs and tax rates as witnessed between the member states of the Bank of the Central African States (BCEAO). Other incentives include transport networks, as in ex-Zaïre, or political uncertainty, as in Burkina Faso during the Sankara period (Igué and Soulé 1992: 112–113).

The strength of trans-state regionalism is intrinsically linked to its lack of transparency, to the extreme versatility of the flows, as well as to its autonomy *vis-à-vis* official circles and policies. The development of the trans-state networks suggests that they possess a clear capacity for responding quickly to the interplay of changing tariffs and fiscal measures, to the shifts in currency demand and supply, and to the changes of world market prices of export crops or of goods that are treated as illegal in other areas on (or outside) the continent. As a result, the composition and direction of the trans-state flows are in constant flux and the articulation and impact of the networks at grass-roots level change over time.

The origins and development patterns of trans-state regionalism

It is often argued that the vitality of trans-state regionalism can be explained in reference to pre-colonial linkages, which traditionally meant a predominance of so-called 'primordial' ties (for example, ethnicity, religion or blood ties) and an emphasis on borderland markets. But these neo-traditionalist interpretations have generally minimized the intrinsic role of frontier differentials in shaping patterns of trade and migration and have underestimated the capacity of trans-state actors to make full use of modern communication, management or transportation techniques. For example, Senegalese traders active on the borderland markets of north-western Uganda get the daily information which they need for the conduct of gold transactions from BBC financial reports (Meagher 1990: 75). In this area, as elsewhere on the continent, trade opportunities may involve transactions of basic commodities as much as sophisticated 'high-tech' products, cars, lorries or even drugs and armaments traded in liaison with extra-continental networks.

It is frequently argued that trans-state integration proceeds 'first and foremost from the will of the populations victimized by the colonial partition, [so as] to safeguard their cultural and historical unity' (Egg and Igué 1993: 1). Under colonial rule, the partitioned populations of the borderlands 'tended in their normal activities to ignore the boundaries as dividing lines and to carry on social relations across them more or less as in the days before the Partition' (Asiwaju 1985: 2). This culturalist vision derives to a large extent from an *a posteriori* reconstruction which overlooks substantial evidence that 'partitioned Africans' were made aware, right from the early stages of colonial occupation, of the range of opportunities and constraints generated by the establishment of boundary lines. Borderland integration was indirectly encouraged along the inter-colonial frontiers, because these resulted in much greater differences than the weaker intra-colonial frontiers.

It would be preposterous to challenge the fact that areas which, at times, were culturally homogeneous or coincided with a single political entity were pulled apart by the partition and the subsequent discrepancies between the policies of the European rulers. The artificial character of African boundaries is clearly demonstrated by the fact that 44 per cent are made up of astronomical lines (meridian and parallels), 30 per cent of mathematical lines, and the remaining 26 per cent of geographical features (Barbour 1961).

The impact of colonialism left a lasting imprint, as demonstrated, for instance, by Asiwaju (1976: 26–32, 134–153) in the case of the Nigeria–Benin boundary. As the colonized territories were progressively integrated into the metropolitan economies, competing communication systems and market centres developed. Distinct currency zones also emerged while restrictive tariff policies attempted to discourage the entry of goods from rival colonial blocs.

Everywhere on the continent, the concomitant processes of territorial differentiation, socio-cultural alienation and ideological legitimation of the new colonial states drastically changed pre-colonial trade and socio-cultural interaction patterns. During the early phase of the partition process, European rulers competed fiercely to establish their territorial claims, with the result that the populations living on the fringes of inter-colonial spheres of influence became particularly prone to intimidation and reprisals. Once a boundary line had been established, colonial policies attempted to restrict contacts. Caravan trade also declined as a result of the emergence of new routes and the introduction of tariff policies designed to consolidate metropolitan and intra-colonial integration (Bayili 1976: 62ff.; Grégoire 1986: 51–62).

But, although they were real, the inter-colonial boundaries had only limited significance. The colonial powers soon discovered that physical enforcement of the boundary lines was in most cases impossible due to their length. Competition and mutual suspicion among colonial rulers further hampered their capacity to harmonize policies; as a consequence of this, 'illegal' trade and migration were able to develop.

The borderland populations may well have perceived boundary lines as arbitrary, but they certainly did not treat them as as meaningless entities. It was soon discovered how the boundary could give access to shelter and protection at places where it demarcated the spheres of jurisdiction of distinct colonial powers. As a result, in Eastern, Southern as well as Western Africa, migration – often towards the British side of the boundary – was very common before the Second World War, either as a protest against governmental policies (such as forced labour and conscription) or as a response to incentives offered by the other side's colonial administration (Bayili 1976; Asiwaju 1985: 141–148; Phiri 1985: 115; Southall 1985: 91–92). Colonial policies, with their distinct pricing systems, monetary regimes and tariff barriers, led to smuggling which, as in the example of the Alur, partitioned by the Uganda/Belgian Congo boundary line, meant 'large profits ... or at least small profits by quite a large number of people' (Southall 1985: 99). Also in West Africa, 'illicit activities' developed to such a degree that, at times, entire villages along the inter-colonial boundaries abandoned traditional agriculture (Mondjannagni 1963).

Trans-state trade flows had little in common with pre-colonial trade routes and patterns. The routes were reoriented so as to take advantage of new and far more profitable trading opportunities which crystallized along the inter-colonial boundaries. The composition and direction of trade varied with factors such as import duties on manufactured goods, transport costs or cash crop producer prices.

The brokerage function associated with borderland trade instilled a sense of shared opportunites and identity which in turn encouraged cultural and ethnic cross-fertilization among the population separated by the frontier-line. The development of trans-state trade and migration encouraged the creation of new settlements within a short distance of the boundary line, often in conjunction with market locations already existing on the other side (Igué and Soulé 1992: 84–87). Since frontier resources were being tapped both illegally and at the expense of a third party, for example the colonial rulers, a sub-culture of resistance came into being.

To conclude, therefore, trans-state regionalism is neither a resurgence nor a legacy of pre-colonial linkages. That some ancient trade routes have stayed in use is a reflection of the fact that they met the requirements of trans-state regional networks. The composition of the flows and the patterns of interaction they nurture are witness to the integrative legacy of inter-colonial frontiers.

The expansion of trans-state regionalism in the post-colonial era

After the end of colonial rule, trans-state regionalism entered a new phase as it underwent an unchecked and spectacular expansion. In the process, it acquired two previously unknown characteristics. First, trans-state region-alism became increasingly focused along former inter-colonial frontier lines and along boundary lines which were previously incorporated into a single colonial bloc, such as in French West Africa, French Equatorial Africa, the Federation of Rhodesia and Nyassaland, and so on. Second, the networks of trans-state regionalism were no longer confined to the borders; they pene-trated the national territories.

After Independence, the dissolution of nearly all colonial blocs, and the subsequent emergence of sovereign states, led to the establishment of different tariff, taxation and monetary policies. Some of the colonial arrangements survived, but most disappeared under the pressure of emerging national interests. Diverging policies created fertile ground for trans-state regional flows. The opportunities for trans-state flows was clearly curtailed when colonial linkages remained in existence, either as a result of explicit polit-ical arrangements, as in Nigeria, or by the establishment of currency regimes (CFA zone, MMA) or customs unions (SACU). Within the CFA zone, trans-state flows could still take advantage of disparities of tariffs and taxation, but they could no longer benefit from the differences between currency regimes. As a result, trans-state flows within the CFA zone were always more limited in scope than those between the member states of the CFA zone and their neighbours from West and Central Africa (Bach 1993).

The expansion of trans-state regionalism was also the result of declining financial capacities and territorial control of the post-colonial states. This was not the result of a voluntary transfer of state sovereignty as it was the case in the European Union (EU) and the North American Free Trade Agreement (NAFTA). As most African countries became independent, the existing boundaries were fully endorsed by the new elites as the basis for the construction of nation-states. The improvement of the '*encadrement du territoire*' ('framing of the territory') (Pourtier 1987: 350; C. Médard 1992) became a priority and stimulated the development of communications and transportation networks (with the aim of connecting peripheral areas to the centre) and the establishment of an administrative grid (development of health, education and housing systems), as well as the emergence of symbols such as the creation of 'national' histories.

During the 1970s, the financial difficulties encountered by a growing number of African states meant that official circuits in large parts of the continent collapsed. The effect of the decline of state resources was compounded by the subsequent trend towards the privatization of the public sphere, both formally and informally. As deregulation policies were undertaken as part of macroeconomic packages, the 'de-institutionalization' of the state and the growth of patrimonialism within state bureaucracies went largely unchecked. Groups of the population which had come to rely on state circuits (health, housing, education, transport and marketing) were compelled to seek alternatives. At times, the territorial control of the states, as the case of the ex-Zaïre illustrates, decreased so as to be redeployed 'on the exploitable areas'; 'fallow areas' began to emerge (J.-F. Médard 1992). Whole sectors of society were falling back on so-called 'parallel circuits' (Mbembe 1992). Trans-state regionalism was no longer the borderland phenomenon of the colonial period and early years of Independence.

The expansion of trans-state regionalism reflects the internationalization of what is often referred to as the informal or the second economy, for example 'activities autonomous from the state' (N. Kasfir cited in Meagher 1983: 351; cf. Maliyamkono and Bagachwa 1990: 26–49), though they were often managed in close liaison with state officials. Trans-state regionalism, like the informal economy, has become an essential resource, either for survival or for accumulation, with the result that its networks have tended to expand far beyond the original borderland areas to cover entire regions and relate to destinations far away from the continent.

The internationalization of trans-state networks may well inaugurate a third phase in the development of flows: their crystallization along the external frontiers of the continent as a consequence of the adoption of rent-seeking opt-out strategies. The consequences will be far-reaching due to the association with highly criminalized circuits based on narco-trade or armament trafficking. Reports released since the late 1980s provide a particularly worrying picture of the development of narco-trafficking and production in Western, Eastern and Southern African states. While South Africa is a major target for arms and mandrax, supplied via Eastern Africa countries, Nigeria emerged as a narcotics redistribution and transit centre for the whole continent (Observatoire géopolitique des drogues 1993: 205–207).

In short, the crystallization of trans-state flows along the external frontiers of the continent is encouraged by the crisis of all but a few African economies. The constant deterioration of living conditions in urban centres, the trend towards the reduction of external tariff barriers and the increasing constraints on currency convertibility are leading to a radical transformation of frontier-management strategies: trans-state flows increasingly relate to the frontier between the African continent and the economically more prosperous European, Asian and Amerian economies.

The deleterious impact of trans-state flows

Field studies on trans-state regionalism have indicated an extreme diversity in the organizational patterns of its networks, as much as in the socio-economic and political circumstances which contribute to their development. As will be argued below, trans-state regionalism has an ambivalent, yet fundamentally destructive and debilitating, effect on populations and states.

Trans-state regionalism is an instrument of socio-economic regulation as a consequence of the decline of alternative resources and the disruption of official circuits. The dynamism of these flows stems first and foremost from the fact that they provide parts of the population with the means for short-term survival. For this reason, state authorities are largely powerless to control their development. States that face the pressure of heavy external conditionalities may even see the lack of formal control on 'illegal' imports as a positive contribution to social peace.

Two radically distinct patterns can be identified with respect to the relationship between corporate policies and trans-state flows. At one end of the spectrum, the development of trans-state flows results from the disappearance of the basic functions traditionally expected from the state. As mentioned earlier, in ex-Zaïre for example, the state 'has opted out and simply ignores much of what is going on' (MacGaffey *et al.* 1991: 158). Situations of severe economic disruptions and impoverishment create a most profitable environment for trans-state networks due to the dearth of available alternatives, as witnessed in Southern Sudan, Mozambique, Angola and Somalia. But it may also be encouraged by state policies. This is particularly so in West Africa due to a unique conjunction of factors, such as the high degree of political segmentation of the sub-region, sharp discrepancies in resource endowments between member states, and the co-existence of inconvertible and (now partly) convertible currencies.

Either way, it provides survival opportunities for large groups of the population. Even when the state has not collapsed, trans-state flows contribute to a vital diversification of urban income sources and play a buffer role when salaries undergo a sharp decline in real terms or, as increasingly happens in the public sector, remain unpaid during substantial periods. Farmers living in areas where state circuits are no longer operational can also find vital outlets for their production in the second economy, as well as pre-harvest cash advances essential for the maintenance of their families and the purchase of tools, seeds and other inputs (MacGafffey *et al.* 1991: 31). In the urban centres of the former Zaïre, the informal economy supplies consumers with food, fuel and manufactured goods, and creates earning opportunities for women in unlicensed trade to supplement the salaries of their husbands to a subsistence level (MacGaffey *et al.* 1991: 152). In their turn, these networks enhance the borderlands' attractiveness for business.

But trans-state flows do not bring about a 'communal redistribution' of resources (Meagher 1996: 6). Access to the resources necessary to participate in the networks is extremely uneven and very competitive: 'the rich and powerful, and those who have jobs, have greater access than do the unemployed, the urban poor, and rural producers' (MacGaffey *et al.* 1991: 154). Small-scale traders have a disadvantage since the economies of scale are 'only for those who can pay the necessary bribes' (Meagher 1996: 6). Most importantly, when farmers participate in the parallel economy, it is 'out of desperation rather than choice' (Meagher 1996: 7). The fact that trans-state regionalism has a visible effect on borderland markets and that it tends to challenge the prerogatives of corrupt and inefficient states should not, however, result in the populist interpretation that the flows lead to redistribution (Meagher 1996). The only 'popular' dimension of trans-state regionalism is to be found in its capacity to adjust to market demands and in the ruthless exploitation of populations that are confronted with a diminishing of alternatives to satisfy their needs. Trans-state regionalism is a fundamentally hybrid phenomenon: although it is separate from state control, it owes much to support from government officials, state bureaucracies and well-established merchant interests (Maliyamkono and Bagachwa 1990: 134–135; Meagher 1990: 8).

The management of frontier disparities on a rent-seeking basis became a vital component of policy in Benin, Togo, the Gambia, Niger and, to a lesser extent, Chad during the 1970s. State revenues, as well as the well-being of the population, came to depend on the capacity to derive resources from the interplay between formal import trade and informal trans-state re-export networks (Egg and Igué 1993: 39–45). The increase of trans-state trade thereby acquired the legitimacy of a development strategy. By 1987, the African Development Bank estimated that Gambia's re-export trade amounted to 40 per cent of the country's imports (Sall 1992: 10). Similarly, in Benin the contribution of trans-state regional flows to the country's budget fluctuated between 60 and 80 per cent until the early 1980s (Igué and Soulé 1992: 26). In fact, this dates from the time of Independence, when these small impoverished states discovered they were no longer insulated from external shocks by the fiscal redistribution mechanisms built into the French West African or Equatorial Federations.

There is little doubt that in West Africa as elsewhere 'parallel markets for goods and foreign exchange promote informal integration' (Azam 1990: 51). These flows often tie borderland areas more closely to neighbouring countries than to the rest of the national territory. The question arises, therefore, whether trans-state integration should be treated as a viable form of 'integration through the market' (Egg and Igué 1993). I argue that to treat it as such is to ignore the fact that it is not the result of any formal trade liberalization scheme. Trans-state regional flows require the preservation of existing frontier lines instead of their disappearance, because they thrive on their existence. For this very reason, trans-state regional flows do not generate viable alternatives to the difficulties of formal integration schemes and are a powerful challenge to the control of states over their frontier lines. They cannot generate alternative territorial formations.

The circumstances surrounding the dissolution of the Senegambian confederation (1982–9), Africa's only post-Independence experiment in political integration, provide a useful illustration of this. The establishment of the confederation resulted from a *quid pro quo* whereby Senegal guaranteed the security of the Gambian regime (threatened by a coup d'état), in exchange for the progessive establishment of an economic union. This, from Dakar's point of view, would make possible the curtailing of trans-state regional flows, which had developed largely at the expense of Senegal. The flows were so significant for Gambia that it eventually rejected the first set of trade liberalization measures in August 1989. As a result, when the deadline for implementation arrived, the economic and financial costs involved with the customs union appeared overwhelming, given Gambia's scarce resources and the substantial income and employment opportunities tied to the re-export trade. Similarly, Togo and Benin were among the most vocal supporters of the Economic Community of West African States (ECOWAS) during the 1970s, although they did not have a clear interest in its trade liberalization or currency integration schemes. For the Benin and Togolese regimes, the maintenance of good political relations with Nigeria was as essential as the avoidance of a reduction of the macroeconomic disparities from which they derived most of their resources.

Trans-state regionalism is also limited as a launching ground for formal cooperation schemes. The patterns of interaction between South Africa or Nigeria and their neighbours are good examples in this respect. South Africa and its non-SACU neighbours are confronted with the disintegrating impact of trans-state regional flows which were once treated by South Africa as an integral component of its external relations. Facing mounting international pressure against apartheid policies, South African public and private corporate actors were until 1990 increasingly linked into regional or international trans-state networks, which related to trade and finance as much as to political lobbying or para-military activity. It was only after the end of the bipolar world and South Africa's internal transitions that the distinction between formal and trans-state regionalism began to make sense in South Africa.

In the totally different politico-diplomatic context of West Africa, trans-state monetary, economic and migratory flows have come to crystallize around the Nigerian territory. Despite some promising initial steps during the oil boom of the 1970s, the development of trans-state integration did not lead to the consolidation of formal cooperation. Trans-state integration between Nigeria, Benin and Niger took place largely at the expense of the Federation, but the losses incurred were treated as marginal. The Federation's resources were expanding and its leadership was committed to building up regional ties (Bach 1988). The establishment of ECOWAS created high hopes. Yet, not one of Nigeria's immediate neighbours was prepared to consider the dismantling of customs and tariff barriers, which were becoming their most valuable resource. Falls in mineral prices increased Nigeria's awareness of the cost of trans-state flows. In an attempt to curb currency trafficking against the naira, banknotes were exchanged (April 1984) and the Federation's frontier lines were closed by the army for nearly two years. Additionally, on two occasions (January 1983 and April 1985), 'illegal' aliens were ordered to leave Nigeria. The most effective measure was the implementation of Nigeria's macroeconomic adjustment package after 1986. The drastic fall of the naira's official exchange rate and the liberalization of external trade brought about a reorientation of trans-state patterns: emigration from Nigeria increased; trans-state networks continued to focus on the Nigerian economic space, but at a growing cost for the states in the CFA zone. By January 1993, a survey of trans-state flows concluded that the very future of Niger and Benin as states was 'being challenged' (Egg and Igué 1993: 3).

To sum up, therefore, trans-state regionalism is an impediment to the abolition of intra-zone customs and tariff barriers. Policies that attempted to revitalize national economies through association with trans-state flows have been confronted with destabilizing boomerang effects and, in the entrepôt states, the deleterious impact of trans-state integration appears increasingly associated with a criminalization of state procedures and policies (Bayart *et al.* 1996).

The 'deterritorialization' of post-colonial states

Trans-state regionalism has also served as an impetus for the de-institutionalization and accelerated privatization of state agencies. The success of these networks depends on their capacity to evade state control or negotiate support from state officials. The rapid pace with which the internationalization and criminalization of Africa's trans-state flows is occurring (Observatoire géopolitique des drogues 1993: 199–224) generates such profits that tailoring the activity of impoverished state agencies to the private needs of trade networks is made increasingly easier.

African states also run the risk of a far more destructive loss of control over their national territory. Trans-state flows contribute to the emergence of new patterns of regionalism, based on the deconstruction of state territories, as opposed to their aggregation. Max Weber's classical definition of the state does not apply in several parts of the continent: in Liberia, ex-Zaïre, Somalia, Angola or Mozambique, the state is no longer the sole agency which possesses the monopoly over legitimate violence in society. The 'deterritorialization' of the state derives from the replacement of the precisely delimited boundary lines inherited from the colonial period by loosely defined frontier spaces. A loss of territorial control is also the result of the resurgence of primordial attachments (for instance, alleged ties of blood, race, language and religion) at the expense of control patterns based on citizenship (for instance, territorial affiliation). While the revival of communal identities has generated overt pressure on the morphology of African states (see below), trans-state flows have challenged their conception as territorially based entities.

However, the sub-Saharan African states are not affected equally by the deterritorializing effects of trans-state regionalism. The impact depends on a country's resources, such as the availability of mineral rents, participation in a currency zone, the importance of donor pledges, and the patterns of governance implemented by post-colonial regimes (the degree of patrimonialism, the allocation of resources). Less tangible factors, such as the capacity of a post-colonial state to manipulate historical traditions, also influence the capacity of the state to resist deterritorialization. Three major areas of resistance to deterritorialization can be identified: the franc zone, the SACU area in Southern Africa and the Nigerian federation.

In West and Central Africa, the CFA monetary unions have led to an '*encadrement*' ('framing') of their member states' territories. Within the two unions, the development of trans-state flows has been hampered by the impossibility of taking advantage of monetary disparities. As incompatibilities grew between adjustment within and outside the zone, trans-state flows increasingly crystallized around the external frontiers of the zone (M'Bokolo 1993). A 50 per cent devaluation of the CFA occurred in January 1994, intending to respond to these pressures. As yet, it is still unclear whether this will alleviate the pressures and enable the reconstruction of integration within the two monetary unions, or if it will rather contribute to their dislocation.

In Southern Africa, SACU and the *de facto* monetary zone that emerges with it has had the effect of shifting the destructive influence of trans-state regional flows along the external frontiers of the member states (*Southern African Economist*, December 1988–January 1989).

And finally, the Nigerian federation provides a case of successful resistance to deterritorialization. It is based on the availability of a substantial mining rent and on the development of infrastructure, education and social services (Philippe 1988; Adamolekun 1991). However, since the mid-1980s, the dramatic reduction of Nigeria's oil revenues and the constraints of structural adjustment have challenged the viability of the country's consociational model (Bach 1997).

In conclusion, therefore, the chief effect of the unchecked growth of network regionalism is likely to be a diversification of state–territory relationships. The classical distinction between the pre-colonial political formations relying on kinship and those based on the occupation of a common territory is being revived. Some African countries might become stateless configurations based on primordial and patronage attachments. Many states *will* be able to survive, but as cores surrounded by peripheries which do not coincide with internationally recognized boundaries. An increasingly smaller number of states may be able to claim permanent and full control over their territory.

Nevertheless, it is important that the diversification of patterns of political control is not misunderstood. The continent may be marginalized from an international point of view, but its integration into the global economy will keep progressing. Accumulation and survival strategies are already increasingly geared towards the 'management' of extra-African frontiers. Africa's comparative advantage in the twenty-first century could well reside in its emergence as a loosely policed frontier-continent between the European, American and South East Asian zones of integration.

Part IV
Conclusion

11 Regionalism across the North–South divide

Wil Hout and Jean Grugel

The new regionalism and the effects of uneven globalization

It has been the intention of this book to assess the way in which the 'new regionalism' is shaped across the North–South divide, how its effects are felt in countries of the semi-periphery and the periphery, and how some of these countries try to link up with new forms of regional networks. In the introduction to this book, we explicitly located the present analyses in the context of the debate on the nature and the impact of globalization. As Holm and Sørensen (1995) have argued, the effects of globalization are 'uneven'. Partly following upon the argument of these authors, we have hypothesized that the extent to which states will be able to resist the effects of globalization is to some degree linked to the position of those countries in the world economic and political order.

The division of the world into a core, a semi-periphery (with a 'strong' and a 'weak' part) and a periphery, following world-system analysis and other structural interpretations of the international political economy, is often linked to the capacity of these countries to react to the forces of globalization. As we argued in the introduction, the world-system approach, by its very nature, nearly always has recourse to explanations at the structural (global) level and cannot account for differences in processes taking place at the national level in otherwise structurally similar countries. For this reason, the deconstruction of semi-peripheral and peripheral countries is called for.

The case studies of the 'new regionalism' in the second part of this book place state–society relations at the forefront of the analysis. They indicate that there is indeed no such thing as *the* semi-peripheral approach to regions and regionalism. In the introduction we postulated that the regionalist outcome is, to a large extent, the result of the *strategies* adopted by semi-peripheral countries. Although these countries are less powerful and have fewer resources than countries in the 'core' of the international political and economic order, we have assumed that they still retain enough leverage to formulate policies aimed at improving their position. In other words, we do not picture the semi-periphery as the defenceless victim of international forces. At the same time, however, we acknowledge that the policy options for the countries in the semi-periphery are limited. In the introduction, we argued that the state strategies of the semi-periphery are conditioned by three factors, which relate to three 'levels of analysis'. These are: the world system position; the relations between state structures and social, economic and political groups; and the policies of other states and regions. The case studies in this volume show that the relationship between these variables is highly contingent and that the specifics of the situation in the different countries and regions explain which policies and 'state strategies' are adopted and what the regionalist outcomes are.

Apart from the focus on semi-peripheral countries and on the role they play in the regionalist project, we have also included three case studies dealing with regions consisting mainly of peripheral countries. Although peripheral countries are less able to influence the outcome of the international political and economic order to the same extent as the countries on the semi-periphery, they are masters of their own fate to some extent. Because of the presumed relative weakness of the peripheral state and the importance of state and non-state actors from outside the region, the region plays a larger role in the case of periphery.

Australia can be seen as part of the strong semi-periphery, as Derek McDougall argued in Chapter 3, because of the structure of its exports, the dominance of intermediate production and its identification with the core. The increased emphasis that successive Australian governments have placed on regionalism is related to the country's changing political and economic circumstances. Economically, East and South East Asia has become increasingly important for Australia, especially after Britain's entry into the European Community in 1973. The Australian state recognizes the consequences of its increasing economic marginalization, leading to its adoption of policies of free trade and financial deregulation. The state's initiatives in the creation of Asia-Pacific regionalism must be seen in the light of its attempts to restructure its relations to the outside world, especially with the dynamic economies of South East Asia. McDougall argues that Asia-Pacific Economic Cooperation (APEC) was not needed to strengthen Australia's relations with the Asia-Pacific, the main function of this regionalist structure being the support of trade liberalization in the Uruguay Round. Thus, economic and political groups tried to get the best of both worlds: on the one hand, they tried to break down the level of protection of the APEC states, while, on the other hand, doing so without discriminating against non-member states (this is the so-called 'open regionalism').

Brazil might be considered as one of the stronger countries in the weak semi-periphery. As Jean Grugel and Marcelo de Almeida Medeiros argued in Chapter 4, Brazil has gone through a process of dependent industrialization, which has taken place largely under the guidance of an authoritarian state. It has a highly unequal social structure and this has given rise to recurrent tensions between the landed elites and the state elites, who have tried to sponsor domestic industrialization. As in the case of Australia, Brazilian regional policies are motivated by its changing relations to the outside world. On the one hand, Brazil's motivation to forge closer links among the countries of the Southern Cone in South America is to be found in its wish to create a sub-regional alternative to regionalism under the aegis of the US through its Enterprise for the Americas Initiative (EAI). On the other hand, the Common Market of the South (MERCOSUR) serves the interests of some influential parts of the Brazilian industrial sector, which can avoid radical reform by remaining only regionally not globally competitive. At the same time, MERCOSUR served a political aim because it placed some South American states in a relationship dominated by Brazil.

Chile is in many ways a typical case among the countries of the weak semi-periphery. Although it has reached an intermediate level of development, a large part of the population works in agriculture and the country remains heavily dependent on primary goods exports. As Jean Grugel argued in Chapter 5, a legacy of the Pinochet dictatorship is that economic policy is still technocratic. Chile's regionalist policies are motivated mainly by economic considerations. While cooperation with the North American Free Trade Agreement (NAFTA) and MERCOSUR is likely to strengthen Chile's place in the community of democratic states, new export opportunities are uppermost in determining regionalist policies. MERCOSUR was originally lower on the list of priorities of Chilean policy-makers than NAFTA, but as the negotiations for NAFTA stalled, associate membership of MERCOSUR became more attractive. Although the *latifundista* sector feared the introduction of free trade measures because these would mean an increase of competition, traditional agricultural interests were no longer, by 1990, in a position to block Chile's affiliation with MERCOSUR.

Turkey belongs to the weak semi-periphery. But it has, nevertheless, developed a strong state sector. A large part of the population is employed in the agricultural sector and most industrial sectors are not competitive at the international level. Mine Eder analysed the regionalist aspirations of Turkey, in Chapter 6, with a focus on Turkey's decision to seek membership of a Customs Union with the European Union. The changes in Turkey's external 'environment' have played a very important role in the shaping of this country's policies towards Europe. Turkey's strategic position changed due to the new geopolitical balance that came about after the end of the Cold War. Turkey's new role was most obvious in the former Soviet republics in the Caucasus, in the Middle East and the Balkans. The increasing awareness among Turkish state elites of the effects of globalization, the ensuing shift of production processes to East Asia, and the effects of the new regionalism in Europe (especially the possible erection of a 'Fortress Europe') were part of the rationale behind the application. Membership of the European Union also remained a top priority because of the desire to establish 'deep integration' and lock in institutional reforms. Although there were major

differences among economic sectors – the textile industry supported associate membership of the EU while the car industry opposed it – economic
considerations did not, in the end, determine the outcome of the processes
at the level of the state elites. Eder ascribed this fact to the traditional *étatiste*
orientation of Turkish politics, which resulted in a very autonomous position of the state *vis-à-vis* society and the economy.

One of the largest and the most populous country on earth, China is
different in a number of important ways from the other semi-peripheral
countries that have been analysed in this book. Despite its size and strength
as an economic great power in the making, China remains fundamentally
a semi-peripheral country. In Chapter 7, Shaun Breslin focused on the
changes that have come about as a result of the economic transformation
in China in the post-Mao era, and on the complicated interaction between
partial economic liberalization and the enduring political power of the party-
state elites. China forms part of a regional division of labour, driven by
foreign investment, with Japan as the core investor and the Asian newly
industrializing economies (NIEs) as intermediate economic actors. Traditionally, Chinese exports consisted of primary products; since the recent
wave of foreign investment in the country, China has become a component
production site for Asian investors. Regional cooperation – in particular,
APEC – has been perceived in China as a possible counterweight to protectionism in Europe and North America. China's state elite is cautious,
however, because too rapid liberalization might harm important sectors of
the Chinese economy. The ongoing process of globalization and China's re-
engagement with the world economy have complicated domestic issues. In
particular, the competition for foreign investment among different actors
within the central state, the increase of the number of relevant actors in the
policy process and the power of external actors over state policy are seen
as the consequences of the internationalization of the Chinese economy. For
Chinese state elites, regionalism is, at the most, subordinate to entry into
the World Trade Organization as this would bring access to important
foreign markets within reach of China, which is clearly on its way to
becoming an export-oriented economy.

In the third part of the book, three major regions were analysed: South
East Asia, North Africa (the Maghreb) and sub-Saharan Africa. In Chapter
8, Chris Dixon interpreted the restructuring of South East Asia as a process
that is driven by changes in the regional division of labour and by changes
in the relation between the different countries of the region with countries
in East Asia, such as Japan and the East Asian NIEs, and non-Asian
countries. The region is composed of countries at different levels of development, thereby making it a mix of peripheral and strong and weak
semi-peripheral units. There were several attempts at instituting formal
regionalism in the region, but the main impetus came with the creation of
the Association of South East Asian Nations (ASEAN) in 1967. Although it
was believed at the time that this would enhance economic growth in the

region, the organization did not contain provisions for the establishment of a free trade area. Regionalism remained a politically motivated endeavour, mainly because the economy of the ASEAN states had little complementarity. Most countries had adopted export-oriented development strategies by 1980, although pockets of import substitution sectors remain very influential in several ASEAN member states (for example, Indonesia, Thailand and Malaysia). These sectors weaken attempts to arrive at full intra-regional trade liberalization. Nevertheless, a regional division of labour has developed, in which transnational corporations based in Singapore take advantage of lower labour costs in other countries in the region; the so-called Singapore–Johore–Riau (or SiJoRi) 'growth triangle' is an example of an institutionalized pattern of production across borders. The restructuring of the region, Dixon concludes, should be seen in a wider Pacific Asian context, which actually brings together a series of regional divisions of labour.

David Seddon, in Chapter 9, dealt with the position of the Maghreb states, which, together, are the African extension of the Arab world. The political and economic development of the region has been dominated by its relationship with Europe. Regionalism in the area can be seen as part of the attempt of the Maghreb to achieve a degree of development autonomous from its previous colonizers. Traditionally, the Mediterranean countries, including the Maghreb, depended heavily on the export of minerals and agricultural produce to Europe. However, the Union of the Arab Maghreb (UAM), created in 1989, failed to forge links between the countries of Nothern Africa. Although the Maghreb states formally subscribed to the objectives of the UAM, the union was eclipsed by attempts to secure bilateral relations with the EU and by an increase of domestic political and economic problems in the 1980s and 1990s. More fundamentally, Seddon argued, the policy aimed at creating horizontal economic ties among the Maghreb countries conflicted with EU policies to maintain the vertical integration of the Maghreb into a European-dominated regional association on the basis of bilateralism. Thus, the Euro-Mediterranean Partnership (EMP), established in 1995, is the consolidation of a 'hub-and-spoke' arrangement based on asymmetrical power relationships between Europe and the non-member Mediterranean countries, including those from the Maghreb.

In Chapter 10, Daniel Bach focused on sub-Saharan Africa, which is composed, mainly, of countries peripheral in the world economic and political order. In contrast with the rest of the book, Bach emphasizes the emptiness of formal regionalism, in contrast to the dynamism of 'trans-state' relations, or what the introduction refers to as regionalization. The analysis of sub-Saharan economic relations makes clear that the 'border' plays a role that is altogether different from that in other parts of the world. In Africa, the existence of borders is often a main source of income for important parts of the population, because they signify the existence of different trade, taxation and monetary regimes. The dominance of trans-state flows has effectively undermined the attempts to institute formal types of regionalism, especially since informal regionalization is increasingly being linked up with criminal activities. The push towards 'deterritorialization' that has been the outcome of trans-state regionalization has been resisted successfully in no more than three cases: the franc zone, the South African Customs Union (SACU) area and the Nigerian federation. The chapter's conclusion is that, in Africa, the distinction between state and territory is increased as the traditional separation between pre-colonial political formations relying on kinship and those based on territorial occupation is revived.

Theoretical implications

In Chapter 2, theories of international relations and international political economy were analysed with regard to their potential contribution to the study of regional cooperation. The analyses of Parts II and III were informed, in particular, by the specific histories as these have unfolded in the regions under study, and not all of them have explicitly addressed theoretical problems. However, despite the theoretical diversity of the chapters in the book, we can draw some theoretical conclusions on the basis of the case studies.

It was noted at the beginning of Chapter 2, that the study of regionalism has traditionally been confined to the institutionalized forms of international cooperation among industrialized countries. We believe that the present volume has made it clear that the scope of theorizing should be broadened to include countries on the semi-periphery and the periphery of the international political and economic order. This section will serve as a reflection on the three issues that were central to the discussion of theories in Chapter 2, namely the role of the state in regionalist projects, the motivations of the actors involved in regionalist projects, and the resulting forms regionalism would be expected to take.

The role of the state

The case studies in this book indicate that it is difficult to generalize about the role of the state in regionalist projects. World-system theory presumes that the state in the core is generally stronger than the state in other parts of the system, while the role of the state on the periphery is weakest. The case studies make it clear that, on the whole, it is important to take into account the constraints from domestic social groups, international capital or other states, within which semi-peripheral and the peripheral states are effectively working. The state in a 'strong' semi-peripheral country, such as Australia, appears to be more capable of setting the agenda of regionalist projects than states in other, 'weaker', parts of the semi-periphery. The obvious exception here is China, which, as an economic great power in the making, occupies an altogether different position among the countries of the semi-periphery. Because China offers so many benefits to international investors, the bargaining position of the Chinese state has increased enormously over the last decade. However, Chile also constitutes somewhat of an exception. In this case, the state has been able to shape the terms of interaction with the other developing member states in MERCOSUR, thanks largely to its relatively strong economy, at least within the regional context, and the effectiveness of its bargaining.

Other countries on the semi-periphery, such as Brazil or the countries in South East Asia, can only aspire to become major actors in regionalist projects if they succeed in working together effectively. In these cases, they may create bargaining positions *vis-à-vis* industrialized countries and aim to lock onto, or even challenge, regionalist projects such as NAFTA or APEC. MERCOSUR and ASEAN/AFTA are 'second-best' options for these countries in a situation where they fail to link up with the core or the terms of the interaction are unacceptable. 'Weak' semi-peripheral countries such as Turkey and the Maghreb countries may be unable to formulate strong bargaining positions, either because of the element of dependence that is inherent in relations across the 'North–South divide' or because of the ineffectiveness of the state. Because they have a weak bargaining position, these states run the risk of being played off against each other and are subjected to unequal, vertical association with the core, as in the case of the Maghreb with the EU.

In situations where the state has lost its grip on society and the economy altogether, as in parts of sub-Saharan Africa, economic regionalization results in a further weakening of political claims over territory. This may eventually result in an almost complete 'deterritorialization' of national political units. In such cases, the state may be reduced to being an instrument for the rent-seeking behaviour of social groups, and, as the situation in ex-Zaïre demonstrates, state power may only be reconquered by military means, for which outside support is needed.

The main conclusion that can be drawn about the role of the semi-peripheral state in regionalist projects is that it should not be seen as a mere reflection of the function of a country in the world economy (as world-system theory tends to argue), nor of political power considerations of states (as neo-realists assume). Neither the neo-marxist position, which sees the semi-peripheral state as necessarily subordinate, nor the globalist position, which accords the state only a marginal role in the era of globalization, are offered much support by the case studies in this book. Rather, these studies show that the role of the state is limited by the actions of social and economic (interest) groups, and that it is an instrument in attempts to lock in the semi-peripheral economy with the core. Thus, concepts and ideas derived from liberal institutionalism and the world order approach appear to be most useful in explaining the role of the state in regionalism across the North–South divide.

The motivations of actors in regionalist projects

The theories that were discussed in Chapter 2 do not appear to be very useful for the analysis of the motivations of the actors in regionalist projects that involve countries from the developing world. On the one hand, some theories argue that a state logic determines external policies more or less separately from the preferences of social and economic actors. For instance, neo-realists assume that 'relative-gain' considerations will predominate, while the neo-institutionalists argue that states will try to aim for policy coordination in order to avoid negative externalities. Similarly, globalism and the governance approach posit, respectively, that regionalism may be a useful counterweight against the activities of distributional coalitions, and that it will serve to protect national values and maintain state autonomy with respect to economic forces. Marxist, world-system and world order approaches tend to see regionalism as an instrument to serve certain economic (class) interests.

The case studies in this volume suggest that, in order to understand regionalism across the North–South divide, we need to disaggregate the analysis to incorporate different group interests. As a result, state policies should not be conceptualized as homogeneous, as if they were the reflection of a *rationale* that is detached from the political process. Of the cases in the book, the Australian one in Chapter 3 is the example of where the *state* led the way towards regionalism. By the 1980s, within Australian political elites, there was a general awareness of the marginal position of the country in international politics and economics. With the changes effected by the end of the Cold War and the rise of the 'dynamic' Asian economies came the fear that Australia would lose out. The APEC initiative might therefore be seen as an attempt to forge close ties between Australia and the other economies of the Asia-Pacific. The Turkish case is rather different, in that bureaucratic and party interests have been able to press for associate membership of the European Union, even though some economic interests have been heavily opposed to the application and stand to lose out from it. In Chapter 6, this was explained as a consequence of the long-standing tradition of *étatisme* in Turkey. The case study of Chile in Chapter 5 made clear that Chilean regionalist policy is the result of the relationship between sectors of the economic elite, especially new export groups, and modernizing technocrats inside the democratic political parties.

Forms of regionalism

As the editors of a recent volume on the political economy of regionalism have argued, the institutional variation among contemporary regional arrangements is a feature that needs explanation (Mansfield and Milner 1997: 14). As in the case of the other two issues discussed in Chapter 2, theories of international relations and international political economy diverge with respect to their expectations of the institutional forms of regionalism. The case studies in this book made it clear that there is no deterministic relationship between the three central variables of the introduction (world system position, state–society interactions and the policies of other states) and the form of regionalism. Countries from highly different levels of development and position in the international order (such as Australia, Chile and China, as indeed the countries in South East Asia) aspire to participate in APEC, which is a very loose organization characterized by 'open regionalism'. On the other hand, a country such as Turkey, which is clearly on the weak semi-periphery, has become an associate member of the highly institutionalized European Union.

Likewise, the nature of state–society relations does not offer a perfect prediction of the form that regional arrangements will take. There are some examples of situations in which processes at the state level have almost autonomously brought about regionalist policies (as in the cases of Australia and Turkey cited in the previous sub-section) in the case studies in this book. On the other hand, in Brazil, the interaction between social groups has resulted in an approach which, when judged by standards derived from economic analysis, will lead to a 'sub-optimal' outcome. Brazilian economic interests have pressed for the membership of MERCOSUR, so that Brazilian industry would be regionally competitive and would avoid becoming subject to international competition too quickly, as would be happening if Americas-wide free trade were introduced. The Chinese and ASEAN cases demonstrate the effect economic regionalization might have on regionalist policies. China and the countries in South East Asia are part of a regional division of labour which is, to an important extent, stimulated by foreign investment. In both cases, regional policies are 'market-driven'. In the case of China, membership of APEC is a stepping stone towards full membership of the World Trade Organization, which would benefit China's export position. In the ASEAN case, sub-regional liberalization might enhance the position of the South East Asian countries within the broader Asia-Pacific economy.

At several points in the case studies, the policies of third states have been an important factor in explaining regionalist policies. The aspirations of the Maghreb countries to link up with the EU can be explained, to an important degree, with reference to the fear that the EU would develop into a 'fortress', with pernicious consequences for the economies of Northern Africa. Likewise, Australia's APEC initiative can be explained in part as a reaction to the dynamism in East and South East Asia. Finally, the policies of Latin American countries such as Brazil and Chile are conditioned by US policy initiatives such as the Enterprise for the Americas Initiative.

Bibliography

Abad, M.C. (1996) 'Re-engineering ASEAN', *Journal of Contemporary Southeast Asia* 18.

Acharya, A. (1994) *An Arms Race in Post-Cold War Southeast Asia? Prospects for Control* (Singapore: Institute of Southeast Asian Studies).

Acharaya, A. (1995) 'Transnational Production and Security in Southeast Asia's "Growth Triangles"', *Journal of Contemporary Southeast Asia* 17.

Achieving the APEC Vision: Free and Open Trade in the Asia Pacific (1994) Second Report of the Eminent Persons Group (Singapore: Asia-Pacific Economic Cooperation Secretariat).

Adamolekun, L. (ed.) (1991) 'Federalism in Nigeria' (special issue), *Publius: The Journal of Federalism* 21, 4.

Alves, M. (1993) 'Something Old, Something New: Brazil's *Partido dos Trabalhadores*', in B. Carr and S. Ellner (eds) *The Latin American Left: From the Fall of Allende to Perestroika* (Boulder, CO: Westview).

Amin, S. (1970) *The Maghreb in the Modern World: Algeria, Tunisia, Morocco* (Harmondsworth: Penguin).

Amsden, A. (1989) *Asia's Next Giant: South Korea and Late Industrialization* (New York: Oxford University Press).

Amselle, J.L., and E. Grégoire (1988) *Échanges régionaux, commerce frontalier et sécurité alimentaire en Afrique de l'ouest* (Paris: Club du Sahel, Ministère de la Coopération, CILSS).

Anderson, B. (1991) *Imagined Communities: Reflections on the Origin and Spread of Nationalism* (London: Verso).

Antolik, M. (1992) 'ASEAN's Singapore Rendezvous: Just Another Summit', *Journal of Contemporary Southeast Asia* 14.

Applebaum, R.P., and J. Henderson (eds) (1992) *States and Development in the Pacific Rim* (London: Sage).

Arat, Y. (1991) 'Politics and Big Business: Janus-Faced Link to the State', in M. Heper (ed.) *Strong State and Economic Interest Groups: The Post-1980 Turkish Experience* (Berlin: Walter de Gruyter).

Arrighi, G. (1994) *The Long Twentieth Century: Money, Power, and the Origins of Our Times* (London: Verso).

Ash, R., and Y.Y. Kueh (1995) 'Economic Integration within Greater China: Trade and Investment Flows Between China, Hong Kong and Taiwan', in D. Shambaugh (ed.) *Greater China: The Next Superpower?* (Oxford: Oxford University Press).

Asiwaju, A.I. (1976) *Western Yorubaland under the European Rule, 1889–1945* (London: Longman).

Asiwaju, A.I. (1985) *Partitioned Africans: Ethnic Relations Across Africa's International Boundaries, 1884–1984* (New York: St Martin's Press).

Australian Department of Defence (1994) *Defending Australia: Defence White Paper 1994* (Canberra: Australian Government Publishing Service).

Axline, W.A. (1995) *Globalization, Marginalization and Integration: The New Regionalism and Developing Countries*, Working Paper No. 950 (Ottawa: University of Ottawa).

Azam, J.-P. (1990) 'Informal Integration Through Parallel Markets for Goods and Foreign Exchange', in World Bank, *The Long Term Perspective Study of Sub-Saharan Africa*, Volume 4 (Washington: World Bank).

Azambuja, M. (1991) *A Politica Externa do Governo Collor* (São Paulo: Instituto de Estudos Avancados).

Bach, D. (1988) 'Les frontières du régionalisme: Le Nigeria en Afrique de l'ouest', in D. Bach, J. Egg and J. Philippe (eds) *Le Nigeria, un pouvoir en puissance* (Paris: Karthala).

Bach, D. (1993) 'Régionalismes francophones ou régionalisme franco-africain?', in D. Bach and A. Kirk-Greene (eds) *États et sociétés d'Afrique francophone* (Paris: Economica).

Bach, D. (1997) 'Indigeneity, Ethnicity and Federalism', in L. Diamond, A. Kirk-Greene and O. Oyediran (eds) *Transition without End: Nigerian Politics and Civil Society under Babangida* (Boulder, CO: Lynne Reinner).

Badie, B. (1993) *Culture et politique* (Paris: Economica).

Baker, R.W. (1993) 'NAFTA and US Political Relations with Australia and New Zealand: Where's the Real Beef?', in R.G. Cushing, J. Higley, M. Sutton, T. Tompkins and S. Weintraub (eds) *The Challenge of NAFTA: North America, Australia, New Zealand and the World Trade Regime* (Austin, TX: Lyndon B. Johnson School of Public Affairs and Edward A. Clark Center for Australian Studies, University of Texas).

Baldwin, D. (ed.) (1993) *Neorealism and Neoliberalism: The Contemporary Debate* (New York: Columbia University Press).

Baran, P.A. (1957) *The Political Economy of Growth* (New York: Monthly Review Press).

Baran, P.A., and P.M. Sweezy (1966) *Monopoly Capital: An Essay on the American Economic and Social Order* (New York: Monthly Review Press).

Barbe, E. (1996) 'The Barcelona Conference: Launching Pad of a Process', *Mediterranean Politics* 1, 1.

Barbosa, R. (1994) 'O Mercosur e suas institucoes', *Boletim de Integrao Latino-Americana* 14.

Barbour, K. (1961) 'A Geographical Analysis of Boundaries in Inter-tropical Africa', in K. Barbour and R. Prothero (eds) *Essays on African Population* (London: Routledge and Kegan Paul).

Barros, R. (1986) 'The Left and Democracy: Recent Debates in Latin America', *Telos* 68, 2.

Bartell, E. (1995) 'Perceptions by Business Leaders and the Transition to Democracy in Chile', in E. Bartell and L. Payne (eds) *Business and Democracy in Latin America* (Pittsburgh: Pittsburgh University Press).

Bayart, J.F., S. Ellis and B. Hibou (1996) *La Criminalisation de l'État en Afrique* (Brussels: Complexe).

Bayili, E. (1976) 'Les Rivalités franco-britanniques et la zone frontière Haute-Volta–Ghana, 1896–1914', Mémoire de maîtrise, University Paris I, mimeo.

Becker, B., and C. Egler (1993) *Brasil: Una Nova Potencia Regional na economica-mundo* (Rio de Janeiro: Bertrand Brasil).

Beeson, M. (1995) 'Australia–Japan Trade Relations: The Coal Industry as a Case in Point', *Australian Quarterly* 67, 3.

Bell, S. (1997) *Ungoverning the Economy: The Political Economy of Australian Economic Policy* (Melbourne: Oxford University Press).

Bernard, M. (1991) 'The Post-Plaza Political Economy of Taiwanese–Japanese Relations', *Pacific Review* 4, 4.

Bernard, M. (1996) 'States, Social Forces and Regions in Historical Time: Toward a Critical Political Economy of Eastern Asia', *Third World Quarterly* 17, 4.

Bernard, M., and J. Ravenhill (1995) 'Beyond Product Cycles and Flying Geese: Regionalization, Hierarchy, and the Industrialization of East Asia', *World Politics* 47, 2.

Bouzas, R. (1996) 'MERCOSUR y Liberalizacion Comercial Preferencial en America del Sur: Resultados, Temas y Proyecciones', in R. Lipsey and P. Meller (eds) *NAFTA y MERCOSUR* (Santiago de Chile: CIEPLAN).

Brand, D. (1992) 'Libre-échange en Amérique-Latine: les perspectives de Succès', *Problèmes d'Amérique-Latine* 7.

Breslin, S. (1996) *China in the 1980s: Centre-Province Relations in a Reforming Socialist State* (Basingstoke: Macmillan).

Brown, D.K., A.V. Deardorff and R.M. Stern (1997) 'Some Economic Effects of the Free Trade Agreement between Tunisia and the European Union', in A. Galal and B. Hoekman (eds) *Regional Partners in Global Markets: Limits and Possibilities of the Euro-Med Agreements* (London/Cairo: Centre for Economic Policy Research/ The Egyptian Center for Economic Studies)

Bugra, A. (1994) *State and Business in Modern Turkey: A Comparative Study* (New York: State University of New York Press).

Busch, M.L., and H.V. Milner (1994) 'The Future of the International Trading System: International Firms, Regionalism, and Domestic Politics', in R. Stubbs and G.R.D. Underhill (eds) *Political Economy and the Changing Global Order* (Basingstoke: Macmillan).

Calder, K. (1995) *Asia's Deadly Triangle: How Arms, Energy and Growth Threaten to Destabilize Asia-Pacific* (London: Nicholas Brealey).

Caldwell, M. (1978) 'Foreword', in D. Elliott (ed.) *Thailand: Origins of Military Rule* (London: Zed).

Cammack, P. (1982) 'Clientelism and Military Government in Brazil', in C. Clapham (ed.) *Private Patronage and Public Power* (Basingstoke: Macmillan).

Cardoso, F.H. (1973) 'Associated-Dependent Development: Theoretical and Practical Implications', in A. Stepan (ed.) *Authoritarian Brazil* (New Haven, CT: Yale University Press).

Carkoglu, C., M. Eder and K. Krisci (1997) 'Turkey and the Political Economy of Regionalism in the Middle East', mimeo.

Cavarozzi, M. (1973) 'The Government and the Industrial Bourgeoisie in Chile', unpublished Ph.D. thesis, Berkeley: University of California.

Cerny, P. (1990) *The Changing Architecture of Politics* (London: Sage).

Cervo, A., and C. Bueno (1986) *A Politica Externa Brasileira 1822–1985* (São Paulo: Editora Atica).

Chan, A. (1996) 'Boot Camp at the Show Factory: Regimented Workers in China's Free Labour Market', *The Washington Post* (3 November).

Chase-Dunn, C. (1989) *Global Formation: Structures of the World-Economy* (Oxford: Blackwell).

Consejo Nacional para la Superacion de la Pobreza (1996) *La Pobreza en Chile: Un Desafío de Equidad e Integracion Social* (Santiago: Editorial Despertar).

Constantin, F. (ed.) (1983) 'L'Afrique sans frontière', *Politique Africaine* 9.

Cook, P., and C. Kirkpatrick (1997) 'Regionalisation and Third World Development', *Regional Studies* 31.

Cooper, A.F., R.A. Higgott and K.R. Nossal (1993) *Relocating Middle Powers: Australia and Canada in a Changing World Order* (Melbourne: Melbourne University Press).

Coussy, J., and P. Hugon (eds) (1989) *Integration régionale et ajustement structurel en Afrique subsaharienne* (Paris: Ministère de la Coopération).

Cox, R.W. (1981) 'Social Forces, States and World Orders: Beyond International Relations Theory', *Millennium: Journal of International Studies* 10, 2.

Cox, R.W. (1987) *Production, Power, and World Order: Social Forces in the Making of History* (New York: Columbia University Press).

Cox, R.W. (1995) 'Critical Political Economy', in B. Hettne (ed.) *International Political Economy: Understanding Global Disorder* (London: Zed Books).

Crouch, H. (1984) *Domestic Political Structures and Regional Economic Cooperation* (Singapore: Institute of South East Asian Studies).

David, S.R. (1991) 'Explaining Third World Alignment', *World Politics* 43, 2.

De Melo, J., A. Panagariya and D. Rodrik (1993) *The New Regionalism: A Country Perspective* (New York: World Bank Publications).

De Paiva Abreu, M. (1994) 'Money Doctors, Foreign Debts, and Economic Reforms in Latin America from the 1980s to the Present', *Journal of Economic History* 54.

Dibb, P. (1986) *Review of Australia's Defence Capabilities* (Canberra: Australian Government Publishing Service).

Dicken, P. (1991) 'The Roepke Lecture in Economic Geography: Global–Local Tensions: Firms and States in the Global Space-Economy', *Economic Geography* 70.

Dicken, P. (1993) 'The Growth Economies of Pacific Asia in Their Changing Global Context', in C. Dixon and D. Drakakis-Smith (eds) *Economic and Social Development in Pacific Asia* (London: Routledge).

Dicken, P., and C. Kirkpatrick (1991) 'Services Development in ASEAN: Transnational Regional Headquarters in Singapore', *Pacific Review* 4.

Dixon, C.J. (1991) *South East Asia and the World Economy* (Cambridge: Cambridge University Press).

Dixon, C.J. (1993) 'The Impact of Structural Adjustment on the Thai Rural Economy', in J. Dahl, D. Drakakis-Smith and A. Narman (eds) *Land, Food and Basic Needs in Developing Countries*, Departments of Geography Monograph, series B, No. 83.

Dixon, C.J. (1995) 'Lessons and Sustainability of Thailand's Economic Growth', *Journal of Contemporary Southeast Asia* 17.

Dixon, C.J. (in press) *Thailand: Uneven Development and Internationalisation* (London: Routledge).

Dixon, C.J., and D. Drakakis-Smith (1993) 'The Pacific Asian Region', in C.J. Dixon and D. Drakakis-Smith (eds) *Economic and Social Development in Pacific Asia* (London: Routledge).

Dixon, C.J., and D. Drakakis-Smith (1995) 'The Pacific Asian Region: Myth or Reality?', *Geografiska Annaler* 77.

Dixon, C.J., and D. Drakakis-Smith (1997) 'Contemporary and Historical Patterns of Uneven Development in South East Asia', in C.J. Dixon and D. Drakakis-Smith (eds) *Uneven Development in South East Asia* (Aldershot: Ashgate).

Dragsbaek-Schmidt, J. (1997) 'The Challenge from South East Asia: Social Forces between Equity and Growth', in C.J. Dixon and D. Drakakis-Smith (eds) *Uneven Development in South East Asia* (Aldershot: Ashgate).

ECLAC (1994) *Open Regionalism in Latin America and the Caribbean: Economic Integration as a Contribution to Changing Production Patterns with Social Equity* (Santiago: ECLAC).

ECLAC (1995) *Policies to Improve Linkages with the Global Economy* (Santiago: ECLAC).

Egg, J., and J. Igué (1993) *L'intégration par les marchés dans le sous-espace est: L'impact du Nigeria sur ses voisins immédiats* (Paris: OCDE/Club du Sahel-CILSS).

Emmanuel, A. (1972) *Unequal Exchange: A Study of the Imperialism of Trade* (New York: Monthly Review Press).

Evans, P. (1979) *Dependent Development: The Alliance of Multinational, State and Local Capital in Brazil* (Princeton: Princeton University Press).

Evans, P. (1992) 'The State as Problem and Solution: Predation, Embedded Autonomy and Structural Change', in S. Haggard and R. Kaufman (eds) *The Politics of Adjustment: International Constraints, Distributive Conflicts and the State* (Princeton, NJ: Princeton University Press).

Evans, P. (1995), *Embedded Autonomy: States and Industrial Transformation* (Princeton, NJ: Princeton University Press).

Falk, R. (1995) 'Regionalism and World Order after the Cold War', *Australian Journal of International Affairs* 49, 1.

Ferrer, A (1996) 'MERCOSUR: Trayectoria, Situacion Actual y Perspectivas', *Desarrollo Economico* 140.

Ffrench-Davis, R., and R. Saez (1995) 'Comercio y desarrollo industrial en Chile', *Estudios CIEPLAN* 41.

Finnery, A. (1991) *Textiles and Clothing in South East Asia: Competitive Threat or Investment Opportunity?*, Special Report Number 2082 (London: The Economist Intelligence Unit).

Fishlow, A. (1992) 'The State of Economics in Brazil and Latin America: Is the Past Prologue to the Future?', in A. Stepan (ed.) *The Americas: New Interpretative Essays* (Oxford: Oxford University Press).

Fottorino, E. (1991) *La piste blanche* (Paris: Balland).

Foxley, A. (1995) 'Economic and Social Goals in the Transition to Democracy', in C. Pizarro, D. Raczynski and J. Vial (eds) *Social and Economic Policies in Chile's Transition to Democracy* (Santiago: CIEPLAN/UNICEF).

Fuller, G.E., and I.O. Lesser (1993) *Turkey's New Geopolitics* (Boulder, CO: Westview).

Galal, A., and B. Hoekman (1997) *Regional Partners in Global Markets: Limits and Possibilities of the Euro-Med Agreements* (London: Centre for Economic Policy Research).

Galtung, J. (1971) 'A Structural Theory of Imperialism', *Journal of Peace Research* 8.

Galtung, J. (1973) *The European Community: A Superpower in the Making* (Oslo: Universitetsforlaget; London: George Allen & Unwin).

Galtung, J. (1976) 'The Lomé Convention and Neo-capitalism', *The African Review* 6.

Gamble, A., and A. Payne (eds) (1996) *Regionalism and World Order* (Basingstoke: Macmillan).

Gao Fengyi (1996) 'Huashengdun Xunqiu Jiaqiang Meiri Anquan Hezuo ['Washington Plans to Strengthen US-Japan Cooperation'], *Guangming Ribao* (17 April).

Garnaut, R. (1989) *Australia and the Northeast Asian Ascendancy: Report to the Prime Minister and the Minister for Foreign Affairs and Trade* (Canberra: Australian Government Publishing Service).

Garreton, M. (1991) 'Political Democratisations in Latin America and the Crisis of Paradigms', in J. Manor (ed.) *Rethinking Third World Politics* (London: Longman).

Gereffi, G. (1995) 'Global Production Systems and Third World Development', in B. Stallings (ed.) *Global Change, Regional Response: The New International Context of Development* (Cambridge: Cambridge University Press).

Gereffi, G. (1996) 'Commodity Chain and Regional Divisions of Labor in East Asia', *Journal of Asian Business* 12, 1.

Gereffi, G., and M. Korzeniewicz (1990) 'Commodity Chains and Footwear Exports in the Semi-periphery', in W.G. Martin (ed.) *Semi-peripheral States in the World-economy* (New York: Greenwood Press).

Gereffi, G., and M. Korzeniewicz (eds.) (1994) *Commodity Chains and Global Capitalism* (Westport, CT: Praeger).

Gill, S. (1992) 'The Emerging World Order and European Change: The Political Economy of European Union', in *The Socialist Register 1992: The New World Order.* London: Merlin Press.

Gill, S. (1995a) 'Globalisation, Market Civilisation, and Disciplinary Neoliberalism', *Millennium: Journal of International Studies* 24, 3.

Gill, S. (1995b) 'Theorizing the Interregnum: The Double Movement and Global Politics in the 1990s', in B. Hettne (ed.) *International Political Economy: Understanding Global Disorder* (London: Zed Books).

Gilpin, R. (1987) *The Political Economy of International Relations* (Princeton, NJ: Princeton University Press).

Goldgeier, J.M., and M. McFaul (1992) 'A Tale of Two Worlds: Core and Periphery in the Post-Cold War Era', *International Organization* 46, 2.

Gomes, M. (1990) 'A Opcao Europeia e o Projeto de Brasil Potencia Emergente', *Contexto Internacional* 11.

Goodman, D. (1995) 'New Economic Elites', in R. Benewick and P. Wingrove (eds) *China in the 1990s* (Basingstoke: Macmillan).

Goulart, L., C.A. Arruda and H.V. Brasil (1994) 'A Evolucao da Dinamica de Internacioalizao', *Revista Brasileira de Comercio Exterior* 41.

Grégoire, E. (1986) *Les Alhazai de Maradi* (Paris: ORSTOM).

Grieco, J.M. (1990) *Cooperation among Nations: Europe, America, and Non-tariff Barriers to Trade* (Ithaca, NY: Cornell University Press).

Grieco, J.M. (1997) 'Systemic Sources of Variation in Regional Institutionalization in Western Europe, East Asia, and the Americas', in E.D. Mansfield and H.V. Milner (eds) *The Political Economy of Regionalism* (New York: Columbia University Press).

Grindle, M. (1986) *State and Countryside: Development Policies and Agrarian Politics in Latin America* (Baltimore, MD: Johns Hopkins University Press).

Grugel, J. (1996) 'Latin America and the Remaking of the Americas', in A. Gamble and A. Payne (eds) *Regionalism and World Order* (Basingstoke: Macmillan).

Haas, E.B. (1958) *The Uniting of Europe: Political, Social, and Economic Forces, 1950–1957* (Stanford, CA: Stanford University Press).

Haggard, S. (1990) *Pathways from the Periphery: The Politics of Growth in the Newly Industrializing Countries* (Ithaca, NY: Cornell University Press).

Hagiwara, Y. (1973) 'Formation and Development of the Association of South East Asian Nations', *The Developing Economies* 11.

Hagopian, F. (1992) 'The Compromised Consolidation: The Political Class in the Brazilian Transition', in S. Mainwaring, G. O'Donnell and J.S. Valenzuela (eds) *Issues in Democratic Consolidation* (Notre Dame, IN: University of Notre Dame Press).

Hatch, W., and K. Yamamura (1996) *Asia in Japan's Embrace: Building a Regional Production Alliance* (Cambridge: Cambridge University Press).

Hawke, B. (1989) 'Challenges for Korea and Australia', *Australian Foreign Affairs and Trade: The Monthly Record* 60, 1.

Hawke, B. (1994) *The Hawke Memoirs* (Port Melbourne, Vic.: William Heinemann Australia).

Hazlewood, A. (ed.) (1967) *African Integration and Disintegration* (London: Oxford University Press).

Henderson, J. (1989) *The Globalisation of High Technology Production: Society, Space and Semi-conductors in the Restructuring of the Modern World* (London: Routledge).

Hershberg, E. (1997) 'Market-Oriented Development Strategies and State–Society Relations in New Democracies: Lessons from Contemporary Chile and Spain', in C.V. Chalmers *et al.* (eds) *The New Politics of Inequality in Latin America* (Oxford: Oxford University Press).

Hesselberg, J. (1992) 'Exports of Pollution-intensive Industries to the South', *Norwegian Journal of Geography* 46.

Hettne, B. (1995a) *Development Theory and the Three Worlds* (London: Longman).

Hettne, B. (1995b) 'Introduction: The International Political Economy of Transformation', in B. Hettne (ed.) *International Political Economy: Understanding Global Disorder* (London: Zed Books).

Hewison, K., R. Robison and G. Rodan (1993) *Southeast Asia in the 1990s: Authoritarianism, Democracy and Capitalism* (St Leonards, NSW: Allen and Unwin).

Higgott, R. (1989) 'The Ascendancy of the Economic Dimension in Australian–American Relations', in J. Ravenhill (ed.) *No Longer an American Lake?* (Sydney: Allen and Unwin).

Higgott, R. (1991) 'The Politics of Australia's International Economic Relations: Adjustment and Two-Level Games', *Australian Journal of Political Science* 26, 1.

Higgott, R. (1992) 'Economic Diplomacy in a Multilateral Context', in F.A. Mediansky (ed.) *Australia in a Changing World: New Foreign Policy Directions* (Botany, NSW: Maxwell Macmillan Publishing Australia).

Higgott, R., and R. Stubbs (1995) 'Competing Conceptions of Economic Regionalism: APEC versus EAEC in the Pacific Asia', *Review of International Political Economy* 2, 3.

Hill, H. (1991) 'The Emperor's Clothes Can Now Be Made in Indonesia', *Bulletin of Indonesian Studies* 27.

Hirsch, P. (1993) 'Thailand and the New Geopolitics of Southeast Asian Resource and Environmental Issues', paper presented at the Fifth International Conference on Thai Studies, SOAS, London.

Hirsch, P. (1996) 'Large Dams, Restructuring and Regional Integration in South East Asia', *Pacific Viewpoint* 37.

Hirst, P., and G. Thompson (1992) 'The Problem of "Globalization": International Economic Relations, National Economic Management and the Formation of Trading Blocs', *Economy and Society* 21, 4.

Hirst, P., and G. Thompson (1996) *Globalization in Question: The International Economy and the Possibilities of Governance* (Cambridge: Polity Press).

Hoang Anh Tuan (1993) 'Why Hasn't Vietnam Gained ASEAN Membership?', *Journal of Contemporary Southeast Asia* 15.

Holm, H.-H., and G. Sørensen (eds) (1995) *Whose World Order? Uneven Globalization and the End of the Cold War* (Boulder, CO: Westview).

Holsti, K.J. (1985) *The Dividing Discipline: Hegemony and Diversity in International Theory* (Boston: Allen and Unwin).

Hopkins, T.K., and I. Wallerstein (1986) 'Commodity Chains in the World-Economy Prior to 1800', *Review* 10, 1.

Hout, W. (1993) *Capitalism and the Third World: Development, Dependence and the World System* (Aldershot: Edward Elgar).

Hout, W. (1997) 'Globalization and the Quest for Governance', *Mershon International Studies Review* 41, 1.

Huntington, S.P. (1996) *The Clash of Civilizations and the Remaking of World Order* (New York: Simon and Schuster).

Hurrell, A., and N. Woods (1995), 'Globalization and Inequality', *Millennium: Journal of International Studies* 24, 3.

Igué, J., and B.G. Soulé (1992) *L'état-entrepôt au Bénin: Commerce informel ou solution à la crise?* (Paris: Karthala).

Innes-Brown, M., and M.J. Valencia (1993) 'Thailand's Resource Diplomacy', *Journal of Contemporary Southeast Asia* 14.

International Labour Office (1992) *World Labour Report* (Geneva: ILO).

International Monetary Fund (1993) *World Economic Outlook* (Washington: IMF).

International Monetary Fund (1996) *Direction of Trade Statistics Yearbook* (Washington: IMF).

Irvine, R. (1982) 'The Formative Years of ASEAN: 1967–1975', in A. Broinowski (ed.) *Understanding ASEAN* (London: Macmillan).

Jeshurun, C. (1992) 'Defence and Security: Introduction', in K.S. Sandhu, S. Siddique, C. Jeshurun, A. Rajah, J.L.H. Tan and P. Thambipillai (eds) *The ASEAN Reader* (Singapore: Institute of Southeast Asian Studies).

Joffe, G. (1993) 'The Development of the UAM and Integration in the Western Arab World', in G. Nonneman (ed.) *The Middle East and Europe: The Search for Stability and Integration* (London: Federal Trust for Education and Research).

Johnson, C. (1982) *MITI and the Japanese Miracle: The Growth of Industrial Policy* (Stanford, CA: Stanford University Press).

Keohane, R.O. (1984) *After Hegemony: Cooperation and Discord in the World Political Economy* (Princeton, NJ: Princeton University Press).

Keohane, R.O. (ed.) (1986) *Neo-Realism and its Critics* (New York: Columbia University Press).

Keohane, R.O. (1993) 'Institutional Theory and the Realist Challenge after the Cold War', in D.A. Baldwin (ed.) *Neorealism and Neoliberalism: The Contemporary Debate* (New York: Columbia University Press).

Keohane, R.O., and H.V. Milner (1996) 'Internationalization and Domestic Politics: An Introduction', in R.O. Keohane and H.V. Milner (eds) *Internationalization and Domestic Politics* (Cambridge: Cambridge University Press).

Keohane, R.O., and J.S. Nye (1977) *Power and Interdependence: World Politics in Transition* (Boston: Little, Brown).

Keyder, Ç. (1987) 'Economic Development and Crisis, 1950–1980', in I.C. Shick and E.A. Tonak (eds) *Turkey in Transition* (New York: Oxford University Press).

Khaw Guat Hoon (1984) 'ASEAN International Politics', in D.K. Mauzy (ed.) *Politics in the ASEAN States* (Kuala Lumpur: Marican).

Krasner, S.D. (1985) *Structural Conflict: The Third World against Global Liberalism* (Berkeley: University of California Press).

Krasner, S.D. (ed.) (1983) *International Regimes* (Ithaca, NY: Cornell University Press).

Krueger, A.O. (1974) 'The Political Economy of the Rent-Seeking Society', *American Economic Review* 64, 3.

Krueger, A.O. (1995) 'Partial Adjustment and Growth in the 1980s in Turkey', in R. Dornbusch and S. Edwards (eds) *Reform, Recovery and Growth* (Chicago: University of Chicago Press).

Kwan, C.H. (1994) 'Disintegration of Russia: Integration into the Pacific', unpublished manuscript, Department of Human and Economic Geography, University of Gothenburg.

Ky Coo (1994) 'Indo-China's Prospects for Stability', *Journal of Contemporary Southeast Asia* 15.

Laban, R., and P. Meller (1996) 'Estrategias Alternativas de Comercio para un Pais Pequeño: El Caso Chileno', in R. Lipsey and P. Meller (eds) *NAFTA y MERCOSUR* (Santiago: CIEPLAN).

Labrousse, A., and A. Wallon (eds) (1993) *La planète des drogues: Organisations criminelles, guerres et blanchiments* (Paris: Le Seuil).

Lafer, C. (1994) 'Brazil in a New World', in A. Lowenthal and G. Treverton (eds) *Latin America in a New World Order* (Boulder, CO: Westview).

Lamounier, B. (1995) 'Brazil: Inequality against Democracy', in L. Diamond, J. Linz and S.M. Lipset (eds) *Politics in Developing Countries* (Boulder, CO: Lynne Reinner).

Lancaster, C. (1992) 'The Lagos Three: Economic Regionalism in Sub-Saharan Africa', in D. Rothschild and J. Harbeson (eds) *Africa in World Politics* (Boulder, CO: Westview).

Lange, P. (1985) 'Semi-periphery and Core in the European Context: Reflections on the Postwar Italian Experience', in G. Arrighi (ed.) *Semi-peripheral Development: The Politics of Southern Europe in the Twentieth Century* (Beverly Hills, CA: Sage).

Lawrence, R.Z. (1995) *Regionalism, Multilateralism and Deeper Integration* (Washington: Brookings Institution).

Leifer, M. (1975) 'The ASEAN States and the Progress of Regional Co-operation in South-East Asia', in B. Dahm and W. Draguhn (eds) *Politics, Society and Economy in the ASEAN States* (Wiesbaden: Otta Harrassowitz).

Leifer, M. (1978) 'The Paradox of ASEAN: A Security Organisation without the Structure of an Alliance', *The Round Table* 27.

Lelart, M. (1993) 'La zone Franc face à Maastricht', *Revue Tiers Monde* 136.

Lesser, I.O. (1993) 'Bridge or Barrier? Turkey and the West After the Cold War', in G.E. Fuller and I.O. Lesser (eds) *Turkey's Geopolitics* (Boulder, CO: Westview).

Levy, J.S., and M.M. Barnett (1992) 'Alliance Formation, Domestic Political Economy, and Third World Security', *Jerusalem Journal of International Relations* 14, 4.

Lieshout, R.H. (1992) 'Neo-institutional Realism: Anarchy and the Possibilities of Cooperation', *Acta Politica* 27, 4.

Lorenz, D. (1991) 'Regionalisation versus Regionalism – Problems of Change in the World Economy', *Intereconomics* 26.

Loveman, B. (1979) *Chile* (Oxford: Oxford University Press).

Luhulima, C.P.F. (1989) 'The Third ASEAN Summit and Beyond', *The Indonesian Quarterly* 17.

Lyon, P. (1991) 'Postwar Regional Co-operation', in K.S. Sandhu, S. Siddique, C. Jeshurun, A. Rajah, J.L.H. Tan and P. Thambipillai (eds) *The ASEAN Reader* (Singapore: Institute of South East Asian Studies). [Abridged reprint of 'ASEAN and the Future of Regionalism', in Lau Teik Song (ed.) *New Directions in the International Relations of South East Asia: The Great Powers and South East Asia* (Singapore: Singapore University Press).]

McCue, A. (1978) 'A Shortage of Workers Pinches Development in Singapore', *Asian Wall Street Journal*.

MacGaffey, J. *et al.* (1991) *The Real Economy of Zaire: The Contribution of Smuggling and Other Unofficial Activities to National Wealth* (Philadelphia: University of Philadelphia Press).

McGrew, A. (1997) *The Transformation of Democracy?* (London: Open University Press/ Polity Press).

Magdoff, H. (1972) 'Imperialism Without Colonies', in R. Owen and B. Sutcliffe (eds) *Studies in the Theory of Imperialism* (London: Longman).

Mainwaring, S., and T. Scully (1995) *Building Democratic Institutions: Party Systems in Latin America* (Stanford, CA: Stanford University Press).

Maliyamkono, T.L., and M.S.D. Bagachwa (1990) *The Second Economy in Tanzania* (Athens: Ohio University Press).

Mansfield, E.D., and H.V. Milner (eds) (1997) *The Political Economy of Regionalism* (New York: Columbia University Press).

Mansor, A. (1990–1) 'Experiences of Economic Integration in Subsaharan Africa: Lessons for a Fresh Start', in Research Group on African Development Perspectives (ed.) *African Perspectives Yearbook 1990–1991* (Münster: Lit. Verlag).

Marks, J. (1996) 'High Hopes and Low Motives: The New Euro-Mediterranean Partnership Initiative', *Mediterranean Politics* 1, 1.

Mbembe, A. (1992) 'Afrique des comptoirs ou Afrique du développement?', *Monde diplomatique*, January.

M'Bokolo, E. (ed.) (1993) *Développement, de l'aide au partenariat* (Paris: La Documentation française).

Meagher, K. (1983) 'How to Survive and Become Rich Amidst Devastation: The Second Economy in Zaire', *African Affairs* 82.

Meagher, K. (1990), 'The Hidden Economy: Informal and Parallel Trade in Northwestern Uganda', *Review of African Political Economy* 47 (Spring).

Meagher, K. (1996) 'Informal Integration or Economic Subvention?', in R. Lavergne (eds) *Regional Integration and Cooperation in West Africa* (Ottawa: IDRC-Africa World Press).

Médard, C. (1992) 'Essai sur la formation du territoire kényan', Mémoire de DEA, University Paris I, mimeo.

Médard, J.-F. (1992) 'Introduction', in J.-F. Médard (ed.), *États d'Afrique noire: Formations, mécanismes et crise* (Paris: Karthala).

Medhora, R. (1997) 'Lessons from the UMOA', in R. Lavergne (ed.) *Regional Integration and Cooperation in West Africa* (Ottawa: IDRC-Africa World Press).

Meller, P. (1996) *Un Siglo de Economia Politica Chilena (1890–1990)* (Santiago: Editorial Andres Bello).

Migdal, J. (1988), *Strong Societies and Weak States: State–Society Relations and State Capabilities in the Third World* (Princeton, NJ: Princeton University Press).

Milner, H.V. (1997) 'Industries, Governments, and the Creation of Regional Trade Blocs', in E.D. Mansfield and H.V. Milner (eds) *The Political Economy of Regionalism* (New York: Columbia University Press).

Mondjannagni, A. (1963) 'Quelques aspects économiques, politiques, sociaux de la frontière Dahomey–Nigeria', *Études dahoméennes* 1.

Montero, C. (1997) *La Revolucion Empresarial Chilena* (Santiago: CIEPLAN).

Moravcsik, A. (1994) 'Preferences and Power in the European Community: A Liberal Intergovernmentalist Approach', in S. Bulmer and A. Scott (eds) *Economic and Political Integration in Europe: Internal Dynamics and Global Context* (Oxford: Blackwell).

Muchnik, E., L.F. Errazuriz and J.I. Dominguez (1996) 'Efectos de la Asociacion de Chile al MERCOSUR en el Sector Agricola y Agroindustrial', *Estudios Publicos* 63.

Nagara, B. (1995) 'The Notion of an Arms Race in Asia-Pacific', *Journal of Contemporary Southeast Asia* 17.

Naisbitt, J. (1994) *Global Paradox: The Bigger the World Economy, the More Powerful Its Smallest Players* (London: Nicholas Brealey).

Nas, T., and M. Odekon (1992) *Economics and Politics of Turkish Liberalization* (Bethlehem, PA: Lehigh University Press).

Nef, J. (1994) 'The Political Economy of Inter-American Relations: A Structural and Historical Overview', in R. Stubbs and G.R.D. Underhill (eds) *Political Economy and the Changing Global Order* (Basingstoke: Macmillan).

Nogami, K., and B. Zhu (1994) 'Quantitative Analysis of the Chinese Economy', *East Asian Economic Perspectives* 6, 4.

Observatoire géopolitique des drogues (1993) *La drogue: Nouveau désordre mondial, rapport 1992/93* (Paris: Hachette).

O'Donnell, G. (1973) *Modernization and Bureaucratic-Authoritarianism: Studies in South American Politics* (Berkeley: University of California Press).

Ohmae, K. (1985) *Triad Power: The Coming Shape of Global Competition* (New York: Free Press).

Ohmae, K. (1995) *The End of the Nation State: The Rise of Regional Economies* (London: HarperCollins).

Okposen, S. (1993) 'The Determinants of Direct Overseas Investment from Singapore', unpublished PhD thesis, London Guildhall University.

Olson, M. (1982) *The Rise and Decline of Nations: Economic Growth, Stagflation, and Social Rigidities* (New Haven, CT: Yale University Press).

Oman, C. (1994) *Globalisation and Regionalisation: The Challenge for Developing Countries* (Paris: Organisation for Economic Co-operation and Development).

Önis, Z. (1995) 'Turkey in the Post-Cold War Era in Search of an Identity', *Middle East Journal* 48, 2.

Önis, Z. (1997) 'The Political Economy of Islamic Resurgence in Turkey: The Rise of the Welfare Party in Perspective', paper prepared for presentation at the BRISMES International Conference on Middle Eastern Studies, St Catherine's College, University of Oxford, 6–9 July.

Önis, Z., and S.B. Webb (1994) 'Turkey: Democratization and Adjustment from Above', in S.B. Webb and S. Haggard (eds) *Voting for Reform* (London: Oxford University Press).

Oppenheim, L. (1993) *Politics in Chile: Democracy, Authoritarianism and the Search for Development* (Boulder, CO: Westview).

Oxfam (1991) *Brazil: A Mask Called Progress*, an Oxfam report by Neil MacDonald (Oxford: Oxfam).

Page, J., and J. Underwood (1997) 'Growth, the Maghreb and Free Trade', in A. Galal and B. Hoekman (eds) *Regional Partners in Global Markets: Limits and Possibilities of the Euro-Med Agreements* (London/Cairo: Centre for Economic Policy Research/The Egyptian Center for Economic Studies).

Palan, R., and J. Abbott, with P. Deans (1996) *State Strategies in the Global Political Economy* (London: Pinter).

Palmer, N.D. (1991) *The New Regionalism in Asia and the Pacific* (Lexington, MA: Lexington Books).

Payne, A. (1996) 'The United States and its Enterprise for the Americas', in A. Gamble and A. Payne (eds) *Regionalism and World Order* (Basingstoke: Macmillan).

Payne, L. (1995) 'Brazilian Business and the Democratic Transition', in E. Bartell and L. Payne (eds) *Business and Democracy in Latin America* (Pittsburgh, PA: University of Pittsburgh Press).

Perry, M. (1991) 'The Singapore Growth Triangle: State, Capital and Labour at a New Frontier in the World Economy', *Singapore Journal of Tropical Geography* 12.

Petras, J. (1969) *Politics and Social Forces in Chilean Development* (London: University of California Press).

Philippe, J. (1988) 'Le fédéralisme et la question économique', *Politique Africaine* 32.

Phiri, S.H. (1985) 'National Integration, Rural Development and Frontier Communities: The Case of the Chewa and the Ngoni astride Zambian boundaries with Malawi and Mozambique', in A.I. Asiwaju (ed.) *Partitioned Africans: Ethnic Relations Across Africa's International Boundaries, 1884–1984* (New York: St Martin's Press).

Pizarro, C., D. Raczynski and J. Vial (1995) *Social and Economic Policies in Chile's Transition to Democracy* (Santiago: CIEPLAN/UNICEF).

Politique Africaine (1983) 'Zambie: La ruée vers l'émeraude', 3.

Portes, A., M. Castells and L.A. Benton (eds) (1989) *The Informal Economy* (Baltimore, MD: Johns Hopkins University Press).

Pourtier, R. (1987) 'Encadrement territorial et production de la nation (au Gabon)', in E. Terray (ed.) *L'état contemporain en Afrique* (Paris: L'Harmattan).

Pusey, M. (1991) *Economic Rationalism in Canberra: A Nation-Building State Changes Its Mind* (Cambridge: Cambridge University Press).

Qi Lou and C. Howe (1995) 'Direct Investment and Economic Integration in the Asia Pacific: The Case of Taiwanese Investment in Xiamen', in D. Shambaugh (ed.) *Greater China: The Next Superpower?* (Oxford: Oxford University Press) .

Ravenhill, J. (1996) 'Trade Policy Options beyond APEC', *Australian Quarterly* 68, 2.

Richards, A., and J. Waterbury (1990) *A Political Economy of the Middle East: State, Class and Economic Dvelopment* (Boulder, CO: Westview).

Rieger, H.C. (1987) 'ASEAN Economic Co-operation: Running in Circles or New Directions?', *Southeast Asian Affairs* 1987.

Rigg, J. (1995) 'Managing Dependency in a Reforming Economy', *Journal of Contemporary Asia* 17.

Rigg, J. (1997a) *Southeast Asia: The Human Landscape of Modernization* (London: Routledge).

Rigg, J. (1997b) 'Uneven Development and the (Re)-engagement of Laos', in C.J. Dixon and D. Drakakis-Smith (eds) *Uneven Development in South East Asia* (Aldershot: Ashgate).

Rigoberto, T. (1992) 'On the Launching Pad: ASEAN Ministers Set Countdown to Freer Trade', *Far Eastern Economic Review*.

Rodan, G. (1987) 'The Rise and Fall of Singapore's "Second Industrial Revolution"', in R. Higgott and R. Robison (eds) *South East Asia: Essays in the Political Economy of Structural Change* (London: Allen and Unwin).

Rodrik, D. (1995) 'Comments', in A. Krueger (ed.) *Political Economy of Trade Protection* (Chicago: University of Chicago Press).

Saez, R. (1995) 'Estrategia Comercial Chilena. Que Hacer en Los Noventa?', *Estudios CIEPLAN* 40.

Sall, E. (1992) *Sénégambie: Territoires, frontières, espaces et réseaux sociaux* (Bordeaux: CEAN).

Seddon, D. (1991) *Politics and the Gulf Crisis: Government and Popular Responses in the Maghreb*, School of Development Studies Discussion Paper, no. 219 (Norwich: University of East Anglia).

Sheahan, J. (1987) *Patterns of Development in Latin America: Poverty, Repression and Economic Strategy* (Princeton, NJ: Princeton University Press).

Silva, E. (1993) 'Capitalist Coalitions, the State and Neoliberal Restructuring: Chile 1973–1988', *World Politics* 45.

Smith, D.A., and D.R. White (1992) 'Structure and Dynamics of the Global Economy: Network Analysis of International Trade', *Social Forces* 70, 4.

Smith, P. (1992) 'The State and Development in Historical Perspective', in A. Stepan (ed.) *The Americas: New Interpretative Essays* (Boulder, CO: Lynne Reinner).

Sola, L. (1994) 'The State, Structural Reform and Democratization in Brazil', in W. Smith, C. Acuna and E. Gamarra (eds) *Democracy, Markets and Structural Reform in Latin America* (London: Transaction Publishers).

Southall, A. (1985), 'Partitioned Alur', in A.I. Asiwaju (ed.) *Partitioned Africans: Ethnic Relations Across Africa's International Boundaries, 1884–1984* (New York: St Martin's Press).

Sriber, M. (1958) 'Le trafic frontalier clandestin entre le Niger et la Nigeria', mimeo.

Stallings, B. (1995) *Global Change, Regional Response: The New International Context of Development* (Cambridge: Cambridge University Press).

Stopford, J.M., and S. Strange, with J.S. Henley (1991) *Rival States, Rival Firms: Competition for World Market Shares* (Cambridge: Cambridge University Press).

Strange, S. (1988) *States and Markets: An Introduction to International Political Economy* (London: Pinter).

Strange, S. (1995) 'Political Economy and International Relations', in K. Booth and S. Smith (eds) *International Relations Theory Today* (Oxford: Polity Press).

Strange, S. (1996) *The Retreat of the State: The Diffusion of Power in the World Economy* (Cambridge: Cambridge University Press).

Sukumbhand, P. (1994) 'From ASEAN Six to ASEAN Ten: Issues and Prospects', *Journal of Contemporary Asia* 16.

Thanat, K. (1992) 'ASEAN: Conception and Evolution', in K.S. Sandhu, S. Siddique, C. Jeshurun, A. Rajah, J.L.H. Tan and P. Thambipillai (eds) *The ASEAN Reader* (Singapore: Institute of Southeast Asian Studies).

Thill, J. (1959) 'Étude de la situation financière du Niger', Niamey, mimeo.

Tsoukalis, L. (1977) 'The EEC and the Mediterranean: Is "Global" Policy a Misnomer?' *International Affairs* 53.

Tsoukalis, L. (1981) *The European Community and its Mediterranean Enlargement* (London: George Allen and Unwin).

Turnham, D., B. Salomé and A. Schwartz (eds) (1990) *Nouvelles approches du secteur informel* (Paris: OCDE).

TUSIAD (1996) *Turkish Economy 1996*, Publication number 96/201.

United Nations Development Programme (1994) *Human Development Report* (New York: United Nations).

United Nations Development Programme (1997) *Human Development Report* (New York: United Nations).

Vaitsos, C.V. (1978) 'L'Attitude et le rôle des entreprises transnationales dans le processus d'intégration économique dans les pays en voie de développement', *Revue Tiers Monde* 19, 74.

Vaitsos, C.V. (1982) *The Role of Transnational Enterprises in Latin American Economic Integration Efforts: Who Integrates, and with Whom, How and for Whose Benefit?* UNCTAD/ST/ECDC/19 (New York: United Nations).

Vallée, O. (1989) *Le prix de l'argent CFA: heurs et malheurs de la zone franc* (Paris: Karthala).

Van Grunsven, L., and O. Verkoren (1993) 'Adjustment and Industrial Change in Southeast Asia', paper presented at the Trilateral Conference on Global Change and Structural Adjustment, University of Amsterdam.

Vatikiotis, M. (1993) 'Market or Mirage?', *Far Eastern Economic Review*.

Vial, J. (1995) 'Policies of Economic Growth and Political Transition in Chile', in C. Pizarro, D. Raczynski and J. Vial, *Social and Economic Policies in Chile's Transition to Democracy* (Santiago: CIEPLAN/UNICEF).

Waldner, D. (1996) 'The Strange Case of Missing Developmental Consequences of Export-Led Growth in Turkey', paper presented at the Annual Meeting of the International Studies Association, 16–18 April.

Wallerstein, I. (1974) *The Modern World-System: Capitalist Agriculture and the Origins of the European World-Economy in the Sixteenth Century* (New York: Academic Press).

Wallerstein, I. (1979) *The Capitalist World-Economy* (Cambridge: Cambridge University Press; Paris: Éditions de la Maison des Sciences de l'Homme).

Wallerstein, I. (1984) *The Politics of the World-Economy: The States, the Movements, and the Civilizations* (Cambridge: Cambridge University Press; Paris: Éditions de la Maison des Sciences de l'Homme).

Walton, J., and D. Seddon (1994) *Free Markets and Food Riots: The Politics of Global Adjustment* (Oxford: Blackwell).

Waltz, K.N. (1979) *Theory of International Politics* (Reading, MA: Addison-Wesley).

Wang Jisi (1997) 'The Role of the United States as a Global and Pacific Power: A View from China', *Pacific Review* 10, 1.

Warren, B. (1980) *Imperialism: Pioneer of Capitalism* (London: Verso).

Waterbury, J. (1992) 'Export-led Growth and the Center Right Coalition in Turkey', in T.F. Nas and M. Odekon (eds) *Economics and Politics of Turkish Liberalization* (Bethlehem, PA: Lehigh University Press).

Wong, J., and M. Yang (1995) 'The Making of the TVE Miracle – An Overview of Case Studies', in J. Wong, Rong Ma and M. Yang (eds) *China's Rural Entrepreneurs: Ten Case Studies* (Singapore: Times Academic Press).

Woods, J. (1995) 'Achieving the 2020 Vision – The Future of APEC and its Impact on World and Regional Trade', paper presented to the 22nd International Trade Law Conference, Canberra, 27–8 October.

Wyatt-Walter, A. (1995) 'Globalization and World Economic Order', in L. Fawcett and A. Hurrell (eds) *Regionalism in World Politics* (Oxford: Oxford University Press).

Yeoh, C., Theng Lau Geok and R. Funkhauser (1992) *Summary Report: Business Trends in the Growth Triangle* (Singapore: National University of Singapore).

Zeitlin, M. (1968) 'The Social Determinants of Political Democray in Chile', in M. Zeitlin and J. Petras (eds) *Latin America: Reform or Revolution?* (London: Fawcett).

Zhang Yifan (1996) 'Mei Yu La Ri Ruhuo Lianshou Chengba Yatai' ['America Intends to Draw Japan Into its Gang to Seek Joint Hegemony in Asia-Pacific'], *Jiefang Ribao* (30 April).

Zhu Li (1987) 'Zijin Fengpei De Zhuyao Gaibian' ['Major Changes in the Distribution of Funds in China'], *Jingji Guanli* 9.

Index

For Product Safety Concerns and Information please contact our EU
representative GPSR@taylorandfrancis.com
Taylor & Francis Verlag GmbH, Kaufingerstraße 24, 80331 München, Germany